BAD BLOOD

BAD BLOOD

A Life Without Consequence

David Brent Roundsley

DBR Design
2020

I have changed names to protect individuals' privacy.

These are my memories and the memories of the people I interviewed during my search. These are told from my perspective, and I have tried to represent events as faithfully as possible as they were told to me.

Copyright © 2020 David Brent Roundsley
Cover Art © by David Brent Roundsley

All rights reserved. No part of this book may be reproduced or used in any manner without the prior written permission of the copyright owner, except for the use of brief quotations in a book review.

To request permissions, contact the publisher through the website:
www.dbrdesign.com

Hardback ISBN: 978-1-7353779-0-2
Paperback ISBN: 978-1-7353779-1-9
eBook ISBN: 978-1-7353779-2-6

Library of Congress Control Number: 2020912741

First Edition September 2020

Published in the United States by DBR Design

DBR Design
P.O. Box 1482
Benicia, CA 94510

Acknowledgements

I have tried to recreate events, locales, and conversations based on 13 years of research, notes, correspondence, emails, photographs, and my recollections. To maintain their anonymity in some instances I have changed the names of individuals and places, I may have changed some identifying characteristics and details such as physical properties, occupations, and places of residence.

There are many people to thank in their assistance on this journey:

First and foremost, my husband David Chamberlain, who without his support and assistance this never could have happened.

> Sarah & James
> Lloyd & Janine
> Delores
> Sue Ellen & Karen
> Father Nikolaev
> Samantha
> Anthony Cardno
> Michael Croteau
> Jen Greenhalgh
> David Hatt

And also, the many family members and friends who listened patiently as the story unfolded over the years and encouraged writing and memorializing this epic adventure.

Finally, a very big thank you to Danni & Alex, in many ways the heart and soul of this journey

Contents

Acknowledgements
The Search – Part I
  Introduction   1
  Chapter 1 – The Beginning   3
  Chapter 2 – Discovery   13
  Chapter 3 – Found and Then Lost   17
  Chapter 4 – Calls and More Calls   19
  Chapter 5 – An Uncle   23
  Chapter 6 – Montana   27
  Chapter 7 – The Private Detective   37
  Chapter 8 – Knocking on the Door   43
  Chapter 9 – Waiting…   47
  Chapter 10 – A New Family   51
  Chapter 11 – More Family   53
  Chapter 12 – Delores   59
  Chapter 13 – First Family Member Meeting   73
  Chapter 14 – A Door Closes, A Door Opens   75
  Chapter 15 – Oregon   79
  Chapter 16 – Sue Ellen   89
  Chapter 17 – Reassessment   93
  Chapter 18 – The Smallest Clue   97
Danni's Story   **101**
  Chapter 19 – Eleanor   103
  Chapter 20 – Danni's Life with Eleanor   107
  Chapter 21 – Kathleen   115
  Chapter 22 – Martin   125
  Chapter 23 – New Hampshire   131
  Chapter 24 – Bad to Really Bad   137
  Chapter 25 – Alex   143
  Chapter 26 – The Accident   151
  Chapter 27 – Alex's Story   155
  Chapter 28 – Danni's Story Continued   161

Chapter 29 – Precursor to the Big Surgery	173
Chapter 30 – The Surgery	177
Chapter 31 – Discovery	183
Journey of a Lifetime	**185**
The Search – Part II	**187**
Chapter 32 – 2010	189
Chapter 33 – New Hampshire	201
Chapter 34 – 2011 Onward	205
Chapter 35 – Sam	211
Chapter 36 – Escape Report	217
Chapter 37 – Letter(s) from a Convict	221
Chapter 38 – Drugs	225
Chapter 39 – 2013…	227
Chapter 40 – 2013-2014	229
Chapter 41 – Brother from Another Mother	231
Chapter 42 – Washington & New Hampshire	235
Chapter 43 – 2017	239
Chapter 44 – 2018	243
Chapter 45 – 2019	245
Chapter 46 – Less than…	249
Chapter 47 – All Men are Created Equal	255
Chapter 48 – Michigan Records	259
Chapter 49 – State of California Reply	261
Chapter 50 – The End?	283
Postscript	285
Selected Song Lyrics	**293**
The Only Path	295
Suburbia	297
Android Dreams	299
Watching You	301
Always Walking	303
Bad Blood (The Ballad of a Bad Man)	305
Goodbye	307
Munich Syndrome Discography	**309**

The Search – Part I

Introduction

Every day I checked the obituaries.

On most days, the first thing I did in the morning was turn on the computer and go to the bookmarked page of the small east Oregon town newspaper and go through the obituaries. Some mornings I'd get distracted with projects or other items and check later in the afternoon. But most days it was the first thing I did.

On Wednesday, June 25, 2009, I had quite a few work deadlines pending and then was further distracted by the unfolding news story: Michael Jackson had possibly died. At first these seemed like a TMZ-type unconfirmed report to get people to click on sites or watch news updates. But little by little, the news was overwhelmed by the story as it was eventually confirmed he had passed away unexpectedly. I continued with the project I had been working on, with one eye on the continuing story, when it occurred to me that I hadn't checked the obituaries that day. I went to the obituary page and staring back at me was a large photo of my birth father, the man I had never met, and the news of his passing.

What should have been the end of the journey I began in earnest February 2, 2007, was now only the beginning.

Chapter 1 – The Beginning

The first Friday of February 2007 was a very cold, grey day. The fog hadn't quite burned off, and the world felt drained of color once all the holiday lights and decorations had been put away. To add to the sense of greyness the year had gotten off to a rather dour start. After what I thought had been a good visit with my adoptive parents, Henry and Dinah, my adoptive sister, and her family in November, we received the family newsletter in December. In it the year was detailed with visits from various "uncles," friends of my sister's from over the years. Everyone was listed as "Uncle Don" or "Uncle Bill." The letter went on for quite a while until the end when there was "and David Roundsley and David Chamberlain were here over Thanksgiving." It made it sound as though my husband and I were missionaries who showed up on their doorstep and they didn't know what to do with us. I was *very* offended. Why weren't we called Uncles? I wasn't sure when, or how, or if, to address it with my mother.

During a phone call in mid-January Dinah asked if everything was okay (my tone of voice was less than happy), and I expressed my displeasure with the newsletter. Her attitude was basically "Well, that's what it was, and that's that." I told her if that was how everyone felt about my presence in the family, then we could just say our goodbyes now and hung up. She called back a couple of times and I let each call go to voicemail. There were no apologies though. We hadn't spoken since, and there was a somber feel to how the year was starting out.

I was working on a fairly easy, but tedious and involved, web design project when the news playing on the TV rolled over to *The Greg Behrendt Show*. I was aware of Greg as a stand-up comedian, but also from his time as one of the few male writers from the HBO series *Sex in the City*. He gained a bit of notoriety in entertainment circles after he had been at a staff meeting where women were commiserating with each other about their dates and men not calling back. They then discussed all the reasons and rationalizations as to why men didn't call back. Greg stunned the room by saying, "He's just not that into you."

Chapter 1 – The Beginning

He went on to write a book with the same name, which I purchased thinking it would be a humorous read. The book turned out to be much more and was quite illuminating for me. The concept didn't have to apply to just romantic situations. It could apply to friends, work situations, and even family. It was a rather freeing concept to realize some friends, co-workers, and even family just weren't that into me.

As I worked away, I heard the topic for the show was adoption and family reunions. Being adopted, and with the recent estrangement from my adopted family, I turned to pay more attention to the show. As it unfolded, it played out like many such human-interest stories where they had a telegenic young woman who was surprised with a family reunion. It was very general and slanted towards a "feel-good talk TV" moment.

I kept the show on but went back to the tasks at hand. As the show was winding down, a woman came on and displayed a website. She explained if you entered your personal information (something I would most definitely *not* do today!), you might be matched with your birth family. This pulled me out of the moment and back to thinking about my childhood and adoption.

When I was adopted, it was coming into vogue to talk about the adoptions and not keep it a secret from the child, as had been the practice for years before. Garden Grove in the mid-1950s was the epitome of southern California post-war suburbia. New homes with new lawns, shiny new cars in every driveway, a swimming pool in the backyard, and families with the requisite two children (preferably a boy and a girl... in that order), station wagon, a stay-at-home mom and a father who left for work every morning at eight, returned after five, and was out doing yard work or BBQing on the weekends.

One of my earliest memories was of me standing in the kitchen with the sun streaming in on the bright yellow linoleum, shiny new appliances, aqua kitchen tiles, wallpaper with herbs and vegetables, and a grey Formica dining room table with black metal legs and gold-plated support pieces holding the legs to the table. I couldn't have been much more than three years old. Dinah was standing over me, looking down as she struck a serious tone of voice saying, "Your birth parents are Daniel and Margaret Andrews, but they didn't want to have children. You were chosen by us, and we wanted you very much."

I didn't think much of this episode and accepted Dinah's statement along with other facts like the sky is blue, grass is green, it's warm in summer, and now my birth parents are Daniel and Margaret Andrews. Of course, this simple statement led to more questions. One thing I've been blessed with is a good memory. If someone tells me something, I mentally file it away. Often people will contradict what they previously said, but I don't generally call them on it. But I file that away as well. With my parents, answers ranged from short and non-committal to longer with more detail. But inconsistencies crept in early. My father and I never had open and honest communications, and seldom had any involved conversations. None of his conversations were about how he felt; they were always about external things like the weather, an event, something on TV. On occasion he'd talk about his childhood, but it didn't always ring true. He would go on about how great his parents were and his childhood, but from seeing the emotionally distant relationships with his two sisters and mother, and the fact all of them fled their very small town in New Mexico as quickly as they could seemed to contradict the idyllic childhood family remembrances.

Dinah was vague, but after a lot of pestering (in ways only very small children can do) she explained my birth mother wanted to keep me (first discrepancy when I was told neither of them wanted a child), but my birth father was a student and felt a child would distract from his studies. The first outlines of these people were my birth mother was a nurse, and my birth father was a student. I once asked my father if he ever saw my birth parents. On the first occasion he said he did. He said my birth father was very handsome. He didn't really say anything about my birth mother. The other two facts they shared were my birth father was of German extraction and he (or they?) were from Detroit. Mine was a private adoption, and my father let loose with an interesting story once. He said the lawyer brokering the adoption had initially thought about adopting me himself, but due to having three sons already, he decided not to follow through with that. My adoptive parents laid out a narrative about not being able to have children, and their various attempts at adoption. The waiting list going through the state/county

Chapter 1 – The Beginning

was apparently several years long. A woman my father worked with at Baker Appliances in Long Beach said she knew someone who was putting their child up for adoption and she introduced Henry to the lawyer. As time went on, the story started to get more detailed. They said in order for the adoption to be signed off on in the courts, there would need to be a social worker report. According to them, the social worker said my birth mother was very unsure of putting me up for adoption, but my birth father was very firm they not keep the child. They insisted my birth mother be absolutely sure this was what she wanted to do. They said the social worker went on to say my birth father was "very self-absorbed, to the point of rudeness." Without saying it directly, they implied my birth father was an arrogant narcissist and the implication was my birth mother was a mousy shadow, capitulating to whatever he wanted.

On the day of my birth, Dinah received a call from the hospital (now a park) in Long Beach. The voice on the other end said, "Congratulations! You're a mother! When you come to the hospital DO NOT go to the nursery, DO NOT ask about infants, recent births, or mention adoption. Go to nursing station #12, ask for Doris, and bring two pieces of identification with you."

Apparently, I was not being held in the nursery, but in a separate unmarked, but secured area. Despite having no medical issues, I was held in the hospital a little over a week. Dinah and Henry took me home, but under a cloud. My birth parents had not signed the adoption papers and could not be reached. While not stated at the time, it turned out my birth mother was a nurse at the hospital I was born in, which complicated matters, and with not signing off on the adoption, there was a real fear there would be an attempt to take me back.

Henry and Dinah had started the process of purchasing a house in a new development in Garden Grove, and the first few months of my life were spent being shuttled between there and Long Beach. When I was about 4 months old, Dinah had taken me and her mother down to the new house. Henry worked late and went to the old house to get some things. As he was pulling out, a car broadsided him. Its lights weren't on, and it immediately took off. While he never elaborated on this incident, the way he avoided being questioned years after the fact, I always had a suspicion he felt the accident was intentional (perhaps by my birth parents?), but at the very least, mysterious. It was telling he never pursued it with the police.

The story Henry and Dinah told me was that around the time of my first birthday, my adoption was still in limbo, and they petitioned the court to request the Los Angeles County Court charge my birth parents with child abandonment. They said that shortly thereafter the lawyer who handled the adoption said that Daniel and Margaret had come into the office unannounced. Surprised at seeing them, he instructed them to sit down and wait while he retrieved the paperwork. Upon his return, they were gone. He was again surprised when an hour later, they walked in, signed the paperwork, and left without saying much. The impression the lawyer had was that Margaret was making one last plea to get back her son.

Starting that day, I was now Henry and Dinah's son legally, but a certain instability and uncertainty had set in that never went completely away.

The first difference that came to my attention (but was seemingly ignored by the greater world) was how I looked with my family. Both Henry and Dinah were large boned with brown hair and dark eyes. I, on the other hand, was slight, a tow-headed blonde, until junior high school, with blue-green eyes. Despite the incongruity, when I was introduced to family friends, the first comment was, "Well, you look just like your father." I did?

The next difference that became (painfully) obvious was I was not the child Henry had hoped for. While he and his side of the family liked to portray themselves as smart, what they were was opinionated (not the same). He was hoping for a rough-and-tumble child, and in reality, I was the polar opposite. I was effeminate, artistic, bookish, and lived in a fantasy world. Henry wanted a son to throw the ball around with and to perpetually hold the flashlight while he did projects around the house. From the start I loved to create detailed and complex fantasy worlds. This would entail me gathering anything and everything within sight (and often out of sight) and cobble together towers, buildings, castles, forts, walls, and whatever, and populate them with the miniature Disney figurines we would pick up during our weekly visit to the Magic Kingdom. Often these fantasy structures would cover 90% of the floorspace in my bedroom. I'd leave just enough room to

Chapter 1 – The Beginning

insert myself into the center of it and direct my fantasy world. One of the biggest components was a piece of cut glass that fell out of a broken pair of my mother's earrings. She threw them out, but I fished the stone out of the trash. I could hold up to my eye, shutting the other eye, and create a laser beam effect, a transporter, or any other fantastical special effect I wanted to visit upon my self-made world.

While this was not commented on most of the time, there would be days when Henry was in an especially foul mood, and he would charge into my room kicking everything in every direction and scream, "CLEAN UP THIS SHIT!" My impressions and main memories of Henry were of him always being angry. He came home and two things HAD TO HAPPEN. He poured a drink first thing coming through the door, and if dinner wasn't ready at exactly 7pm, there would be hell to pay and he'd sulk for the remainder of the evening.

Dinah indulged me for the most part, and the tradeoff for her was that she got a social partner that she didn't have with her husband. Instead of going to Disney films, I have countless memories of my mother taking me to less child-friendly fare: *The Children's Hour*, *Suddenly Last Summer*, *Some Like it Hot*, *The Innocents*, etc. Our family was out of sync with the other families on the street. Something I didn't notice at the time was how different our house was from the other new homes on the street. The color choices from that era were brown and beige. My parents on the other hand had a living room painted in a very deep, vibrant turquoise. Their bathroom had bright pink tiles, and they painted it a deep lurid purple. Not being able to find matching curtains my father hung up deep purple towels as drapes. The main bathroom was a vibrant, almost-electric blue. Something else about my mother I didn't notice at the time was the elaborate amount of make-up she would wear from the very moment she got up. A thick, almost theater-type pancake foundation with heavy eye make-up and lipstick always at the ready. I have many memories of accompanying my mother to local upscale department stores. She would try on (and buy) evening gowns and dresses. Her closet was full of dresses, that in hindsight, were flashy and were more like something seen in the movies at the time, not the types seen out and about every day in Southern California. For me, seeing Donna Reed making a meal in a nice dress seemed rather ordinary. Henry and Dinah were older, and because they couldn't have children, by the time they adopted me, most of the families on the street not only had the requisite two children, often they had three or four. Most of them had older children who could handle babysitting, but as I was younger Dinah, or both parents, took me along to everything they did. Be it drinks with the girls, ballroom dance lessons, bowling league, or the rare dinner out. There were never any children my age at these places or events, so I was inserted into very adult conversations from a very early age. I must not have caused too much of a fuss as they continued to bring me along, and it seemed like I was invisible to the adults, who would talk freely and openly about the transgressions of their friends and neighbors. (And there were a LOT of transgressions)

Another indication I wasn't the ideal fit was Henry's family. His father had died in a mining accident – he was the chief engineer of the mine and almost never went into the actual mine. On the one occasion he did, something ignited, and he perished – and his mother immediately moved to San Francisco, moving into a one-room residence hotel in the Tenderloin. His older sister shortly moved out to Richmond on the other side of the bay from San Francisco. From very early on I knew the family did not approve of me, and I later found out I was viewed as a mistake that didn't work out. To describe Henry's mother and sister, I will paraphrase a joke Lily Tomlin once made about the Nixons. Her joke was "We made ice sculptures of the first family. Pat never melted." The same could be said for my adoptive grandmother and aunt. My grandmother was cold and very indifferent to me. My aunt, on the other hand, was always smirking and making sarcastic asides. My first clear memory of my father's sister was going to her house for dinner. She served something that didn't appeal to me as a young child. I wrinkled my nose. She made a very loud pronouncement, "Well, if you don't like this then you're not really a Roundsley." (I didn't, and apparently, I wasn't.)

As I got older and edged out of my fantasy world, music, song, and dance caught my attention. My recollections of my first five years are that I was unself-conscious and overall happy and upbeat. Dinah had been a light opera singer in high school but walked away from it when she went to college. She was feted and considered a star in her high school. When graduation was approaching, she approached her musical director and asked if she should pursue a career in opera, or light opera. His reply was "Maybe you should take secretarial courses in case this doesn't work out." I think this adversely affected Dinah and all her future decisions and choices in her life. What she did was forego the singing altogether and pursue secretarial skills. She was an incredibly fast touch typist (pre-electric typewriter days) and could type 125 words per minute – including numbers!

Dinah's sole indulgence with music was to buy all the soundtracks to musicals and sing along with them in the house. If a song struck me, I'd get up and sing along, too. Unfortunately for me, at least in Henry's family's eyes, the songs were usually sung by women. I didn't think of them in those terms. I just liked the song and would sing along. Once when they were visiting my mother felt I really got into the spirit with one song and put it on.

My adoptive aunt smirked openly, and Henry's mother said, "You'll probably have a career in the *theater*" which was code for gay (or in their world, a more pejorative term).

They did little to withhold the smirking, and my aunt piled on with "*You're SO theatrical!*"

When I was nine years old, I truly found out how Henry's family felt about me when my parents adopted my younger sister. Dinah wanted a second child and wanted to adopt a daughter. While Henry always kept a roof over our heads and food on the table, being short at the end of the month was a regular occurrence. When it came time to do the adoption, Dinah wrote my father's mother a letter asking for a "loan" (which would go unpaid) to start the adoption process. In her reply, Henry's mother referenced the fact, "David hasn't turned out the way we had hoped, so maybe we shouldn't go down this road a second time." My mother shared the letter with me. While I can see now how cruel that was, I believe her objective was to have an ally against my father's family. Oddly, it didn't upset me, as I already knew how they felt about me and where I stood in their world.

I had one very good friend down the street, Barb, from the ages of two through five. She was a year younger, but we were best friends, very carefree,

Chapter 1 – The Beginning

and I can't recall any childhood fights. Her family was very gregarious, and Henry and Dinah socialized with them. I think it was the happiest I saw my adoptive parents when they went out with Barb's parents. When I was five and just about to start school, Barb's family moved. I was crestfallen, but I started kindergarten and I don't recall any anxiety or worries moving into the next educational level, other than being reluctant to get up early on a daily basis to go to school. But the biggest thing I noticed after the fact, was my parents didn't really seem to have any friends or socialize much after Barb's family moved. They NEVER had anyone over for drinks, let alone dinner, or even a BBQ. And other than Dinah going out with former co-workers for lunch, or bowling leagues, there was little to any socialization.

But something shifted for me between kindergarten and first grade. I was actually looking forward to first grade. I had been reading on my own for quite a while and I was anticipating this new adventure. I recall shopping for long pants and getting a new Voyage to the Bottom of the Sea lunch box and thermos, along with a school bag and supplies. Class started and when we hit lunchtime, as I stepped out of the classroom, the principal (we were introduced at a school-wide meeting at the start of the day) came charging around the corner, face red and contorted with rage, running as fast as he could. I had no idea why, but I had the feeling it was me with whom he was angry and I took off running, only to trip, falling on my knees, ripping my new pants, bloodying my knees as my new lunch pail fell to the ground, contents scattering and my thermos breaking. It turned out a dog had gotten onto the school grounds and he was chasing it. Why did I assume he was angry and chasing me? The look on his face and the anger was a perfect mirror of Henry, and it was the only conclusion my young mind could arrive at.

All these things went through my mind as I was pulled back to the TV show and the website they were now displaying on the TV screen. I grabbed a pen and jotted the website information down. The show was over, and I turned the TV off. I went to the website, and there was a form to fill out. I entered my birth parents' names, the hospital I was born in, and the day and year. I entered the information, closed the browser window, and went back to work.

Chapter 2 – Discovery

After filling out the form on the website displayed at the end of the Greg Behrendt show, I pushed the thoughts of my adoption and the past out of my mind and got back to the repetitive web project I had started earlier. Around 11 AM the phone rang. I looked at the Caller ID and it said it was from Tennessee. I didn't know anyone in Tennessee and my first inclination was let it go to voicemail. I assumed it was a telemarketer or even a wrong number. But something compelled me, and I picked up. The voice on the other end was a woman who introduced herself as Martha Davis. Being a musician and heavily into music, my first thought was "Oh, it's Martha Davis, of the band *The Motels*, calling to thank me for buying their albums and supporting them." (Of course, I knew this wasn't *that* Martha Davis, but that's what flashed through my mind.) She said she saw my information posted on the website and explained she was a "Search Angel." She went on to explain she felt she could connect me to my birth parents based on the information I posted. To say I was stunned was an understatement.

In that moment I flashed back to 2001 when my husband and I had our wills done. As it turned out, our lawyer had adopted a son and we were discussing what a paid search would cost. He said it could run upwards of $20,000. Back in the early 1990s I had petitioned the state of California for the information they *could* release. Adoption records are sealed to protect the identity of the birth parents. The information provided stated both my birth mother's parents were dead at the time of my birth (she was 24) and my birth father was an orphan (he was 27). What this information conveyed to me was no one on either side of my birth family lives very long, and the probability of finding them alive was improbable in 2001, so we declined to pursue the paid search.

I pulled myself out of my thoughts and focused on what Martha was now saying. I asked how much this would cost. She said it would be $250 to start. My mind went back to the costs we were told in 2001, and my tone became wary as I said, "And to finish…?"

Chapter 2 – Discovery

She said, "That would be $250 to close. Oh wait, you're in California. There's a surcharge."

I thought, "And here it comes" and I said, "And…?"

She said the surcharge was $100.

This was significantly less than the first prices we heard. I asked if I could confer with my husband and get back to her. I called my husband, Dave, and he said "Well, the odds of her closing are slim, so go ahead and start." I called her and said, "Let's do it!" I sent her the deposit via PayPal, and she said, "I already know your mother's maiden name. It's Van der Westhuizen. That's a very rare name. If there are Van der Westhuizen's out there, you are probably related. There are some relatives in Southern California I want to check with first. I'll call you back in a couple of hours."

At this point, every cliché I've seen in a movie, on TV, or read in a book about everything spinning about you seemed to be happening to me. I recalled snippets of my childhood, things people said, spinning around me like a video tornado, and an image would come into focus, the memory would replay, and then the whirling vortex continued. I flashed to my elementary schoolyard and one of the boys from the local church. I (foolishly) shared that I was adopted, and he took on a very nasal taunting tone saying, "Wow, you must have been a horrible child for your own parents to not want to keep you." The images and memories were coming fast and furious now.

I was now transported back to the early 1990s. One of the things I've found over the years is, for whatever reason, I tend to meet other adoptees. It just seems to surface in random conversations. A co-worker, also an adoptee, had joined an adoption search group. She asked me to accompany her, but I was resistant. To my way of thinking, as it was a private adoption and *if* my birth parents were still alive and at all interested in meeting or finding me, they would have. It felt like searching was only going to give me a second shot at rejection. She told me the majority of people who search are women, and men seldom look. The group really wanted a man to attend. I reluctantly attended the group. I was the only male in the room. The group was mixed between adoptees and people who had put their children up for adoption. At this point in time, the image in my mind of my mother was a

Chapter 2 – Discovery

washed-out grey visage of a cold indifferent woman, incapable of making her own decisions. For my father I imagined a professorial type sitting in a dusty attic apartment surrounded by books, wearing a tweed jacket with elbow patches, but also cold and indifferent.

As I sat in the group, I heard stories of regret, anger, sadness, loss, and parts of their lives they were hoping to find or reclaim. I was very taken by the stories of the women who had put children up for adoption. Circumstances, timing, loss, and regret… I attended a few more meetings. This was when I applied to the State for what open information I could get. It was during one of these meetings the group was introduced to Neal. Neal was unable to attend in person but had the group leader share his information. Neal was an ex-FBI agent who had put a child up for adoption years ago and had come to regret the decision. He was recovering from heart surgery but wanted to make his resources available to the group should they choose to search.

After some soul-searching, I made the decision to utilize Neal's services. I called Neal and he was very personable and a good listener. I gave him the information I had, my birth parents' names, the year I was born, and what scant information my adoptive parents had shared with me. Neal spent about a week pouring through public records and city directories but at the end of a week he said he couldn't find *anything*. He said it was like witness relocation or alien abduction. He floated the theory the names my parents had given me might have been fictious. He obviously felt badly but said there wasn't anything he could provide.

Now with the information Martha provided I googled "Van der Westhuizen" and the first hit was a company in Grand Rapids, Michigan. Recalling my parents saying Daniel was from Detroit, I began to think perhaps they had given me the right information after all, and this might lead to something. It was now late afternoon, and it felt as if barely five minutes had passed.

The phone rang shocking me out of my recollections. It was Martha. She informed me I was NOT a Van der Westhuizen. My birth mother had been adopted herself. She then said she was remarried with the last name of Birtwistle and living in Montana. Remarried. That was something that had

Chapter 2 – Discovery

crossed my mind. "Had they stayed together after my adoption? Montana? How did she get from Michigan to Southern California to Montana?" flickered through my mind. Martha went on to say her social security number was still active, but she wasn't answering her phone. Martha told me to relax and she'd touch base with me on Monday.

Relax? Now my mind was going a million miles an hour.

Chapter 3 – Found and Then Lost

The first thing I did was google Margaret Birtwistle + Montana. The first hit was her obituary. While the rational part of my mind was unsurprised, I was desolate. I had just found my mother and lost her within a matter of hours. This obituary was run by the United Methodist Church of Anaconda.

```
Margaret M. Birtwistle
    ANACONDA — Upon her prearranged request, no
services will be held for Margaret M. Birtwistle,
73, who died Monday of natural causes at her
Georgetown Lake home.
    However, a memorial recognition will be conducted
for her at the conclusion of Sunday's service at
United Methodist Church of Anaconda. Private
inurnment will be in the Southern Cross area,
Georgetown Lake.
    Margaret Mary was born Feb. 9, 1932, in Grand
Rapids, Mich. She was adopted by Sam and Lucille
(Smythe) Van der Westhuizen. She grew up in Grand
Rapids, graduating from Ottawa High School in 1950.
She received her registered nurse degree in 1953
from Butterworth Hospital and Nursing School in
Grand Rapids.
    She worked as a registered nurse for 20 years,
retiring in 1972, due to an accident, as nursing
supervisor at Galen.
    Margaret came to Montana in February 1965, moved
to Mill Creek in 1980 and to Southern Cross and
Georgetown Lake in 1986.
    She married Daniel Andrews, they later divorced.
While camping at Lost Creek State Park, Margaret met
Stanley "Stan" P. Birtwistle and on Oct. 25, 1978,
they were married in Deer Lodge. Stan died April 12,
1997.
    Survivors include a cousin, Barbara Johnson of
Caledonia, Mich., and many dear friends in Anaconda
and Deer Lodge.
```

Chapter 3 – Found and Then Lost

```
    Cremation arrangements are under the care of the
MJ Funeral homes.
    Memorials: Thompson Pets, Anaconda.
```

The posting of obituaries by the church only went back 18 months. If she had died a month earlier, I probably would not have found the online obituary. Seeing this made what had previously been a rather abstract concept more real. Equally confusing was the sense of loss. Could you feel deep loss for something you never had? And there was anger. Anger it had taken this long for things to fall into place, to finally find this information and get a sense of where my life began. Also, in reading the obituary, there was no mention of children. While I wouldn't have expected mention of a child placed for adoption, surely had she had any other children, it would have been mentioned? There was no clue as to where or when she and Daniel divorced. Was it shortly after the adoption? At this point, I now had more questions than I had when the day began.

Chapter 4 – Calls and More Calls

Saturday was spent digesting what I had uncovered, talking with friends, and trying to make sense of what I had found, and figuring out what the next steps and path forward would be. After some deliberation, and in spite of Martha's advice to wait until Monday, on Sunday morning I called the church that posted the obituary. I *knew* someone was there – it was Sunday after all – but I got an answering machine. I left a concise message referencing the obituary they had posted and stated I was Margaret's son. I left my name and number.

There was no return call.

I spent the rest of the weekend putting the locations from the obituary into Google maps, looking at the satellite views trying to get a frame of reference for Anaconda and Georgetown Lake. They seemed impossibly far away, and my mind cast about for how Margaret spent the last years of her life in these locations.

On Monday with no call from Martha or the church, I decided to call the church back. A man answered. I explained I had called Sunday and left a message. His tone of voice shifted, and his wording seemed to be puzzled and unsure. He said he had received the message but wasn't sure how to proceed. He explained that while Margaret showed up at the church from time to time, she had kept to herself. Some days she'd just show up, pitch in, help with whatever project was underway, and then abruptly leave. He couldn't think of any close friends in the congregation. When I explained I had been put up for adoption, he exhaled and said he had no idea she could have had a family. After a bit more pondering on his side, he suggested I call Sharon at the funeral home. He said they had taken care of the proceedings. With the phone number in hand I called and asked for Sharon. A friendly and perky voice answered, and Sharon asked me what the call was about. I explained it was in regard to Margaret Birtwistle and that I was her son. She let out a whoosh of air and said, "No shit! Margaret had a son?" After chatting for a bit, she suggested I talk to Tom Johnson at the bank. He was the executor of her estate.

Chapter 4 – Calls and More Calls

Armed with the new phone number, I called the bank. A rather officious woman answered identifying the bank. I asked to speak to Tom Johnson. She asked what this was regarding. I told her it was about Margaret Birtwistle. Her voice seemed to get haughtier and said, "WHAT ABOUT MARGARET?"

I said, "I am her son and was told to talk to Mr. Johnson."

At this point, I could hear a hand partially cover the mouthpiece as the woman yelled to someone nearby, "MARGARET HAD A SON!" and then came back on the line, more composed and said, "Please hold."

After a very brief wait, a man came on the line and identified himself as Tom Johnson. I explained who I was and the chain of calls that had led me to him. He then said he was most surprised to hear of me. He had known Margaret for several years and had been her benefactor when she hit difficult challenges, guiding her through times of uncertainty. He explained to me she had been homesteading a pasture near Georgetown Lake where she lived in a trailer with a large menagerie of animals. Her animals were her family, and in fact while she was always getting calls from credit card companies, she always budgeted money for and had left a small annuity for her animals after she passed. He shared stories, with a chuckle, about times she'd tromp into the bank and her boots would be caked with mud and cow manure, but she'd trudge in regardless. When her car no longer worked, he found her a replacement, but she was insistent he make sure no one else get the malfunctioning car she had as she didn't want anyone put into danger. Despite being a character, she was beloved by everyone and was missed.

He then suggested I call Sarah Durand. ("Great," I thought, "*Another* call!") who was her best friend. I thanked him for his time and dialed the new number. Sarah picked up on the third ring. I explained the call was about Margaret Birtwistle and I was her son. Sarah surprised me by saying, "I know who you are. I might be the only person she ever talked to about you." This was yet another moment where movie clichés of images, memories, and moments swirling about kicked in, and for a brief moment, I felt weightless while all this information swirled about me.

We spent quite a bit of time on the phone and Sarah explained how Daniel and Margaret had come into their lives. There was a small building in

Chapter 4 – Calls and More Calls

the back of their home that they had converted into living quarters and they were renting it out. Eventually Margaret came over to inquire and Margaret and Dan agreed to move in.

Sarah and her husband James had several children and they all referred to Margaret as Aunt Margaret and Daniel as Uncle Dan. That is until Daniel left. She thought Margaret and Daniel had arrived in Montana in the early-to-mid sixties, with Margaret working as a nurse, possibly in Billings. James seemed to recall Daniel wasn't working when they moved to their property but was studying. This would turn out to be a recurring theme and would continue to crop up as my research expanded. While the details aren't precise, James worked briefly at the prison in Deer Lodge and in talking with Daniel found out Daniel was ex-military. The prison apparently had a higher success rate with employees if they were ex-military, so Daniel applied. From all accounts he was very successful and climbed the ranks rather quickly, rising to become Captain of the outside guard. In fact, he was referred to as "the whiz kid."

By this point in time, senior staff were provided with housing by the prison, and Daniel and Margaret were living in the back of what was formerly the prison toy shop. Everyone said this time was good for the couple. Daniel was doing well, rising through the ranks, and Margaret was a well-respected nurse at the local hospital. Folks said all their furniture was new, and Margaret was buying her clothes at the better shops. But come late 1970 and moving into 1971-72, things changed. Margaret was attacked by a patient and suffered a severe back injury, ending her nursing career. Around this time Daniel ceased working at the prison. They lived in an apartment in town for a while and eventually moved to Red Lodge after Daniel become an assistant deputy sheriff.

It was at this point Sarah was unsure if she should share something with me but pressed on. She said Margaret became aware Daniel was having an affair. Margaret wasn't happy about it, but for whatever reason, tolerated it. She then became aware Daniel had gotten the woman pregnant. She was very distraught as she had always wanted to and hoped to eventually have children with Daniel. (this did cause me to think "umm, she DID have children with him. ME!") One evening after she had taken her pain

Chapter 4 – Calls and More Calls

medication for the back injury and was drifting off to sleep downstairs in a recliner, she became aware Daniel had poured the remains of her pain medicine down her throat. As she explained it to Sarah, she said she felt the effects of the medicine (this is where it gets a tad weird) but felt the presence of a ghost or spirit in the house imploring her to wake up. She did wake up and utilizing her nursing training she expelled the remaining drugs and called her friends to come pick her up.

She returned to Deer Lodge and initiated divorce proceedings against Daniel. She said she wasn't looking forward to the court date or seeing Daniel with this new woman and their newborn daughter. (I had wondered and sensed there might siblings, or half-siblings out there, and now I had confirmation.) Another aspect of the divorce was they had had work done on the house they lived at in Red Lodge after moving there, and the contractor was suing them for non-payment. Margaret ended up on the hook for these bills.

At this point, I was getting a much clearer image of Margaret, but only a somewhat shadowy picture of Daniel, my birth father. But what I had heard about Daniel synced with the statements from the social worker and my adoptive parents prior to my birth, as well as Daniel and *studying*.

At this point, James and Sarah offered to mail me two photos of my parents. They mentioned that when a camera came out Daniel always seemed to be out of the room or area, but they had a couple of candid shots taken during Christmas 1972 when their daughter Nancy received a camera. Along with these shots they also included the two obituaries they had clipped and a random sampling of photos of Margaret taken after she left Daniel up until a few months before she passed.

At the conclusion of this conversation, Martha called back. She had located Margaret's brother (also adopted), and he had (very reluctantly) agreed to speak to me. It was at this point that I updated her with the news of Margaret's passing in September 2005. She was quite surprised, as Margaret apparently wasn't listed as deceased with Social Security.

Chapter 5 – An Uncle

With the various calls and information I had accumulated in a short period of time, I was a bit overwhelmed and anxious when I dialed Margaret's brother's number. One of the provisions of the call was that Margaret couldn't know her brother had provided any assistance or information. Of course, as she was deceased, this was no longer a consideration.

Initially wary and warning me he was a bit hard of hearing, Lloyd sounded both surprised and saddened to hear Margaret had passed. As we spoke, I could tell he was digesting the new information, both of my existence and of Margaret's passing.

Lloyd explained that he changed his last name from Van der Westhuizen to West when he started teaching, as his students kept mispronouncing his name.

What was welcome and unexpected was how candid and open he was about their upbringing, their lives, and their shared history. His father started a business with his brother and met his mother in Grand Rapids. After they were married their mother found out she could not have children, so they adopted. Lloyd was adopted first, and Margaret a few years later. Lloyd was quite frank saying he was not very aware of his sister when they were growing up. He explained the reasons as they were interested in different things, but the larger part being that Lloyd was spoiled and selfish. (that last bit of information left me speechless)

Lloyd was very open about the fact that their mother favored him to the extent both were affected. Margaret grew up with feelings of inadequacy, and Lloyd was instilled with the feeling he should get things his way. Other than a possible appendectomy when she was an adolescent, he was not aware of any health issues with Margaret.

Lloyd had a better memory of Margaret when he was in high school. His recollections were that she was reasonably happy but couldn't really verify that as they didn't communicate much. There was still a discrepancy in how they were treated. Even though both got passing grades (mostly C's), Margaret was made to do homework every night, while Lloyd was excused.

Chapter 5 – An Uncle

Margaret also had to get up an hour earlier than Lloyd to help with chores, and she was tasked with making Lloyd's bed once he was up.

After graduating from high school and under pressure from her mother, Margaret applied to and was admitted to a program for registered nurses at Butterworth Hospital in Grand Rapids. Lloyd was married and living in Kalamazoo at this point, so they saw little of each other. Margaret did rotations at the state mental hospital in Traverse City as well as at hospitals in the Detroit area. It was in Detroit working in a tuberculosis ward that she met Daniel Andrews. Her family believed Daniel to be quite a bit older than Margaret, but they had apparently developed a relationship, and after she graduated, they got married.

Daniel and Margaret were staying with her parents in Grand Rapids when Lloyd was on holiday visiting. They announced their intention to wed and move to California, which came as a shock to everyone. Margaret's father offered to take Daniel into the family business, which had expanded and was doing well, and her mother was seriously upset. For the previous couple of years, the relationship with Margaret had (seemingly) been closer. Asking her why they were moving to California, Margaret said she didn't want to go, but Daniel was adamant. They knew Daniel had been married before and had a child (another half-sibling), speculating that he wanted to put distance between himself and his earlier life and possibly avoid child support.

For the first three or four years after they went to California, Margaret sent Christmas presents to Lloyd's children, and in the few years, her parents went out and visited two, possibly three, times. The last visit went very badly according to Lloyd. Previously Daniel had not been impolite, but during the last visit he was openly hostile. He acted as though he resented them and their efforts to keep in contact with Margaret. Appearing angry, he sat with a revolver on the table next to him as he glared at them.

In the next few years, Margaret called her parents to ask for money for a plane ticket home on more than one occasion. The first time they sent the money, but she didn't come home. The next time she called, her father offered to send the ticket, but not money. Upon hearing this she hung up. Sometime later Margaret called saying that she was in some kind of

Chapter 5 – An Uncle

unspecified trouble. Her parents contacted their minister and asked him to have a minister of their faith who lived in the area check on Margaret. It's not clear what he found out, but from various sources it came out she had lost her nursing license and Daniel threatened the minister with a gun when he showed up.

Sometime after this, mail was returned with no forwarding address. There were no calls and Lloyd completely lost contact with Margaret. Sometime in the late 1970s Margaret called to say she had remarried, to Stanley Birtwistle. When her father became ill and was in the hospital there were calls made. When he passed away, a ticket for a flight was sent to her and she returned to Grand Rapids the day before the funeral.

That night Lloyd and Margaret met, and she filled them in on some of the happenings in her life since contact was lost. The details weren't clear, and there were gaps and things she did not want to go into. She did speak at length about the numerous places she had lived with Daniel and how they would get behind in the rent and move out at night, skipping out on the rent. She said Daniel would often get connected with county or town law enforcement as a reserve officer, enjoying owning several guns and intimidating people. She mentioned their migration northward through California. She declined to describe how they parted and never mentioned putting a child up for adoption.

After many years the details were no longer clear, but several aspects of her story strained credibility. What grabbed everyone's attention was when she produced a 20-gallon trash bag and dumped out on the floor a huge array of medical paraphernalia, including bandages, tape, over the counter medications, prescription pills, etc. She went on and on, accusing her mother of treating her unfairly. While true, it was ill-timed.

After the funeral Margaret was anxious to learn the terms of the will and was visibly disappointed to learn that everything went to her mother. Before she left, Margaret wanted to know if Lloyd wanted her new mailing address and phone number. Lloyd told her he didn't need it since not knowing where she was had worked quite well for the past 20 years. He saw now how cruel that was, but the truth was she was different and had character traits he

Chapter 5 – An Uncle

disliked. He couldn't imagine a positive outcome from continuing communications and chose to not get involved.

There was no contact for four to five years until their mother had a stroke that left her bedridden. When she had a second stroke that left her in a coma, Lloyd called Margaret. (Their mother had kept Margaret's number.) Tentative plans were made for her to fly in for the funeral as death was thought to be eminent. Margaret's mother hung on for another 10 days so there were a few calls to reschedule the flight. The last time Margaret complained about the inconvenience of these changing plans. Lloyd asked if she'd rather have the money the tickets would cost and save the trouble of travel? She said to send the money.

The money issues had hurt her parents, and they were angry that she had broken off contact and avoided ongoing interactions. When they made out their will it directed the entire estate go the surviving spouse, and when the survivor passed, Margaret would get $1,000 and the rest of the estate would go to Lloyd. After their father passed, Lloyd had a long talk with his mother and convinced her to change the will. It then read that Margaret and Lloyd's three children would each receive ⅛ and Lloyd would receive ½.

Lloyd shared with me that his parents never told him he was adopted. He only found out by accident after he was married. He needed a copy of his birth certificate for a passport and the state mistakenly sent him his original birth certificate. He attributed the lack of disclosure on his parents' part as a sign of love and affection. He said he and Margaret never talked about adoption, but he assumed she knew they were both adopted.

He closed with what a sad tale it was. The fact that from the time she got married until their parents died there was almost no contact, interaction, or even communication.

I deeply appreciated the candor and honesty. It was a very sobering and sad tale, but at least I had now heard from Margaret's brother as well as the friends that knew Margaret and were in her life the last years of her life. While she had become estranged from her family, her friends in Deer Lodge were her real family, and that made me feel a bit better about the saga that was unfolding.

Chapter 6 – Montana

The next few weeks seemed to dissolve into a surrealistic blur. I no longer felt tethered in time. It felt like I was inhabiting several streams of time concurrently. While I could see everything unfolding in real time, I also felt like I was seeing the life Margaret and Daniel led back in the day.

Two letters arrived around the same time. One was from Lloyd summarizing the conversation we had on the phone and a series of copies of photos of Margaret from the time she was an infant up to a shot of her working in the area she homesteaded towards the end of her life. The other letter that arrived was from the Durand's. This contained two photos of Daniel and Margaret taken on Christmas Day 1972. One had Daniel looking down at a toy one of the Durand children was holding, while Margaret looked on. The other was the two of them standing in front of a truck. Daniel had a big pair of dark sunglasses on and Margaret was by his side, wearing a neck brace. I could definitely see a resemblance between myself and Daniel. Margaret's photos were the bigger surprise. She had red hair! I had always assumed both my parents had blonde to light-brown hair.

Words can't really describe what it was like for me after 50+ years to actually see what my birth parents looked like. I found myself spending a lot of time trying to correlate the pictures I was holding with the various stories that were relayed to me.

With continued calls to Montana, it was becoming clear we should go there and meet these incredibly generous and nice people face-to-face.

On Saturday, May 26, 2007, we went to the Fillmore in San Francisco to see Marianne Faithfull. It was somehow appropriate to sit in the fabled Fillmore auditorium and listen to songs of longing, loss, regret, and redemption before setting off on this journey. Very early Sunday morning, we departed for Montana.

Taking Route 80, we headed north towards Wells, Nevada, where we planned to stop for the night. On the way we stopped at Lovelock, Nevada, for lunch. The terrain and people had started to shift. In Lovelock I was fascinated by the rows of slot machines and with mostly senior citizens either in wheelchairs, on oxygen, and more often, both, parked in front. We arrived

Chapter 6 – Montana

in Wells early evening and checked into the motel. We had done some research online and found a highly rated Basque restaurant, Bella's Restaurant & Expresso. The reviews turned out to be accurate, and we turned in early.

We arrived in Deer Lodge early the next afternoon and checked into Scharf's Motor Inn as it was recommended by James and Sarah. The people at the front desk were very friendly and couldn't have been nicer, but the first thing we wanted to confirm was the wireless network advertised on their sign. The room they had reserved for us was to the right of the office, and when we turned our laptops on, there was no signal. They could not have been more accommodating as they gave us the keys to rooms further down at a right angle, within sight of the office. In some ways it felt like Goldilocks trying to find the right bed, but after two or three rooms, and some aiming of the router in the office, we finally achieved a useable signal!

I called Sarah to let her know that my husband Dave and I arrived, and she invited us to their home. We drove over, taking in the town on the way. A small town with a Main Street, the town seemed well kept and had a cozy small-town charm. In some ways it reminded me of growing up in Garden Grove in the 1950s. We arrived at James and Sarah's house and I was a bit surprised to see clumps of snow on some of the shrubs outside their house with it being late May. Sarah welcomed us in and told us James was at the cemetery putting flags up for Memorial Day. Two of her children (all of them now adults) were home and introduced themselves but went into another room to leave us alone.

We made small talk until James arrived and then we all gathered in the living room. They talked about meeting Margaret and Daniel for the first time, how both had become part of the family, and how after Daniel left, Margaret was still "Aunt Margaret" and very much a part of the family. While they racked their brains, some specifics (like who Daniel hooked up with once they moved to Red Lodge) escaped their memories. We talked for quite a while, or rather, they talked, and I'd interject with a question or two. I finally felt compelled to ask them who they thought I resembled most, Margaret or Daniel? There was a bit of hemming and hawing, and James kind of looked away saying, "When you smile, I can see a bit of Margaret." I took this translation to mean I favored Daniel, but I hoped they weren't going to hold that against me. We didn't stay too long as we were both tired from two days of driving. We crashed early and had a very solid night's sleep.

Tuesday was the real start of the visit. We made our way over to the bank to meet Tom Johnson. He brought us into his office, and we chatted for quite a while about Margaret. He didn't meet her until years after she divorced Daniel, so he had no knowledge or recollection of him. Margaret was living on a very fixed income, and on more than one occasion, Tom had stepped in to help her out of certain situations. The main takeaway from the conversation was Margaret was a character, but a likable one. He did say, if you got on her bad side, she would look right through you and keep going. One point of interest was that Tom had a box of Margaret's belongings. A selection of handmade wallets her husband had made for her, as well a very nice purse (tan suede with brown alligator skin trim and accents), and a notebook. The notebook was of particular interest. On the pages were the various amounts of money she owed various credit card companies, along with a page for each month where she would write the names and phone numbers down of a handful of close friends. It almost like she sensed something would happen and should someone come upon her and these notes, the appropriate people would be notified.

After taking up more of Tom's time than we should have, James had arranged for us to have lunch with John Murphy and Tony Smith at the restaurant in Scharf's. Both had worked with Daniel at the prison. John had been the lead investigator there and turned out to be a very friendly and funny man. Tony was equally outgoing, but John was definitely in his element and enjoyed hearing the 'dirt' on Daniel as well as telling stories of their time together. Neither of them really knew or interacted socially with Margaret.

Scharf's is across the street from the historic prison Daniel worked at with these men, and as they told me about their time there, I'd look over and catch a glimpse of the prison. The main street and town haven't really changed a lot, and I could easily picture Daniel entering or exiting the prison, or Margaret picking him up at the end of the day.

One thing that dawned on me was that Daniel vanished rather abruptly and left a lot of unanswered questions in his wake. Tony and John shared

Chapter 6 – Montana

anecdotes about Daniel and how, despite having a solid working relationship with him, they always felt something was off.

As John and Tony reminisced, they both started chuckling recalling a prank they had played on Daniel. During the time they all worked at the prison often there would be high-profile mob members and criminals held there while they were being transported for trial or incarceration elsewhere. One day someone noticed a big shiny black car parked out front. This prompted one of them to go up to Daniel and whisper in his ear, "Daniel. Did you see the big shiny black car parked out front? Two guys wearing dark suits with white ties sitting in the front of the car? They said they wanted to talk to you." At this point both John and Tony worked very hard to keep from laughing, saying Daniel turned white, and started looking about wildly. Daniel abruptly got up and headed for the back entrance of the prison. He didn't say a word to anyone and left. What made it stranger was he called in sick for the next few days, and stranger yet, he asked the warden to station an armed guard at the end of the driveway of the former toy shop where Daniel and Margaret now lived.

Tony said it was around this time he recalled the head of the machine shop had come up to him. The machine shop kept the vehicles for the prison running and Daniel had approached the head of the shop asking if they could modify his car with a switch, so he could turn off his brake lights. He said if he was being followed at night, he'd like to be able to turn his brake lights off so no one would see where he was driving to. This was brushed off as a joke. But it was one of the many quirks that stood out in their memory.

John said they often said Daniel was an enigma wrapped in a cipher locked inside of a puzzle.

A lot of the people who had worked at the prison now worked at the prison-turned-museum as docents. After lunch we were given a personalized tour of the prison by James. He explained where prisoners were kept, where social activities were held, showed us where Daniel's desk was, and walked us through what an average day there would entail.

While this was going on, John Murphy thought he could find some of the past issues of the prison newspapers with photos and stories of events he knew Daniel attended. He also went into the archives to see if he could locate Daniel's personnel file. As we were wrapping up, he had a furrowed

Chapter 6 – Montana

brow. He said in looking at the various photos and stories, he realized Daniel had managed to get out of the camera range for each. He was also puzzled that there was no employee photo in Daniel's basic file.

Wednesday was spent driving around Deer Lodge and the surrounding area. We spent time in the library researching newspapers and then drove out to Anaconda. A short distance from Deer Lodge, Anaconda was smaller than Deer Lodge and very picturesque. We drove out to Southern Cross Road at Georgetown Lake. It was a few miles out of town and was very scenic. We weren't sure exactly where Margaret had lived on the road but drove up the road and eventually turned back. We noticed a small diner on the corner and came back for a quiet dinner in Deer Lodge.

Thursday, we arranged to meet James and Sarah's oldest daughter Nancy in Helena. We took a scenic drive up to Helena – Montana is very beautiful – and drove around the city a bit. We stopped for lunch at the Brewhouse Pub & Grill and then went to the mall until it was time to meet Nancy at Perkins Restaurant.

Nancy was incredibly nice and shared many stories of Margaret. It was very obvious she had a deep affection for Margaret and still missed her. She also shared some stories of their time with Daniel. She said he taught her, and some of her siblings, to drive. She recalled him sitting out back and telling her the story of him being an orphan and growing up in an orphanage. He said one night in the orphanage he suddenly felt a presence from another world and his bed suddenly rose into the air, spinning round and round, finally coming back to the ground with a crash. She implied he wasn't telling the story to wind her up or scare her but seemed to really believe what he was telling her.

She went on to tell us about the last family gathering they had the summer before Margaret passed away. The entire family was at the lake, and Margaret had come down. They spent a lot of time together talking and Margaret was expressing care and concern for all the kids.

The next day James and Sarah met us in Anaconda. We had gone out earlier, drove around to get a feel for the city, and stopped at the church that ran the obituary. We didn't go in, as I didn't have a sense that they'd be able

Chapter 6 – Montana

to provide any more information than I received when I spoke to them on the phone.

We walked around downtown, and I was trying to envision my mother during the last years of her life interacting with the people here. James and Sarah eventually showed up and drove us out to Southern Cross Road off Georgetown Lake. We saw the small diner on the corner again, and a large field area across the street. We followed them as we went about a quarter mile up the road to a gate and what almost looked like homemade fencing. Behind the gate were two trailers, one with a porch/room built out of the front, a light pole with single halogen light and an unkept area. This trailer was where Margaret lived the last years of her life and where they found her body.

Apparently after divorcing Daniel she rented a room in downtown Deer Lodge, but at some point, she went camping where she met Stan Birtwistle. Stan was barely 5' tall and apparently had done rodeo riding in his younger years, even appearing in a movie, but the name now escapes me. He stood on top of the saddle; twirling his lasso as he rode. Apparently, they hit it off and it was not uncommon to see their truck barrel up to a restaurant in Anaconda and have them spilling out with two or three big dogs, laughing hysterically over something. Stan was quite a bit older. At first, they lived out on the old copper mine in Anaconda. One of the people we met referred to it as "the poor farm." There wasn't running water. They'd need to get a wheelbarrow and bring it up from a stream or well. At some point, the EPA showed up and said there was arsenic in the ground and water from the old copper mine, and they'd have to leave.

This was when they asked an acquaintance if they could homestead the area off Southern Cross Road, where they put the trailer down. This was where they had a huge menagerie of animals. Margaret was even in one of the local papers when they photographed her feeding a very large moose. Fish and Game had warned her to stay away from the animals as they migrated through as they could be dangerous, but she ignored the advice and fed each and every animal that crossed her path.

The gate was padlocked, but easy to jump over so we entered the property. We walked over to the trailers and I expressed interest in looking inside. Both James and Sarah got a bit of a pained expression and said I didn't want to go in. I appreciated their concern but crawled in through an open window. Sarah said when Margaret was alive, the house was pretty messy and dirty, with the exception of the bathroom, which was spotless. There was a potbellied stove that Margaret would keep stoked in the winter. She'd sleep in a recliner she kept nearby and would leave the door open so the goats, dogs, cats, or whatever could come in to stay warm. There was little left in the make-shift front area or trailer, other than debris that had accumulated since after Margaret's passing.

There was a cat prowling about the second smaller trailer. Sarah commented that it very was very likely one of the ones that had kept Margaret company. James and Sarah also took us out to a grove of trees a few hundred feet from Margaret's homestead. They said this was where they scattered her ashes. Margaret said lightning had stuck the area once, killing a cow in this location. Margaret was very taken with this section of the land and that's where her ashes were scattered. There were no real words to sum up how it felt being in this grove of trees knowing the woman who had given birth to me was now scattered here and I would never really get to know her or hear her own take on her life and history.

Shortly after the last family gathering at the lake Sarah said Margaret asked her to call and check on her daily. She didn't really say why, but it was obvious she felt something was up. Margaret shared with Sarah that the doctor wanted her taking Lipitor for cholesterol and come in for a medical procedure. On Labor Day weekend Sarah called, but didn't get an answer. She assumed Margaret might be out running errands, or possibly cleaning houses, which she did to pick up some extra money. When she didn't answer the next day, they contacted the sheriff's department to do a welfare check and they found her body. What was ironic was the samples of Lipitor her doctor had given her were unused, but her refrigerator was full of various medicines for her animals.

They also shared that Margaret had become somewhat fearful and paranoid the last couple of years before she passed away. She claimed she had spotted someone on her property at night and was afraid it might be Daniel. She had even gone so far as to get a gun. This frightened everyone. While she didn't talk about Daniel a lot, she checked in with Social Security to see

Chapter 6 – Montana

if he was alive and if she could claim any additional benefits, but they always said no.

James and Sarah headed back home, but we stopped off at the diner on the corner. It was a bit rough around the edges and was full of regulars. A very gruff older woman was filling coffee cups for people when she came up and asked if we were ready to order. I asked her if she knew Margaret, who had lived up the way. She got a suspicious look on her face and she said, "Yes" warily. I told her I was Margaret's son. She broke out in the biggest smile and said, "Are you going to inherit the trailer?" I explained that "No, but we were here to find out as much about her as possible." She said she didn't see Margaret that much: on occasion she'd come in and say she forgot milk or something from the store and ask to buy some from the diner.

While it was a bit disconcerting to see how rough things were at the end of her life, it was obvious everyone we spoke to had genuine affection for her.

We had made plans to take everyone out to dinner Friday evening to thank them for their generosity with their time and memories. While we were dining and discussing things, John Murphy said, "Oh, did you talk to Father Nikolaev?"

James and Tony both nodded and said "Yes, you should talk to Father Nikolaev."

I asked who he was. They explained he was a Catholic priest that came down and worked at the prison for a few days at a time each month. They thought he might live in Great Falls. They said he would stay with Daniel and Margaret for the weekend after he finished his week at the prison. My husband Dave sleuthed online and found three or four possible phone listings for Nikolaev and left messages. At this point, our plan was to leave first thing Saturday morning and head home.

As we were loading the car and getting ready to leave Saturday morning my cell phone rang. A big booming voice said, "Is this David Roundsley? Daniel and Margaret Andrews' son?" It was Father Nikolaev.

I replied, "Yes," and explained how we came to hear of him and that we were just about to leave Montana. He insisted he *had* to meet me and asked us to change our plans and drive up to Great Falls where he lived. We discussed the options for a few minutes and decided to change our plans.

Chapter 6 – Montana

We agreed to meet at a 24-hour coffee shop in Great Falls. We arrived about when we thought we would, and we were met by a big bear of an older man. He gave us both a hearty hug and said he was very pleased to meet us. We got a table and he was smiling and said, "Your father was a *very good friend* of mine." This was the first time during the entirety of my quest that anyone had come close to saying anything remotely good about my father or referred to him as a friend. He explained when he was no longer working at the prison, Daniel and he continued to talk on the phone on occasion. He was unaware of the reasons why Daniel left the prison, but he was in touch with both Daniel and Margaret when they moved to Red Lodge. Once when Margaret was up at Great Falls for a doctor's visit, Father Nikolaev arranged for them to go to a tea-leaf reader. He said when they read Margaret's, they said, "I see you in a large house full of children." He said Margaret was very pleased, as she was still holding out hope to one day have children and a family with Daniel. He said that was the last time he recalled seeing or talking to Margaret.

He also had with him a small oil painting. He said it was from Daniel and Margaret, but it was Margaret who had picked it out. It wasn't a particularly well-done painting, but it was oddly prophetic of where Margaret eventually lived, as it showed a solitary building in a large meadow surrounded by tall trees. Father Nikolaev insisted I keep it.

A short time after that, Daniel called him and said he had gotten involved with something he didn't know what to do about or how to get out of. His tone was worried, but he didn't go into any of the details. After that they lost touch. Father Nikolaev went on to say he and Daniel hit it off *very well* when they first met and whenever he was there doing the rounds he'd often stay with Daniel and Margaret during the weekend and head home the following Monday. By the time he met my father Daniel had already been promoted to Captain of the outside guard. When they'd do rounds inside, Daniel would go up to one of the many big-name mob prisoners and introduce Father Nikolaev to them on a first-name basis. There was a bit of a glint in his eye as he described Daniel's familiarity with some of the bigger names in organized crime. He suggested I track down a book about Las Vegas in the

Chapter 6 – Montana

1950s called *The Green Felt Jungle*, saying I might find some of the information useful in my search.

He said I definitely took after my father in looks but commented my father was much slimmer. The few pictures I had seen showed a very slim, possibly too slim man. We left and were made to promise to stay in touch and keep him posted on anything I might uncover about my father.

It took two very long days to drive home to California. After driving through the nether depths of Idaho with our windshield almost opaque with insects, we decided to stop in Elko, Nevada. We were going back through Wells when police lights went off behind us. They said we didn't come to a complete stop at the stop sign. We explained the long drive, and the officer saw Dave was a veteran, so he let us off with a warning.

We got home late Sunday night, thoroughly exhausted, but feeling the trip had been more than worth it.

Chapter 7 – The Private Detective

I kept in continuous contact with Martha attempting to find out what became of Daniel after Margaret divorced him. While she was able to zero in on Margaret instantly, Daniel Joseph Andrews became a very different proposition. I'm not sure how her search methodology worked, or what data she had, but nothing was forthcoming. At this point, I went to a couple of websites and was overwhelmed with the number of Daniel Andrews out there.

I talked with Sarah and James several times and with each conversation, different pieces of information came to light. While they didn't know who Daniel had fathered a child with after moving to Red Lodge, or even where he was, James recalled Daniel coming through Deer Lodge around 1979 trying to contact Margaret. Daniel called James, and James, somewhat taken by surprise informed Daniel that Margaret had passed. This would have been amusing, as James projected a very Jimmy Stewart type of honesty. Apparently, this wasn't believed, and Daniel eventually tracked down her phone number and contacted her. Margaret relayed she wasn't quite sure what it was he wanted from her when he called, but she was remarried at this point. And then Sarah recalled he was going through the area on his way to the Tri-Cities area in Washington! This didn't really resonate with me, but I relayed this to Martha. It was the breadcrumb she needed and took things to the next level. She quickly located Daniel in Kennewick, Washington. She informed me that he had remarried.

I went to an online background check company and filled in the data that I now had. A massive file came back showing several addresses, and what appeared to be two bankruptcies. No phone numbers were listed – just addresses and bankruptcies! At this point in time, I didn't have a good feeling about Daniel at all but felt it necessary to push through. I sent a letter to the last address listed from my search results, introducing myself, not going into much detail about what I already knew and had discovered, and sent my contact information. Days passed and there was no reply. I then sent a registered letter, with essentially the same information. When I received the

Chapter 7 – The Private Detective

proof of delivery card, it said it was signed for by Lisa Peterson. That name didn't show up in the background searches. Again, days passed with no reply.

While I had the option to head up there in person, after sending out several dozen letters to various Daniel Andrews around the country (and getting a few replies that they weren't the Daniel Andrews I was looking for), I wasn't 100% certain this was the right Daniel Andrews. I wasn't ready to make the trek up to Washington. Yet...

In the meantime, my adoptive father called, and we worked our way through the newsletter issue. But when I told him I had found my birth parents, and Daniel might be in Kennewick, Henry blurted out, "STAY AWAY FROM HIM! HE'S A BAD MAN!"

This was new! Especially after decades of vague statements, the worst being he was self-centered and didn't want to be bothered with a child. I asked what he meant, but he said he needed to go and abruptly hung up. When we talked a few days later he denied saying that but cautioned me to think about it and to go slowly.

While it seems a bit fantastic in hindsight, after discussing it with my husband, we thought we should see if we could engage a private investigator local to Kennewick to confirm if this was indeed the Daniel Andrews I was looking for.

I searched online and amazingly found a private investigation agency one town over. I called the office and talked with a (what I assumed to be a young) man named Marlon. I explained the situation, we discussed fees and I engaged him.

Two days later I received a call from Marlon. Marlon said he went to the address I had provided. He said the house stood out from the others in the neighborhood. They had a fence with "Beware of Dog" along it in regular intervals, a locked gate leading to the door, security cameras, and a doorbell by the garage. He rang the bell and he said a stern woman came out from behind the security screen. He explained who he was and that he was representing Daniel's son who had been placed for adoption. She said "this isn't a good time. Please go away." What was interesting was she didn't say, "You have the wrong Daniel Andrews" which she very easily could have done.

Chapter 7 – The Private Detective

What then began was a regular stakeout of the residence. What Marlon noted was the woman left around 8 in the morning, but often returned around lunch, then left again, returning sometime in the afternoon. After establishing this pattern, Marlon waited until she left and rang the doorbell by the garage. There was no answer. He continued doing this sporadically over a period of days. One day he reported an older man was seen near the house walking a German shepherd. Marlon followed the man as he returned to the house but was unable to catch up to him before he entered the building. Again, no answer to the doorbell. The house in question was on a corner, and the way the house around the side was banked, he could walk up and get a clear view of the backyard. He said he observed the man who he assumed was Daniel sitting out back with the dog, staring off into space.

By this time, we were now in to almost a month. I explained to Marlon we couldn't have surveillance go on indefinitely. Daniel and who I assumed was his new wife were obviously aware of Marlon and not going to engage. I told him he should find a woman to try and make contact. Two days later Marlon notified me he had a co-worker who went by. When she arrived, a young woman was sitting in the front yard with the German shepherd. His operative arrived smiling and casually said, "Oh, is Daniel home?" The young woman on the lawn said, "Oh, they went to the store. They'll be home this evening." The operative smiled and said, "Okay, I'll try then. Bye."

I knew Marlon and his co-worker were going to go back that night, but I cautioned him to be *very* careful. I explained Daniel had a history of having guns and had pulled them on people, including clergy. Marlon said he'd take care. He also asked me to send a current photo of myself. We had recently done a photography class that had us do headshots as part of the course, so I faxed him the most current photo I had of myself.

Along with the photo I sent a letter for Marlon to present:

```
Dear Daniel.
    My name is David Roundsley and I am the child you
and Margaret Van der Westhuizen-Andrews put up for
adoption in Long Beach, August 1955.
    Through a search I did on the internet, I was put
into contact with people who knew you and Margaret
```

Chapter 7 – The Private Detective

> in the Deer Lodge area of Montana and they directed my search to the tri-city area of Washington, and you.
>
> I discovered Margaret had passed away in September of 2005.
>
> If you would be so kind, I would like to talk to you when it is convenient, or if you wish, meet you in person.
>
> The couple that adopted me provided a solid home environment and I've had a good life.
>
> I am a graphics designer, with my own web design company, and a musician, having released an album last year.
>
> If possible, I would like to know a bit about my birth parents' life and health history.

Martha had also offered to talk to Marlon and gave him some guidance on what to say and proceed with Daniel.

And I waited.

… and waited.

After three days, and sincerely worried something bad had transpired, I finally heard from Marlon. He hemmed and hawed a bit and explained what had happened. On the night in question Marlon and his associate went back. There was no evidence of a dog out front and the porch light was on. Bypassing the buzzer by the garage and jumping over the gate they went directly to the front door. The door was answered on the first ring, and Marlon said the man standing in front of him was without a doubt my birth father and the man he had seen earlier. In looking at my picture and seeing the man standing in front of him, the resemblance was overwhelming. At this point in time my hair was cut in a flattop as was Daniel's. Marlon said they talked for about 15 minutes.

My father indicated they didn't keep me because he said Margaret was involved with three other people. (I didn't believe this statement for a moment, as Daniel had gotten very possessive of Margaret with her own parents and no one who knew them could imagine him tolerating her talking to someone else, let alone getting involved, unless he was involved) He said he was having marital problems, and things weren't stable in his home life. He also indicated there were some medical issues but refused to elaborate.

Marlon said Daniel seemed to tear up looking at my picture as Marlon informed him of Margaret's passing. When asked if there were any other children, Daniel said I was the only child he knew of. (again, I knew he had a daughter with a woman in Montana, as well as the first child referenced in Lloyd's first conversation with me) (though this could have "technically" been the truth if he was referring to any other children with Margaret) Marlon said Daniel did not want to take my photo, letter, or Marlon's card, but after pressing it to him one final time, he took the items.

Marlon explained he hadn't called me sooner as when he has done similar attempts in the past, the people usually relent after a couple of days and call requesting a meeting. But Daniel did not call back, and Marlon said he was sorry.

In the meantime, I updated Father Nikolaev and several people in Deer Lodge. While they knew some of the darker aspects to Daniel's past now, a few people volunteered to write Daniel letters directly. He never replied to any of them.

I thanked him and called Martha to update her. She was very understanding and felt that if she could get Daniel on the phone, she'd be able to change his mind.

At this point, I knew I would need to go there in person.

Chapter 8 – Knocking on the Door

My husband and I decided to drive to Kennewick and knock on my birth father's door. As we were now into fall, the end of October felt like the right time to go. Not only was my birth father's birthday on the 23rd, so was the wedding anniversary of my adoptive parents, so we decided to go to where Henry and Dinah now lived, take them to dinner for their anniversary, and then head over to Kennewick.

Thankfully, the weather was clear, and we did the drive straight up to the hotel in a little under 12 hours. We let my parents know we had arrived and crashed. The following day, the 23rd, we went over to their home and spent the day with them and then took them to a restaurant they had heard good things about. It was an overall pleasant evening, but there was an undercurrent of tension during the visit. It could have been a byproduct of the fallout over the newsletter, or it could have been they now knew I was going full-on into my birth search and would be leaving to try and meet my birth father the following day.

We finished dinner, dropped them off at home, and went back to the hotel. I was entirely too wound up to fall asleep easily, and when I did it was fitful and full of dreams. I woke up an hour before the alarm. I got up, logged into my computer, and reviewed all the notes and reports I had acquired since February 2nd.

We hit the road late morning and drove east towards Kennewick. The weather was clear, traffic was light, and we made very good time. We rolled into Kennewick around 12:30. We were too early to check in to the hotel, so we decided to drive by the address I had for my birth father. There was an SUV parked in the driveway, so we assumed his wife, the one who had barred communications with Marlon, was home. We kept driving, exploring the town a bit. We had lunch and were able to check in to the hotel a bit early.

As it was the day after my birth father's birthday, I had purchased a birthday card and wrapped up a CD of my debut album I had released in 2006. Not knowing if someone would answer the door or not, inside the gift bag was a simple note wishing him a Happy Birthday and letting him know

Chapter 8 – Knocking on the Door

we had come to Kennewick in hopes of meeting and included my cell phone number.

Late afternoon we drove over again, and the SUV was no longer parked in the driveway. We parked across the street. I stopped and paid more attention to the neighborhood and house. While not the most upscale neighborhood, it was a well-kept and nice street. I looked at the house and didn't see the forbidding signs Marlon had described. There was a fence around the front, but it was a simple white picket fence made of a vinyl composite. There were no "Beware of Dog" signs visible. I also didn't notice any of the security cameras he had described. Had he invented these to make the task of surveillance seem more pressing? There was a doorbell/buzzer on the garage by the gate though.

We opened the gate and walked up to the front door. There was a security screen, and on it was a brass plaque that said, "The Home of Mr. and Mrs. D. J. Andrews". There was a lawn swing on the porch, a few pots and a sign hanging by the door saying "Trick-or-Treaters Welcome" with a pumpkin design. My heart was beating hard, and my breathing was far too rapid. I could not recall a single moment in my life when I was as nervous and tense as I was when I pressed the doorbell. I strained to listen if I could hear the bell ring. I'm not sure if it was my nerves, the rush of blood pumping in my ears, or what, but I didn't think it had made any noise. While I didn't want to lean on the bell annoyingly, I pressed it one more time. The neighborhood was very quiet. No traffic had gone by, and no one was out on the street or in front of the other homes. We stood there and waited. Finally, after what felt like an eternity, I knocked vigorously on the door frame, being unable to open the security screen and knock on the door itself. I stood back a bit from the door and held my breath.

There was no reply and the stillness of the neighborhood seemed to have an oppressive weight. After what was probably only five minutes (but felt like hours), I left the gift bag with my CD, birthday card and note at the front door and we left. Unsure of how things would go, we drove to the local mall and walked around. I kept checking my phone to see if I'd receive a call, but it remained silent. We went out for dinner, where I picked at my food. We decided to drive back by the house after dinner. Twilight was fading into

Chapter 8 – Knocking on the Door

night, and as we drove by, we saw the outside lights on. The entire yard looked like an athletic field with very high-powered lights all around. We could see the backyard was very visible. We could also see my package was still sitting at the front door. We drove back to the hotel, where I had another very fitful night's sleep.

The next day there was no call. We drove by the house, and the package was still sitting at the front door. We went for lunch and spent some time walking around the mall. We went into the Burlington Coat Factory and found two very nice trench coats with removable liners that would be good for winter weather.

After killing some time, we went back to the house late afternoon. The package was gone! I checked my phone to see if I had missed a call, but it was empty. We parked the car and we made our way up to the front and again my heart felt like it was beating a million miles an hour as I steeled myself to ring the bell again. As I was about to do this, Dave stepped to the side and was peering through the blinds on the picture window on what was probably the living room. I hissed at him, "What are you doing?" He calmly said, "The place is empty."

It didn't really register at first. I said "what?" and I walked over and peered in. Indeed, there wasn't a stick of furniture in the place. All sorts of scenarios played through my head. Were they having the carpets cleaned? Repainting? Ordering new furniture? I found it puzzling as in the front their name was still on the doorplate and there was outdoor furniture and the Halloween sign up.

We went back to the hotel, and I immediately entered the address into Google. In a matter of seconds, the page showed the house had just sold and showed the listing agent. From what I could gather the house hadn't been publicly listed. But it showed the home sold. I called my sister whose birth mother was a realtor. I asked if she could ask Jackie to look up the transaction and give some insight on the sale. Jackie was disinclined to get involved, but my sister offered to call the realty office and inquire for me. She called back a few minutes later and said she called the agent and explained I was Daniel Andrews' son and had come to town to meet him. The agent seemed friendly and said she'd relay the message and asked that I call the office in an hour. I

Chapter 8 – Knocking on the Door

waited and called. Whoever answered the phone said the agent was unavailable. I asked if I could leave my number and they replied that it wouldn't be necessary. I suspected she contacted my birth father, and he told her not to relay any information back to me. While disappointed, I can't say I was surprised. I suspect between my two letters, the private investigator and the various letters from old friends from Montana, it was obvious Daniel did not want to be found or contacted.

An exhaustion like I had never felt before set in as we left the next morning to head home. We drove south, entered Oregon and made our way back home.

The first thing I did when I got home was to start a string of searches online and it showed Daniel Andrews was now listed as living in Pendleton, Oregon. In looking at the map I realized we had not been all that far from where they were as we were heading home. I also realized there would be no point in either going to his new address or writing any more letters. He would not respond.

What I did was find the local newspaper online, and bookmarked the obituaries, as I felt that was going to be where I'd find my birth father.

Chapter 9 – Waiting…

As 2007 rolled into 2008 some things surfaced about my birthparents, but for the most part it was relatively quiet. I would do searches online from time to time, but it wasn't something I thought about continuously. Around mid-2008 I started a public blog. I was curious about both my birth parents and decided to post all the pertinent information I had up until that point. Their names, ages, dates, and locations of where I knew they had lived, and what key life moments I had confirmed. I asked if anyone knew about the life and times of Daniel and Margaret Andrews to contact me.

One of the highlights of 2008 was the chance to meet Margaret's brother Lloyd, his wife Janine, his son Rob, Rob's wife Nancy as well as their daughter, her then-husband and two friends of Lloyd's. They had come out to California to tour wine country, and as it turned out, a former student of Lloyd's lived in the same city my husband and I lived in. Lloyd contacted us and the plan was to meet at the home of his former student. I extended the offer for them to come up to our place, but I was told (quite firmly I might add) we were to meet at the original location. I wasn't sure what to expect, and it was a tad intimidating to join such a large group, feeling outgunned and outnumbered. After a couple of glasses of wine, the afternoon became quite convivial, and as more wine was consumed at a Mexican restaurant in Palo Alto, it turned into a lovely day.

A few months after the blog was up, I was surprised to get a note from Sean Roberts. It turned out he had dated Margaret when she was in nursing school. They had gone out a few times and he was sufficiently smitten with her that after he was called into the service, he tried to keep communications open by sending letters. He said she replied at first, but the responses dwindled off quickly to become few and far between until there wasn't any correspondence going on at all. Upon his return home he looked her up, only to be told she had run off with a man she met while doing a nursing rotation. Sean was very nice, and he gave me the name of a woman who was Margaret's roommate in nursing school. When he and Margaret were first dating, he had been to Margaret's family home and had met Margaret's brother Lloyd about the time Lloyd married Janine.

Chapter 9 – Waiting…

I did a search for the woman who roomed with Margaret and found a phone number in Michigan. I called it and left a message but received no reply. A couple of months later, when I least expected it, I received a call from her. She explained she had been unwell and had spent some time in the hospital when I called. I could tell she was trying to frame her remembrances and wording carefully, but the essence was that Margaret enjoyed partying and men once she was finally out from underneath her mother's tyrannical thumb. "Fun" was the first thing that came to mind when she thought about Margaret during that time. I sensed hesitation about going into too much detail, but what came through was Margaret wasn't having any problems attracting attention from the opposite sex and was enjoying the freedom to explore this.

She said the pivotal moment for Margaret came while they were still roommates. Margaret went home for a weekend but when she came back there was a change. She knew Margaret's relationship with her mother was strained, but during the weekend a fight happened, and her mother exploded and said "you're not my daughter! You were adopted!" This started a whole reassessment of who she was and her place within the family. As she had to get up an hour earlier than her brother, make his bed, she now felt like she was adopted just so they'd have "help" around the house. And this also cast a new light on her relationship with her brother. She now could see why they treated him like the little prince while she was treated like a second-class citizen.

She explained their time together wasn't that long after they started doing rotations in various hospitals around Michigan and after Margaret met Daniel and they left Michigan, there hadn't been any further correspondence or contact. She always wondered if she would have run off with Daniel had that horribly mistimed fight and outburst had not taken place.

I received a note from a woman in the Georgetown Lake region who had known Margaret and she put me in contact with another woman who had also known Margaret. I contacted her and she didn't have too much more to add to what Margaret's friends had already shared. But she did have one new story. She said Margaret had spoken about being adopted and had searched for her birth mother. She said Margaret had found out her mother had come from a fairly well-to-do family, but the scandal of having a child out of wedlock was not welcome, so she was put up for adoption. What was even more interesting was shortly thereafter I was connected to another woman online from Montana, and she relayed a similar story, but with a big difference. She said Margaret had sought out her mother and found she came from a very poor farming family who couldn't shoulder another mouth to feed as the Great Depression had begun. Margaret said it was ironic her mother had put her up for adoption thinking she'd have a better life with the well-off family that adopted her, but she said she would have been much happier living a simple life on a farm.

The most interesting conversation took place around June. I received a note from a man who was the Deputy Warden at the prison in Deer Lodge at the time Daniel worked there. I asked for his phone number and settled in for a nice conversation. Roger Davis said he had been at the prison for a while when Daniel was hired. He rose very quickly through the ranks and was made Captain of the outside guard.

As was the practice with officers, Daniel and Margaret were invited to dinner with his wife. As everyone started the first course Roger asked what had brought Daniel and Margaret to Montana? Daniel looked at Margaret and said, "Should we tell them?" Margaret nodded. Daniel then said, "We were living in Southern California, and I was servicing vending machines at the time. One of my larger clients was an aerospace firm. I found it easier to fill the machines at night after the company had closed. It must have been sometime around 10 or 11p.m. when I was filling the machines. All of a sudden, a door opened and out stepped a middle-aged man. He had rolls and tubes under his arms, some of the rolls looking like blueprints, along with an attaché case. He turned, startled to see me standing there and gasped. His sudden appearance startled me as well. As the man scurried off down the hall, tossing glances back at me as he made a hasty retreat, I realized I had probably just witnessed espionage! Shortly after that, I felt that I was being followed and watched. I was also sure someone had broken into our apartment and had been going through our things. When Margaret came home from work, I presented her with my suspicions and findings. We felt the only option was to disappear. We gathered everything we could carry and

Chapter 9 – Waiting…

placed it in the car, and took off in the dead of the night, leaving the lights on in our apartment." No one knew quite what to say at this point during the dinner, and conversation was quickly diverted towards more mundane and acceptable dinner topics.

Things continued to go well with Daniel's career at the prison. He got involved with several initiatives and wrote up a few propositions to better the prisoner environment and trying to improve the efficiency of operations. As time went on, Daniel's behavior started to change. He became moody and seemed to be under some type of stress.

"Shortly after Christmas 1972, Daniel showed up at my office. In a very somber tone, he asked if we could speak privately. I asked him to step into my office and shut the door. Daniel sat down but didn't make direct eye contact. He was visibly upset so I asked what was up. He replied in a somewhat shaky voice, 'You didn't give me a Christmas card this year.' Stunned and surprised I said, 'Daniel, all of the officers received Christmas ***gifts***. Only the rank-and-file received Christmas ***cards***.' Daniel's voice caught, and I sensed he might be tearing up, then he said, 'It's just not the same.'"

After talking this through a bit and taking into account other changes in Daniel's behavior Roger had noticed, it was suggested the job might not be a good fit at this point and Daniel might be better off looking for employment elsewhere.

Shortly thereafter, Daniel tendered his resignation and eventually found a job as an assistant deputy sheriff in Red Lodge.

Sometime after this I was in communication with Lloyd and shared the story of Daniel's dramatic narrative of leaving southern California. Lloyd broke out laughing. He said Daniel had probably been embezzling from the vending machine company and they were on the brink of pressing charges. They left in the dead of the night to avoid prosecution and/or paying their rent.

Chapter 10 – A New Family

Towards the end of 2008, Dave's father became ill. His health was going downhill and in February of 2009 he passed away. We spent a lot of time in Arizona as his dad went into hospice care, then afterwards to try and help get his mother settled.

In the meantime, my mother had her own health issues. She had fallen and broken a hip and was diagnosed with breast cancer after that. She had undergone a double mastectomy and was quite frail. We were often up in Washington or down in Arizona visiting our mothers.

Opening the browser window to the obituary page had become routine. While it was a daily ritual, and I obviously had some expectation of what I'd eventually find, seeing my birth father's picture and obituary on June 25, 2009, still caught me by surprise. The picture staring back at me was certainly the same face I had seen from the pictures James and Sarah had sent, but obviously older. His face was thicker, he was wearing what looked like a late-1970s checkered blazer, and his hair was *much* darker than the pictures from 1972. He wasn't smiling, but looked like someone had asked him to, which resulted a (very) slight uplifting on either side of his mouth, but still maintaining a stern gaze. What followed in the obituary was even more surprising:

```
Obituaries – Daniel Joseph Andrews
   October 23, 1927 – June 24, 2009
   Pendleton – Daniel J. Andrews, 81, died
Wednesday, June 24, 2009 at The Pines in Pendleton.
A funeral service will be held at 11 a.m. Saturday,
June 27, at Smith Mortuary Chapel in Pendleton.
Vault interment will be held at 1 p.m. Monday, June
29, in the Pomeroy Cemetery in Pomeroy, Wash.
   Mr. Andrews was born Oct. 23, 1927 in Detroit,
Mich., to Alex Frederick and Beatrice Bagnowski
Andrzejewski. He joined the Navy Seabees and
following basic training he served on the Battleship
Texas in the Pacific and Hawaii during WWII. He was
honorably discharged in 1946.
```

Chapter 10 – A New Family

```
    His occupations included California State Patrol,
Montana Deputy Sheriff, chief security officer in
Deer Lodge, Mont., and customer service
representative for Pitney Bowes, from which he
retired in 1993.
    Mr. Andrews is survived by his wife Sue Ellen;
sister Myrtle Schmidt; stepdaughters Lisa Peterson
(I now know who signed for the registered letter I
had sent earlier) and Karen Robbins; four
grandchildren; three great-grandchildren; and
numerous nieces and nephews.
    He was preceded in death by his brother Donald
Andrzejewski and sister Kathleen Jones.
    Memorial contributions may be made to the
Salvation Army in care of the Smith Mortuary of
Pendleton, P.O. Box 123, Pendleton, OR 97801
    Smith Mortuary of Pendleton is in charge of
arrangements.
```

What happened to him being an orphan? No mention of Margaret or the woman he hooked up with while still with Margaret. No mention of a daughter, and now there's a father, mother, and three siblings? Unlike the experience with Martha or talking with the people in Deer Lodge and elsewhere, this was no swirling vortex of memories. The first identifiable emotion was anger. While I had a suspicion the man was a compulsive liar, there was evidence now to support that in front of me.

Seeing Daniel's obituary on a Thursday with the funeral planned for Saturday, we had a discussion about if we should try to attend or not. Having made the trips to Montana, Washington, and Oregon, we knew it would mostly likely entail two long days of driving. And the fact Daniel's wife, Sue Ellen, had rebuffed the private investigator, not notified me of his passing, or notified the daughters he had, I felt my presence would be viewed with hostility. At this point I had little warmth or kind regards for the man who was my birth father and felt meeting him for the first time at his funeral would not have accomplished much.

Chapter 11 – More Family

I went to Ancestry.com. I had been on the site before, but believing my father was an orphan and my mother's parents were deceased, I hadn't even bothered to attempt creating a family tree. Armed with the information from the obituary, I created a family tree. As anyone who has worked on this site knows, it can start matching *hints* that show up as a small leaf next to the person's name. I immediately got a hint for Daniel.

It brought up the name Delores June Todd as possible wife to Daniel! Was this the woman he attempted to kill Margaret to be with? Was this the woman he had a daughter with? After months of not much new being revealed, I was now submerged in a heady crush of information.

The first thing I noticed on the information tethered to Delores' profile was it indicated she was deceased. But it also pointed to another tree, the *Smith* family tree. There it indicated Delores and Daniel had a child, Arlene. But again, it indicated *she* was also deceased. I couldn't help wondering if perhaps what Daniel hadn't been able to accomplish with getting rid of Margaret, he had with these two women?

I searched online for information on Arlene, and a Facebook profile of a man, whom I (correctly) assumed was her husband came up quickly. Up to this point, I had not been a Facebook user and really had little interest in joining, but the only way to look at this page was to become a member. So, I signed up for a Facebook account. I searched the page of Arlene's husband looking under friends there was Arlene. There was no mention of Arlene being deceased, so I went to that page. It looked like she might be alive, but other than a handful of friends, there were no pictures or information to tell me much about this Arlene.

What happened next probably should go down as one of the more unfortunate Facebook moments in history. Here I was a new user, with that generic icon, no friends, no history, nothing, and I sent a direct message, "Were your parents Delores Todd and Daniel Andrews?" Immediately I received a reply "Yes." I replied with "Daniel has passed away and I believe I'm your half-brother." The moment I hit "Send" I knew it was monumentally bad, but I was caught up in the moment. What surprised me,

Chapter 11 – More Family

was almost instantly I received a reply, "Interesting. I'm off work in two hours call me at…"

As surprising as it was to confirm I had a half-sister, what followed was even more so. She didn't sound surprised at hearing of Daniel's passing or of the existence of a half-brother. There was a 'been there, done that' tone to her voice. She sounded mildly interested at the information I presented, but not overly so. She *was* offended and justifiably angry at not being notified of his passing or mentioned in the obituary.

What unfolded over a couple of hours was her long and at-times harrowing tale of growing up in a continually shifting and unstable environment. When I mentioned it was quite startling to now have a half-sister, she replied, "No. You have three." She went to explain Daniel had one more daughter after her with her mother, Audrey, but the most intriguing part of the story was an older third sister. (this would be the child Margaret's family assumed Daniel was trying to avoid child support for) Apparently, Daniel had left the family for a time after Audrey was born. After relocating to Washington, he contacted Delores and asked her to join him so the family could be together. They joined him in March of 1978, but by December Daniel had asked for a divorce.

What followed was Delores going on a rampage to obtain as much information as she could about the "orphaned" and very secretive Mr. Andrews. The first thing Delores uncovered once they separated were phone records, quite a few, all calling the same number in Michigan. She soon discovered this was his sister, Myrtle. This triggered further digging and she happened upon a criminal complaint. Daniel had been married and had a daughter, Danielle. In the complaint, Danielle had been severely scalded. At the time of the complaint, it was looking like she would not survive and if that were to happen, Daniel would be charged with murder! From what Delores could find, Danielle didn't succumb, and charges weren't pressed. But what happened afterward remained a mystery.

At first, I wasn't sure if Arlene and I were connecting, but it became apparent her favorite topic of conversation was herself. She indicated her younger sister liked to keep a very low profile and had changed her name. She also indicated she and Delores (who was NOT deceased) were not on

Chapter 11 – More Family

the best of terms. The conversation started to feel like a riptide, where you're pulled under and are struggling for your footing and oxygen. There were no pauses or conversational openings. After a rather long conversation (which felt like the world's longest run-on sentence), I needed to call an end and we agreed to speak again shortly.

Looking online a second obituary had appeared with much less information. I shared both obituaries with Arlene, and presumably she shared them with her sister and mother. I did start to look for Danielle but found absolutely nothing online. Had she passed due to her injuries? Was she disfigured due to what Daniel theoretically did to her? I wasn't finding anything.

I told Arlene to share my contact information with her sister and mother but hadn't heard from either of them. After talking with Arline over several days, she casually mentioned she had *forgotten* to pass on my information. I was mildly annoyed but not totally surprised as I had a feeling, she was trying to keep me and the information I had provided to herself. A couple of weeks later I received an email from Audrey, and we set up a time to talk on the phone.

Audrey was much more grounded than her older sister and supplied more family history, background and context on their dysfunctional upbringing. Both girls were saddled with an unstable upbringing from their father *and* their mother. Both had challenges to overcome, but I sensed Audrey had done better with the circumstances handed to her.

I definitely felt more of a connection with her, but I also sensed both women had a much narrower and more provincial outlook on life.

By this point, with the information provided by both, I was confirming conclusions about Daniel and his life. As I had previously had success with people from his and Margaret's past contacting me, I updated, expanded upon, and even threw in some conjecture on my blog. I had a fax line I seldom used, so at the bottom of the blog I included that phone number, now connected to a message machine, and asked anyone who had known Daniel or Margaret to please contact me.

By this point in time Arlene, Audrey and myself were brainstorming about how to make actual contact with Sue Ellen, and hopefully get some

Chapter 11 – More Family

answers in the wake of the many questions now laid before us. Upon returning home one afternoon, I noticed the message machine attached to the fax line was blinking. We NEVER received calls on the line, not even wrong numbers or telemarketers.

I pressed play for the message. A woman's voice came on in a very terse clipped tone, "David? This is Sue Ellen Andrews, Daniel's wife. I saw your blog. Call me at…" One of the challenges had been to find a phone number for the Andrews household. I knew from the stern tone of her voice it was not going to be a friendly call. As I had already spent a fair amount of time and money trying to contact them, I wasn't in a rush to return the call. Considering how much effort, time, and expense had gone into the search, I felt it best not to reply, but to think about it long and hard before responding.

I shared this information with Arlene, and she jumped at the chance to reach out. She had briefly lived with Daniel and Sue Ellen during a troubled spell with her mother. She also mentioned Audrey had spent a week with Daniel and Sue Ellen when she was much younger. She called the number and left a message but received no reply. After several days I gathered my copious notes, cleared my head, and worked on grounding myself before dialing the number.

There were only two rings before the phone picked up. The same voice and tone on the answering machine said, "Hello." I identified myself and there was forced pleasantry as each of us asked how the other was doing. Once we had gone past the pleasantries, Sue Ellen got right to the point. "I saw your blog and I want you to take it down." While I had anticipated this, I had a flash of anger what with being rebuffed and ignored when I reached out to them, knowing Daniel's two youngest daughters had been denied closure or acknowledgement, so I calmly replied "No. I've been looking for Daniel now for over two years, I've interviewed countless people from all over the country, and I have carefully researched it all and stand by everything I've included in my blog."

Sue Ellen replied she found the blog very upsetting. I told her I could see why it would be. After a pause she said, "I'll make a deal with you. Take the blog down and I'll answer any and all questions you have." This was

Chapter 11 – More Family

something I had not anticipated. I immediately started weighing the pros and cons. On one hand, the blog had actually been a success in finding people who knew both my birth parents and I was immediately concerned there might be more people out there who might find it and contact me. On the other hand, I had also purposely slanted the narrative to paint Daniel in the absolute worst light possible... though keeping within the facts that had been presented to me.

I took a deep breath and recognized this opportunity would probably never come again, so I agreed to this Faustian bargain. I could hear give a sigh of relief and I began asking questions about health. One of the biggest holes in your life when you're adopted comes to light every time you see a doctor. The first question is always, "Does this run in the family?" I found answering, "No, I'm adopted" didn't always register as an answer, so I learned to circumvent it with, "I am an orphan."

What started out with general health questions slowly became more personal. What started out with a wife defending her husband's honor started to reveal doubts, uncertainties, and showed the marriage was not always a smooth and happy one. Some of the things relayed to me were surprises. Sue Ellen said she and Daniel got up every morning and studied the bible. Here was a man who had lied and cheated on his wives, scalded a daughter, left children fatherless across the country, and now is studying the bible. Really??!!??

She also relayed a story of one time there had been an argument and Daniel got in his car to leave. Instead of letting him leave, she jumped on the hood of the car and hung on until he came to a stop. This certainly fit the narrative of a man who was prone to leaving. When questioned about the exclusion of Daniel's daughters in the obituary and the lack of notice about his passing, I received a rambling excuse about being unprepared for his passing and things happening so quickly. Oddly, she did say she considered contacting me as she kept the letter and picture the private investigator had given to Daniel. I also asked if she knew where Danielle was. She indicated this was the first she had ever heard of an older daughter of Daniel's. At the end of our call I thanked her for her time and answers and agreed to remove the blog. Very reluctantly I removed the narrative of the blog and exchanged

Chapter 11 – More Family

it with a high-level outline of the timeline of my birth parents' lives and places they lived and worked.

A few days after speaking to Sue Ellen, I realized I still had questions. I called her back and to my surprise, she answered my new round of questions. What I thought would be 'just one more call' turned into a series, and over time the wariness both Sue Ellen and I had given way, and a real friendship started to develop.

Chapter 12 – Delores

And then an email arrived from Delores. Up until this point, Delores had been more of an abstract concept instead of an actual person. Arlene didn't talk about her a lot but was very dismissive of her when she did. Audrey on the other hand seemed to have a more complex relationship. Of the two, she was definitely closer to her mother and talked about still visiting her in Montana from time to time.

On a Saturday afternoon in July we had just gotten back from running errands when I checked my in-box and there was an email from Delores:

```
Hello David, what a pleasant surprise to find out
about you.
    I'm going to put on my "thinking cap" and write
down things I remember about your biological father,
Dan. I can imagine you want to know as much as
possible about him, but I have to warn you, not much
of it is pleasant to hear, and it's not easy going
back down memory lane to remember everything because
I've put it out of my mind for so long.
    I met him in the fall of 1974 when I was being
physically abused by my then husband, Ted, and Dan
was the deputy Sheriff. Dan and another deputy
responded to my urgent phone call and they made sure
I was allowed to leave the home with my two sons, in
a safe manner. At the time I lived south of Laurel,
MT just across the line in Carbon County. Red Lodge
is the County seat of Carbon County.
    For some reason, Dan kept in contact with me and
even went so far as to call a beet farmer in Silesia
who agreed to rent me one of his "shacks" where the
Mexicans lived when working for him in the summer.
Dan dropped in on me every day or so to check on me
since I didn't have a phone way out in the country,
and he was my HERO because I was terrified of Ted.
    Dan told me he was living with a woman, in
Joliet, MT, but they were parting ways, who I later
found out was your biological mother, Margaret, and
that he was not married to her. In fact, he said he
```

Chapter 12 – Delores

had never been married, never had any children. He also said he was 4 years older than me, which I found out was untrue – he was 14 years older.

I found a job in Billings, MT, after living in Silesia for a couple of weeks (those beet shacks are COLD) and rented a tiny apartment in Laurel, MT. By the time I got my divorce, I was relying heavily on Dan as a friend and continuing protector since my former husband, Ted was still threatening to kill my two boys and me. Ted even tried to run me off the road, but I managed to escape. Then Ted found out where I worked and left a threatening note on the windshield of my car; I planned on leaving Montana to get away from Ted, but Dan asked me to move in with him at the Joliet house and I did. He told me the woman he had been living with had moved back to Deer Lodge where they had lived when he was a guard at the prison.

Dan was secretive about his past, saying he did not know his parents and been raised in an orphanage in Detroit, Michigan. He said didn't know if had brothers or sisters. He maintained throughout our relationship that he had never been married nor had any children, which I later found out to be untrue.

I was without a vehicle of my own at this time and borrowed his older blue pickup to go into Laurel for a doctor's visit.

I have to admit that I never loved Dan Andrews and that I lived with him for protection at first and then because he was the father of my girls. I want to mention here that Dan was never loving or kind to my sons, Bruce (age 2½) and Harvey (age 1½). He basically ignored them and if they wanted to sit on his lap or hug him, he pulled away. He often said things like, don't touch me, your hands are dirty, or your hands are sticky even when they were fresh out of the tub. I'm getting a bit personal here, but Dan was extremely under-sexed. The average of being intimate was approximately once every six months. He told me about deviant (in my mind, not his) sexual behaviors that he and Margaret had engaged in while

Chapter 12 – Delores

living in California and when he asked me to do these things, I refused.

    This was probably the reason I didn't "turn him on". He was a VERY needy person, expecting me to wait on him hand and foot and be at his beck and call at all times. Things changed dramatically once I became pregnant, with Arlene. He said he wanted to kill my son, Bruce who is mentally slow which got on his nerves, and even went so far as to show me how it could be done without suspicion, i.e., Dan wanted to push him down a high stairway from the upper bedroom. I didn't take him seriously and he dropped the subject. He was very unhappy when I got pregnant with Arlene and asked me to get an abortion, but I refused.

    I borrowed his old blue pickup one day to go to Laurel for a doctor's appointment. As I pulled to the curb in front of a store in Laurel, the brakes went out. There were no cars in front of me, so the pickup coasted slowly to a stop. The ford garage was a block away, so I went there, and they hauled the pickup into the shop and put it on the rack. The repairman checked things and then told me, "Lady, someone is trying to kill you cuz the brake lines have been cut." I called Dan who came to get me, and he said someone was after him and trying to do him in. At the time I didn't suspect him of trying to kill me but after we divorced, I realized he was in fact trying to get rid of me, my two boys and our unborn child. I will admit to being naïve and too trusting.

    One day when I was in the upstairs bedroom, where the boys slept in the Joliet house, Dan came upstairs which was unusual. When I went to go down the stairs, he attempted to push me, but I held tightly onto the rail and then insisted he go down first – I think we stood up there for 20-25 minutes before he finally went down ahead of me. He said he had tripped and fallen against me – he said he did not push me although I was suspicious at the time, he talked me out of it. After all, he was a deputy

Chapter 12 – Delores

sheriff and what were the odds I'd end up living with another man who wanted to do me harm?

A few days later as I was walking across the living room, he ran up behind me and pushed me very hard – I almost went to my knees but ran and managed to keep my balance. I was very upset with him for doing this and that day I went to Laurel and rented a small apartment for myself and the boys, having a lady friend come and get me and to move our few possessions into town. We had no furniture, just a few toys, clothes, etc.

In a week or so, Dan too moved into Laurel, renting a very nice, big apartment over a store. Luckily my tiny two-room apartment was fully furnished but I had to go on welfare to live, since I was pregnant and could not work. Then Dan lost his job as a deputy sheriff (he wouldn't tell me why) and he found a job at the Mall that was being built in Billings as a night watchman. He eventually talked his way back into my life and we moved into a small three-bedroom house. He was on his best behavior and even smiled at my boys and was pleasant to all of us.

However, one night a woman with a stocky build and long black hair came to our house when Dan was gone. She was angry and threatened to harm me unless I'd let Dan marry her. She said her name was Shari Green and she worked nights at a bar south of Laurel and she and Dan had been dating for several months. I didn't believe her until she showed me Dan's wedding ring on HER finger, wrapped w/tape so it would fit her. I was truly shocked. When I told him about her when he came home, he tried to deny it but her having his ring on her finger pretty well said it all. She came back again when he was there and he went out and talked to her, out of my hearing, and she never came back. I don't know how long he had known her, but he did tell me I didn't want mess with her (talk to her) cuz she was tough – got into bar fights, etc. He would not tell me any details about her – how long he had known her, etc.

Chapter 12 – Delores

He was at work the night Arlene was born in October. A day or two after she was born, my ex Ted came to the house saying he wanted to see his sons. Dan was so jealous he insisted we get married. (we had wedding rings but hadn't worn them as hadn't gotten married). As I said, I didn't love the man but in order to give our first child together legitimacy, I agreed. We were married in Cody, Wyoming on Nov 6, 1975. Once our daughter was born, Dan made over her and insisted on feeding her and would sit and stroke her face with his little finger, which totally surprised me. However, once Arlene got older, he ignored her.

I got a job in Billings and we lived in a nice mobile home in Laurel. I became pregnant with our second daughter during this time. Then we moved into Billings where we rented a lovely and expensive 4-bedroom duplex two blocks south of the hospital. Dan now had a job with Pitney-Bowes as a maintenance/repair man. He had the northern route and would leave Monday morning and go as far north as Glasgow, coming back Friday evenings. In the summer of 1976, Dan told me we had to file bankruptcy since he had not paid the bills for the considerable work done on the Joliet house, which he wasn't making payments on. He had told me Margaret was going to move back into that house and make payments, so I had not been concerned but obviously that never happened. We filed bankruptcy, which ruined my excellent credit, February 1977, a few days before our second child was born.

By this time, Dan and I were barely speaking. He adamantly insisted over and over that I have an abortion and I steadfastly refused. He told me if I didn't, he would move out. When I went into labor with Audrey, he and I took the kids to the babysitter in Laurel and then he took me to the hospital, leaving me on the doorsteps. He would not go in with me nor stay with me during labor. I was alone when Audrey was born and when I asked afterwards if Dan had come back or called, I was

Chapter 12 – Delores

told no. The next morning around 6 a.m. he called and snottily asked me, did I have ANOTHER girl? I said yes and he hung up. I didn't hear from him again and when I went home from the hospital, a lady friend took me to Laurel to get the other kids and then took me home to the duplex. All of Dan's things were gone and so he had meant what he said. The rent was due within a week and I called the bank to check on the balance and was shocked to find the account was empty. Dan had not only moved out, but he had taken all of the money in our joint account. As I recall, I had about $20 in my purse. I called my mother in Olympia for help and she sent money, and my dad came up from Sidney, MT, and helped me with groceries and more money. I couldn't pay the duplex rent.

I was desperate but was able to find a low-income rental within a day or two and my lady friend and grown son moved all of our things. I went back to work when Audrey was only a couple of weeks old, having convinced the Dr. to OK my return to work because of my financial situation. I don't know where Dan was, and he didn't call or come around. I found out later he had lived in an apartment for 3-4 weeks and then moved to Richland, WA through a transfer with Pitney-Bowes. He did not write or make contact until the end of February of the following year, 1978. I was quite surprised when he called from WA to tell me he wanted the kids and I to move there and be a family again. At this time, I had a good paying job with an oil company and didn't want to move but I was foolish enough to let him talk me into doing so AFTER he came to Billings and spent a week with us. He said he had accepted Jesus as his savior, was going to church, reading the bible (he read it while he was there in Billings) and he seemed a changed man, to the point where at his suggestion we renewed our marriage vows in church prior to moving to Richland.

We moved to Richland, WA, in March 1978, renting a two-story home. I worked from April through

Chapter 12 – Delores

December and one day when I came from work, all of Dan's things were gone. I had been suspicious prior to this because he'd say he had to work over-time... on a Sunday, for example, at the Pitney-Bowes office. Not only did he not answer the phone but when I drove by to check on him, his car was not there. This man could lie so well you couldn't help but believe him – believe me, I was duped enumerable times. He finally admitted he had been involved with a someone at a hospital, Sue Ellen, and that he wanted a divorce so he could marry her. I readily agreed to the divorce and at his request, I filed and went to court in 1979 – he didn't show up nor did he pay child support nor call to check on us or see the kids. Nothing. I was quite bitter back then. I quit working and ran a day-care for kids in Richland until we moved to Sidney, MT, in 1981.

    I hired an attorney to get child support, but he made such unreasonable demands that I cancelled things. We moved to Sidney, MT, and during that time I would occasionally check with Social Security to see if he was collecting disability or was in fact still alive and thus found out he WAS on disability. When filling the paperwork, he had claimed no children so Social Security was quite surprised when I furnished proof of Arlene and Audrey's existence. The girls were able to collect under his disability.

    There was no contact until the time Arlene was having emotional problems and running away from home. As a last-ditch effort, I called information for Dan's phone number and was told it was unlisted. The operator agreed to call Dan and give him a message, saying it was urgent he call me. Surprisingly, he did and he even agreed to have Arlene come stay with him for a while. She can tell you about this experience, but I can say it wasn't long before she was back home with me once again. Audrey also wanted to meet her father. I had his phone number from having called Arlene and she talked to him. He refused to talk to me and shortly thereafter I got a letter from his attorney wherein

Chapter 12 – Delores

I was advised Dan had agreed to Audrey's visit. He sent a plane ticket but not trusting him to return her in a week, I insisted he sign and send me an agreement to the effect he would not keep her against my will. He refused, I insisted, and he capitulated but unfortunately, I did not get the agreement until late afternoon of the day of her early flight to WA, so she didn't get to go. She did spend some time with him in 1992, which was disastrous. I'll let her tell you about it.

What I've told you will probably bring up enumerable questions on your part and I will do my best to answer anything you want to know.

In my opinion, Dan was a hard, cold, unloving man who showed little emotion – it was an unusual day when he smiled. He was not affectionate in any sense of the word. He wanted someone to take care of him, to be at his beck and call and when that wasn't forthcoming, he'd pack some clothes and his toothbrush and move in with a guy friend for anywhere form a few days to a couple of weeks. He never told me where he was and during the time away, he never called.

He didn't like getting his hands dirty and in fact, I dumped the garbage 99% of the time. When he did, he made a big fuss about it and would wash his hands quite thoroughly. Same with the kids – if he touched them, he had to wash and wash. He loved sugar, despite the fact it gave him gout at times. His favorite was STORE BOUGHT white cake with white frosting and he did not like homemade cake. He would get home before I did and make his own dinner – when I came home, I cooked for the kids and myself, plus did the dishes. When he was upset with me, which was often, he would often go to bed before me and when I'd come to bed, would switch to the couch. He would go days without speaking to me or the kids.

After the divorce I got to wondering about a lot of things – so much didn't add up. The first thing I did was check for a divorce decree and lo and behold, I found one between Dan and Margaret. The

Chapter 12 – Delores

decree said they had been married in Nevada – I forget the date – so I wrote and got a copy of that as well. I had found out his TRUE AGE when I was reading the VA paperwork when he bought the house in Silesia and was truly shocked to find out he was 14 years older, not 4. He denied it, said the VA had birth year wrong but I didn't believe him. I also found out at that time that Dan's given name was Andrzejewski and that he legally changed it to Andrews when he lived in Deer Lodge, so I wrote Detroit for a copy of his birth certificate in that name.

   This was before all the privacy issues and I was able to get it. It showed Joseph Andrzejewski as his father, mother's name (Beatrice Bagnowski??) and that he was the 4th child! Surprise, Surprise. I don't remember HOW I found out about your sister, Danielle but welfare sent me a copy of paperwork about her – Dan had been married to I think it was Mary who was a nurse but she had TB, which she gave Dan. He had to go to solarium (??) for treatment and I guess this is where he met Margaret, who was a nurse there. I didn't find out about this until my girls passed on that info to me from your website. Anyway, Danielle had suffered severe burns form boiling water and both Dan and Mary gave her up for adoption to Dan's aunt Eleanor Andrzejewski.

   I spent a lot of time at the library (this was before computers) and wrote enumerable letters to Andrzejewskis in the Detroit area – only got a few letters back saying, sorry, don't know Daniel or Eleanor, etc. I was able to find names of Dan's siblings, Myrtle, Kathleen and forgot the brother's name. Unfortunately, I gave these papers to my youngest daughter a few years back and she can't find them. I really want to find Danielle which I was unable to do but luckily found out about YOU, which is a blessing.

   David, I want you know that you were only one of four kids (that I know about) that your father had nothing to do with. I know from my girls' how heart

Chapter 12 – Delores

breaking this is, and also from personal experience because my own mother left me when I was 4½, and took my brother, 2 years younger, to remarry and have another daughter – who is 9 years younger. She had very little contact with me – no phone calls, a meager present at birthdays and Christmas. I actually saw her once when I was 12 and took me to Sidney for a day visit where she totally ignored me. Also lived with her for a couple of months when I was 15, which did NOT work out at all… I won't go on and on about how hurt I've been by her uncaring and indifference, but just want you to know I empathize and sympathize with how you must feel.

When I was little, I cried for her many nights, missing her and wondering how she could leave me… then I figured out it must have been because I was such a terrible person. After all, she took my little brother. Then I graduated to hating her when I was in my late teens. I first started talking to her when I was in the abusive relationship with Ted, but I could tell she wasn't interested in my problems. She did LOAN me money at times which I always paid back. I didn't see her for years—I'd ask to come to Olympia, and she had enumerable excuses, all of which proved untrue until I finally surprised her with a visit 3 years ago in Sept., 2 days after her birthday. She was in early stages of Alzheimer's and had cancer—she died the following January 2 ½ years ago. I went back for her funeral and thought I would literally die from the emotions that coursed through me… didn't realize how rejected I had been throughout the years – I'm one who always thinks things will get better, the forever optimist – Audrey calls me Polly Anna. Despite everything, I still remain P.A. ha-ha

Anyway, this is not supposed to be about ME but about your father, but I guess things get intertwined.

The good things about your Dad is that he didn't drink – he did smoke. He paid the bills on time, when he was with me at least. He was a dependable and responsible worker and never had a problem getting a job. He never beat me, but I do feel he wanted to kill me on those two occasions (stairs and brakes on pickup). He was neat and clean-well dressed – showered daily, kept nails clean and neat, wore his hair in a crew cut until after he moved to Richland and then let it grow out. His hair was thin and hard to keep in place – used hair spray. He also shaved under his arms—and used deodorant. Always looked neat and clean.

    I honestly feel he NEEDED to be taken care of – Mary was a nurse; Margaret was, and Sue Ellen might have been one too. I have the personality of a care giver but with little kids, could not devote as much attention to him as he needed. He would actually be unreasonable about attention – for example when I was pregnant with Arlene and he worked the night shift – he would call me repeatedly during the night and be angry that I wasn't awake and thinking about him. I was up all day with the boys and a woman is especially tired when expecting.

    He loved to buy tools, but they would sit in the packages unwrapped – he never used them.

    After he and I were divorced, I wondered at his secrecy – was he involved in the Mob? Did he do a crime and was hiding for that reason? There has to be some reason that his sister won't talk about Dan's past and why he lied to me about things. I doubt any of us will ever know WHY now that he is gone.

    I hope you won't take all the negative things I've said about Daniel to heart – you are a special entity of your own.

    I used to ask God, WHY did you give me the parents I have? (My father wasn't who would have asked for and then I ended up with the wicked stepmother from hell, like in the story of Cinderella when I was 8). Then I read a wonderful book that changed my outlook on being left behind.

    I have a few pictures of your father which I would be happy to copy and send to you. I'd also

Chapter 12 – Delores

```
like to send you a copy of the book that changed my
life.
    Audrey said she gave you my phone number. Please
feel free to call and visit. If you want pictures
and it's OK, I'll send you the book, you could give
your address then. I'll only have the internet for
about another week.
                                    Sincerely, Delores
```

I was stunned by the amount of information and the candor of Delores's email. I had to reread it several times for it all to sink in. I printed a copy out and let my husband read it. I called her that afternoon to thank her and we ended up talking for over two hours. We hit it off immediately. From that point forward, we often exchanged at least one email each day, often more, and spoke on the phone several times during the week.

I called Father Nikolaev and shared the discovery of Delores and her very candid letter. One of the things that came out of this phone conversation was Father Nikolaev had been reticent to share with me previously, but Daniel and Margaret were swingers during their time in Montana. From what Daniel shared with him, this behavior started when they were still living in Southern California, where it was easier to find like-minded people. When they had migrated north, he said he believed they relied on an underground magazine where people could post personal ads. While this disclosure didn't surprise me, what did surprise me was the lack of judgement in Father Nikolaev's voice.

Upon sharing Father Nikolaev's information that Daniel and Margaret were swingers with Delores, she paused, took a deep breath and then said, "Your father enjoyed having people *relieve themselves* on him in the bathroom. This was something I was ABSOLUTELY NOT about to indulge, tolerate, or encourage. He never brought it up again after I expressed my disapproval."

For some reason, hearing these aspects of my birth parent's past were not surprising or shocking to me. By this point I would have been more surprised if had been told they worked with the poor or disadvantaged.

Between the things Delores shared in her initial note and the various conversations along with Lloyd's summation that Daniel *was* a sociopath, I was not sleeping well. It wasn't uncommon for me to wake up at 2 or 3 o'clock in the morning. When this occurred, I'd get up, see what was on the TV, and then search the web for more clues or information. One night I woke up and scrolled through the guide to see what was on and it was a documentary about the Zodiac killings in San Francisco. I had the volume on low and I was going through my notes when part of the program caught my attention. This part of the story was focused on the killing at Lake Berryessa. A man wearing a hood tied a couple up and attempted to kill them. The woman died, but the man survived. While the Zodiac was tying them up, he talked to them and he said he had escaped from the prison in Deer Lodge, Montana! I immediately flashed on his propensity to intimidate people, his personality, and for a fleeting moment, I wondered if Daniel could have been the Zodiac killer? In all likelihood he wasn't, but the fact he was in Southern California when they suspect the first killings took place, migrated north up to Montana, a small part of me still wonders. There were many superficial things that didn't dissuade me from thinking Daniel might be the Zodiac. The sketches, rough as they were, could easily be Daniel. The only different item was glasses, which could have been an effort in disguise. The flattop haircut was something Daniel wore from his time in the military until his passing. Also, the personality traits discussed in the documentary matched (a bit too well) those of Daniel's, from his enjoyment of intimidating people and the need for recognition for his brilliance.

Chapter 13 – First Family Member Meeting

My mother's health was declining rapidly in 2009. After a visit in May where we needed an ambulance to take her to emergency, my father and sister felt assisted living was necessary. We came up a couple days before my birthday in August and went out to visit her in the care facility they had selected. It appeared this was one of those "McMansions" that sprang up during the dot-com boom, then fell into foreclosure when the bottom fell out of the market. The home was run by a Romanian family. They had a very gruff demeanor, and I sensed they were doing this as a last option vs. any desire to offer meaningful care. My mother looked incredibly frail and didn't always seem to be with it. My father seemed visibly uncomfortable being there. I wasn't left with a good feeling about her care, but this was a decision my father had made.

With three-way communications going on between my half-sisters and their mother, we had discovered Audrey lived less than three miles away from where my adoptive family was living. We made arrangements to meet her and her family for lunch that Saturday. While I wasn't nervous, it felt very surreal as we waited at the restaurant. I had never met anyone I was physically related to and didn't know how I'd feel or react. A short while later, an attractive woman with an older husband and a teenage daughter walked in. We hugged (a tad awkwardly, as I later learned Audrey wasn't a hugger) and asked to be seated. We were shown a table with one side against the wall with a built-in bench, and chairs on the other side. The host offered one of the chairs facing the wall to Audrey and she strongly replied she never sat with her back to the room and sat on the bench facing the room. At first, I thought she was kidding. She was not. This caused me to pause and think about some of the things I'd come to learn about Daniel, but we sat down and had a pleasant meal.

Audrey was articulate and funny with an acerbic edge. Her husband didn't say much. I learned he was not the father of her daughter, who didn't seem very interested in the meeting or meal.

We discussed what I had discovered about Daniel, learned more about Audrey's life in Montana growing up with Arlene, and about her eventual

Chapter 13 – First Family Member Meeting

marriage and move to Washington. I thought the meeting went well and we agreed to stay in touch.

Chapter 14 – A Door Closes, A Door Opens

As August rolled into September, Dave and I were on the way back home from a memorial for his cousin George. My phone rang and it was my adoptive sister. She was with my mother and my mother was trying to communicate with me, but her dementia had progressed to the point it was hard to figure out what she was trying to say.

About a week after the call my sister called to inform me my mother had fallen, was in the hospital and fading pretty fast. I got the first plane up to Washington the next morning. It turned out the attendant at the home my mother was in put her in a wheelchair but didn't secure her while they got the shower going. She fell and bruised most of her left side and face. I hadn't had a good feeling about the facility when I was there before, and sadly my suspicions were now confirmed with this level of negligence. I went to the hospital and my mother was unconscious. I sat with her for quite a while and finally said, "It's okay for you to let go". Around 2 a.m. that night, the call came that she had passed away.

Dave had driven up that day, bringing my laptop, a scanner, and anything we might need, as the plan was to continue on over to Great Falls, meet Delores in person, and also introduce her to Father Nikolaev. We spent a couple of days in Washington, and then headed out for Montana. The one thing we hadn't planned on initially was the weather in Montana in early October: snow! We stopped by a local department store and purchased two overcoats, plugged in our GPS, and headed out. We started climbing through the mountains in late afternoon and soon realized along with the snow, we no longer had a cellular signal. We also noticed almost no traffic. While the roads were clear enough not to be a hazard, we had mild concerns that should something happen, we'd have no way to reach help.

We pulled into Great Falls just as evening started to descend. When we booked the hotel, we asked for an upgraded room. The hotel clearly dated from the 1940s or 1950s (at best!). We made our way to our room, which had definitely seen better days. But the oddest feature was, as we entered, where there had clearly been a wall by the bed, was now an open space, that led into an area that had clearly been a bar / lounge at some point in the

Chapter 14 – A Door Closes, A Door Opens

hotel's history. The bar was still there, along with stools, but no alcohol, drinks or glasses were there. They had added a couch, but it gave the overall space a very odd, incomplete feeling. The only effort to modify the room, other than removing the wall, was to seal the door that went out into the hallway from that area. Otherwise, the room was pretty much the way it probably was when it was a lounge. You almost expected to see Dean Martin come in and could visualize a piano in the empty space that now existed by the window. In looking round the room, it had a serious "The Shining" vibe going on. Every time I went around the corner into the "lounge" portion, I half expected to see a bartender from a bygone era standing there offering me a drink.

I sent a message to both Delores and Father Nikolaev to let them know we had arrived safely and made plans to meet the following day. Downtown Great Falls was not particularly busy and almost had a deserted feeling to it that night.

The next morning, we went out for breakfast and checked out the downtown area. It was still rather deserted and seemed like a movie set from a bygone era. Delores came down and met us. I told her about our oversized room and welcomed her up to chat, but she said she was uncomfortable doing that, so we agreed to go for coffee. After being thrown off by her discomfort about coming up to our room (I have no idea what she thought might transpire), she relaxed when we settled in for coffee. She marveled how much I took after Daniel and shared much more about her time with him, her own upbringing, and the challenges she had raising her four children – essentially by herself. She told us about (yet another) unfortunate relationship she got into once she knew things were over with Daniel. At this point, it seemed she had exclusively been involved with less than great partners. She explained she was currently married but was in the process of getting a divorce. She explained they had been divorced previously but reconciled and remarried. I was mildly amused when she told us she had asked her soon-to-be-again-ex-husband, "Should we use the same lawyer we used last time?"

She asked a lot of questions about what I had discovered and uncovered, and some of the answers triggered memories she recounted to us. As the day

Chapter 14 – A Door Closes, A Door Opens

wore on, she seemed to relax more and more. After we finished lunch, we asked if she'd like to join us for dinner. She said she would. We also asked if she'd like to meet Father Nikolaev. She said she had something she had to do first but would meet us later at his home.

I called Father Nikolaev, and he was fine with Delores coming later. We drove over to his home, checking out more of the city. I'm not sure why, but to me, Great Falls felt like time had passed it by more so than the other areas of Montana we had visited so far. It just felt like the clock had stopped at some point. We found his home and made our way from the street up some perilous, cracked concrete steps, through a seriously overgrown border, and to the front door. We rang the bell and eventually Father Nikolaev appeared. A large man when we last saw him in 2007, he seemed much heavier and not well.

He beckoned us into an overcrowded living room: it wasn't quite an episode of "Hoarders" but working on getting there. The house was quite warm, and there was a distinct cat box odor, making it a bit uncomfortable. Other than the outward changes, Father Nikolaev was as vibrant and upbeat as when we first met him. He was anxious to hear all I had discovered and about the ill-fated trip to Kennewick. Delores showed up a bit later, and she was visibly more uptight than she had been at lunch.

They both shared their stories with and about Daniel, and the fact there was this connection between the two of them and they had lived within the same town for all these years, but never crossed paths. We were probably there an hour or longer, but it was apparent Father Nikolaev had gotten a bit winded. We invited him to join us for dinner and gave him the address and time we'd be there, and we all left.

We went back to the hotel, and I jotted down notes from the many topics covered over the course of the day.

We cleaned up and headed out for dinner. Delores met us promptly, but we kept waiting for Father Nikolaev to show up. I called his number, but it went to voice mail. He never showed up, and when we touched base later, he said he had misheard the information about dinner. I suspect he was more winded from our meeting than he let on and just didn't have the energy to join us. We had a nice meal, talked some more about Delores' life, how her

Chapter 14 – A Door Closes, A Door Opens

two older sons were doing. Bruce, the oldest, was just going into a half-way house for the developmentally handicapped and her second child, Harvey, was doing time, ironically, at the new state prison in Deer Lodge, for a serious felony charge.

We called it a night and went back to the hotel. The plan was to drive down to Deer Lodge and visit James and Sarah. It was surprisingly snowy on the way down and it took longer than we anticipated. We arrived around 4:30, but it was already getting dark. We checked into the hotel, unpacked, and met James and Sarah for dinner.

We met at the restaurant across the street from the motel and caught up on what had been going on in our lives. As the meal was winding down a woman, slightly older than myself, was making her way by the table. James called out to Brenda and asked her if she remembered Daniel and Margaret Andrews. Brenda immediately stopped, and in a rush of words, without catching her breath, she started recalling Daniel having an affair with one of two sisters. She couldn't make up her mind which of the sisters Daniel was having the affair with and was seemingly almost talking to herself as she tried to work through who Daniel *was* sleeping with. In the midst of this, with both James and Sarah looking a bit uncomfortable, James cleared his throat and introduced me as Daniel and Margaret's son. She stopped, smiled, said it was a pleasure to meet us and then went on to recount how Daniel almost made her an alcoholic. She said at that time they had the apartment above her, and around five o'clock each night, Daniel would flush the toilet twice as a signal for her to come upstairs and start drinking. Both Dave and I thought she was hysterically funny, but James and Sarah seemed uncomfortable. She never figured *which* sister Daniel was seeing, but said it was nice meeting us and cheerfully went on her way.

We stayed the night and then headed out early the next morning for Oregon.

Chapter 15 – Oregon

As we were going to be returning home via eastern Oregon, it made sense for us to stop and actually meet Sue Ellen. While our conversations had thawed considerably, there was still a bit of tension that hadn't completely resolved itself. After all, I had written a blog that painted her "beloved Daniel" as a man who left a trail of wrecked relationships and destruction. For the most part she had been painting a rather idyllic picture of their almost 30 years together, but each time we spoke, something would come out, or creep into the conversation. Sue Ellen was shocked by the items I had posted online (and had now removed) and challenged me on how I could know such things again. I explained to her the vast number of people I had spoken to on the phone, met in person, exchanged correspondence with, and how all the various stories and remembrances fell into place, syncing with each other, despite seeming unrelated.

One thing Sue Ellen did was send me the eulogy for Daniel. This had my eyes crossed and head spinning while I read and reread it several times to take everything in:

```
A Brief Synopsis of the life of Daniel J. Andrews
Read by Lisa Peterson at Daniel's Memorial Service
     June 27, 2009
     Daniel was born and raised in Detroit, Michigan.
He was cared for and schooled by the Catholic Nuns
from the time he was 6 months old until he went into
high school. They favored Daniel because of his
beautiful "Palmer Method" handwriting. He would sit
in the back of the school room copying work for
them.
     The high school he attended was a big square gray
building and referred to as the "brain factory."
Thus, those attending were a privileged group of
young people and had to attain a B average, or they
were immediately dismissed.
     Daniel remembered the day Pearl Harbor was bombed
and started scheming as to how he could enlist. He
was only 16 at the time, and finally convinced a
```

Chapter 15 – Oregon

stranger on the street to go with him or bribed would be a better word. Daniel bought him a new shirt and tie and slipped him some "coin" and Daniel was off to basic training. Following basic training they were put on a train and headed for California. Daniel remembers that the Salvation Army was on board and offered everything "free" to the solider boys; never forgetting their generosity and repaying them a monthly tithe until his death.

He boarded the Battleship Texas and off they went to Hawaii. The one thing that always impressed Daniel, upon departure, was hearing one of his favorite songs Ave Maria. He along with those, that never got seasick, would ride the big 16" guns during severe storms.

Following his stint in the service he signed up for the Korean War, however, was never called to service.

He went back to Michigan, traveling to New York and Chicago earning enough money to keep himself in pocket change ending up in California. Taking several small jobs, such as painting and working maintenance for an apartment building, always looking to better himself and thus working for 3-M setting up and managing vending machines on Marquart Air Force Base utilizing his talents to get Pepsi and Coke in. He was always proud of his negotiating ability to bring in a company the size of Coca Cola.

Daniel always the thrill seeker, listening to the police scanner, and encouraged to apply for law enforcement. He applied for the academy and joined the rank of officers to serve in the San Bernardino Sheriff's Department. He found a dog named big Sam, who would follow the school children, riding the school bus and Daniel identified him as "street smart." Thinking the impossible he found out who owned big Sam (A cross between a German Shepherd and a St. Bernard.) The owner told Daniel that he could not do anything with him, so Daniel told him that he would like to have him trained as a K-9. The owner was more than thankful to have him taken off his

Chapter 15 – Oregon

hands. This initiated the love Daniel had for German Shepherds, owning 3 during his lifetime. Big Sam and Daniel went off to K-9 school and became a successful team. However, during a liquor store holdup one late night, Daniel and Sam pulled up, and big Sam knowing that the man coming out of the liquor store had a gun, jumped in front of Daniel taking a hit, and dying in Daniel's arms. To this day, Daniel could never tell this story without crying.

Daniel found reason to leave California and headed through the Dakota's and ended up in Montana. Working as a Deputy Sherriff and afforded the opportunity to apply to work at Deer Lodge State Prison. Never failing to once again better himself, working his way to the Captain and Chief Security Officer. He loved working in this type of environment, always trying to make life a little better for the cons. He brought in a library, worked them on a fire team, and had a Christmas party for them and their spouses, a first for the prison. In face he has a letter written by the con's thanking him for his trust of them to do this.

Daniel had more than nine lives. He was shot, stabbed twice, rolled many cars in high speed chase, rear-ended time and time again, held hostage for 5 days hand-cuffed to the steel springs of a bed, yet still loving every minute of it.

He left law enforcement, thus sending him out job-seeking one more time. He applied for a position, using the expertise he had gained when working for 3-M accepting an offer from the world-wide company of Pitney Bowes. He worked 17 more years as a customer service rep. making sure everyone had the best possible customer service ever.

One thing Daniel always told me was that the Sisters taught them to sew, and iron as well as instilled in them the knowledge to always learn 2 jobs, just in case one never worked out.

Chapter 15 – Oregon

> Daniel and I met in February of 1978, when he visited the office that I worked for setting up a Pitney Bowes copier. I would never ever call him for service on the copier, thus always tearing the machine down the last nut and bolt fixing it myself. Until one day in December of that same year, he stopped by and asked me out to lunch. I moved to the Tri-Cities and went to work for the Sisters of St. Joseph of Carondelet the very best place I ever worked, and meeting friends for a lifetime. We married in October 1979.
>
> Daniel wanted once again, to have a German Shepherd, so we purchased a female that we named SamiSu. She was a wonderful friend and companion and her ashes have been placed with Daniel for a ride along side-by-side to heaven.
>
> Our second German Shepherd came 10 years later, this one being 12 weeks old and sired by a long-haired shepherd brought over from Berlin, following the cold war. KoJo together with a German guard daily walked the fence between the east and the west. This shepherd we named Tsar Bear Cyr-Newton Andrews. A beautiful companion and life-long friend, and so smart we had to spell names we were talking about, or else he would get so excited thinking they would be on the door step any minute.
>
> When Daniel was admitted to St. Anthony's this last time, Tsar grieved himself so, he didn't want to be alone without Daniel. Tsar died peacefully June 12, and Daniel never knew that Tsar had gone on ahead to be there to meet him.
>
> I will take Tsar Bear's ashes with me to join my beloved husband and friend as Daniel has taken SamiSu with him.

My head, eyes, and anything else were spinning after reading this. So very much of this did not jibe with what I'd heard from the people in Deer Lodge, his ex-wife Delores, and many others. It was obvious Daniel had created a very different (false) narrative of his history.

Chapter 15 – Oregon

I shared Daniel's eulogy with Delores, and she said there was absolutely no way Daniel was ever shot or stabbed. He had no scars on any part of his body and was VERY averse to the slightest bit of physical pain. Reading he had been rear ended also brought up the realization that he most likely lost his job with the Sheriff's Department for continually rolling and wrecking police cars.

Delores also said there was no evidence of Daniel donating to Salvation Army or any group whatsoever during their time together.

Along with the eulogy Sue Ellen had also included a copy of the letter she had sent to Daniel's sister Myrtle. What I couldn't wrap my head around was the fact Daniel's sister was listed in the obituary, but the eulogy said Daniel was an orphan. I'm not sure how Myrtle felt about the eulogy (or complete exclusion of her and her family), and never heard what her reaction to this letter was.

```
July 8, 2009
Dear Myrtle, Clyde, and Family
   I want to write and tell you how many wonderful
years (30) I had with your brother. He was just the
best in so many ways. He was a wonderful husband and
stepfather to my girls, and they loved him so.
   My granddaughter made a DVD, which I am enclosing
of his younger days, which all of the grandbabies
and great grandbabies. Then, you can see such a
difference in both of us this Thanksgiving. I'm all
bent over and very overweight, due to the long time
caring for him. He was very ill, and yet we did not
know the significance of his illness until we
hospitalized him June 7. In January he had a full
body scan and it came back negative, telling us his
prostate cancer had never left his prostate. Yet, on
June 7, a cat scan was done on his right femur and
it was found to have a 5cm lesion (rapidly growing)
which had eaten through both the top and bottom of
the bone. How he never broke it was a miracle. The
doctors could not believe that he had fallen twice,
been in this horrible pain for weeks, yet still
walked and functioned.
```

Chapter 15 – Oregon

He was to have been one of the toughest men on earth. His last days of suffering were horrific. When he coded on the operating room table, in bringing him back they broke his sternum. Now, combine that with the bone cancer, and possibly lung cancer, it was unbelievable.

Both of my daughters were by his side constantly. They took time form work and loved him through all the heart and sorrow caused from the cancer. I could not have asked for them to have been any better to him.

Our love was like we were glued together with "super glue". We laughed, and cried together, and talked endlessly. Daniel would talk my ears off. He never stopped talking. I so wanted to write his life's story, but never got the chance, as these last two years took its toll on both of us. I did write a short synopsis of his life to read at this memorial service. Lisa did the honors. Please note that I did not go into any detail of his early years and tried to summarize the first paragraph to the best of my ability.

Our dog Tsar Bear brought such joy to our lives. He always made us laugh. He was such a sweetheart, and we both loved him so. He was like a small horse in the house and was as smart as any dog could be. I still cannot believe that they both are gone. Daniel did not know that Tsar had died. I'll bet he was so surprised to see him already on the other side waiting for him.

Please know that I loved your brother with my whole heart and soul and miss him terribly. He was good to me. For years he cooked, cleaned, and did the laundry. I would come home from work and all I had to do was sit down and eat, and of course, do the dishes.

In the end he would ask me over and over if I was tired of taking care of him. My answer was always, no. I finally told him that when we married and took the vows of through sickness and in health to love and to cherish till death do us part was a true vow,

Chapter 15 – Oregon

and I would never leave him nor forsake him. I would tell him as long as he gave me a couple of days to recover, then I was good to go for another stint. It was hard, I do admit because of my bad back, but I would never have given up caring for him until the doctors told him he would be bed-ridden for the rest of his life, and that I could no longer care for him. I know this broke his heart as it did mine. I so wanted to just pick him up and bring him home. He really wanted to die at home, but it was just not to be.

The nursing home was good to him. The young people that cared for him were remarkable. They were attentive and careful as they could be. He was in so much pain it made it difficult to care for him. He would stroke out and hit at them saying, no, no, no. And, why are you doing this to me? Just moving him was awful. We gave him "comfort" care which consisted of 10mg of morphine, both under his tongue and by injection every hour. It seemed to only make a difference for a short period of time.

Lisa, Karen and I have spent hours purging our souls and crying for him. We also share the good life we all had together and laugh too.

Did I share with you how God intervened and sent Deacon James, from the Catholic church to the nursing home…looking for a man named Daniel? I asked him to come in Daniel's room and explained the situation he was in. That he was born, baptized and raised into the Catholic Church and that during our time here in Pendleton we had been unable to attend any church because of his illnesses. I told him that we had been married in the Episcopal Church and that Daniel had joined that church when we married. Deacon Omar asked me if I would like for him to have Father Clemons come and perform the sacrament of healing. I, of course, said yes. It so happened that Father Clemons had come and blessed our home and Tsar Bear when we first moved here. Deacon Omar returned with Father Mike Fitzpatrick in tow. Father Mike performed the sacrament of healing, and this

Chapter 15 – Oregon

```
act alone settled Daniel down for the first time
since the surgery. It was a miracle, and then Daniel
passed the next day June 24 at 12:19 PM.
   As a result of this I was able to have Father
Clemons participate in the memorial service and
Father Mike at the burial. Both services were just
the best. The navy, marines, and Oregon National
Guard (my grandson TJ) presented me with the flag.
It was a very moving ceremony and touched the hearts
of all in attendance. Many tears were shed that day;
however, the day we buried him was a joyous day. All
3 great grandbabies were there, as well as Father
Mike's Pekinese dog, Cookie. Both days were
beautiful and sunny. The girls and I picked out a
gray blending into black for his coffin. He was
dressed in a gray conservative suit, with a black
shirt and beautiful gray with purple swirls tie. He
is laid to rest next to my mother and father, and I
too, will be buried next to him.
   Three doctors told me that I now needed to take
care of myself. I have joined the Racquet Ball Club
here in Pendleton, where Lisa has worked for some 17
years. She is starting me out slowly and I am
already losing weight. My blood pressure the day
before he passed was 200/100. The doctor added one
more (3) blood pressure pills and it is helping to
take the swelling out of my system, even though I am
up at night often. I pray I can get into shape and
maybe be able to cut back on some of these pills and
be able to enjoy all of my family for some time to
come.
   Just know that I loved him so much and we had a
wonderful 30 years together.
   My love to you and his family,
   Sue Ellen
```

Again… reconciling this and the eulogy and all I had come to learn, was mindboggling. Nothing would do, but Sue Ellen insisted we stop and see where Daniel was buried. Frankly, I didn't want to. There wasn't much affection for him going into this search, but at this point, I so openly disliked him and everything he had inflicted on so many people, it was bordering on open hatred.

Reluctantly we punched the new address and directions of the cemetery into our GPS and headed to Pomeroy, Oregon.

Arriving in Pomeroy we saw a very picturesque, but incredibly small town that seemed more like a movie set for a period piece, set decades in the past. It was a sunny clear day, and we eventually found the small cemetery. We had the directions Sue Ellen had provided, as there was no marker where Daniel was buried. The cemetery was not fancy but was well maintained. As I stared down to where Daniel laid, I was struck by the differences between his and Margaret's lives and how they both ended. The feelings I had looking down at Daniel's plot versus how I felt in the in the grove where Margaret's ashes were scattered contrasted sharply. I had a feeling of sadness and loss, but also a small measure of comfort with Margaret, knowing she had friends who truly cared for, loved, and missed her. With Daniel I was overcome with feelings of anger knowing, other than some medical issues towards the end of his life, he had essentially lived a life without consequence. He had always been able to bail and run when it suited him and had never had to answer for the results of his self-centered actions.

Chapter 16 – Sue Ellen

We meandered west through Washington as we made our way to Pendleton, Oregon. The town was hilly and picturesque and once again, I found myself trying to envision the life Daniel had during the last couple of years of his life living here. We checked into our hotel, which was in the heart of the downtown area. The vibe of the hotel and surrounding neighborhood was *sketchy*. There seemed to be an awful lot of people meandering in the parking lot with little to do with checking in or out of the hotel. We took our luggage up but kept our computers, cameras, and the scanner in the trunk of the car. The lock on the door seemed almost decorative, and not overly functional. We said a prayer and headed over to Sue Ellen's home.

The drive was much hillier than expected, with a few sharp turns. We pulled up to a very well-maintained home. And now on display were the video cameras Marlon had told us about when he had attempted contact when Daniel and Sue Ellen lived in Kennewick. Again, not totally sure what to expect, I rang the doorbell. A smiling young woman answered the door and ushered us in. This was Karen's daughter. Scanning the room, I saw a very traditionally furnished and cozy living room. One item – a small electronic organ – caught my eye. Was Daniel musically inclined?

Sue Ellen came around the corner and introduced herself. There was a formality that was a bit difficult to shake off. She asked if we'd like anything and then very kindly offered us a seat at the dining room table where she had a very large collection of photo albums and items of Daniel's. I explained I wanted to scan pictures and documents, and she was fine with that. At first, she sort of made herself busy in the kitchen, shooting glances our way, and then little by little I'd ask a question about a photo or item in a scrap book. She eventually came over and explained things about their life together.

In the many albums were pictures of Daniel as a small boy, with his brother Donald (Don) and his sisters, Kathleen, and Myrtle. While I didn't comment, this completely flew in the face of the "being raised by nuns from 6 months to high school" obituary. Among the many photographs there were also cards and letters Daniel had given or sent to Sue Ellen over the years. I was rather surprised at the romantic and kind sentiments expressed

Chapter 16 – Sue Ellen

in these items. There was never a mention of anything like this with Delores or from Margaret's friends. For an *orphan*, there was far more of a childhood contained in these albums than anyone could ever have guessed. While there were some childhood pictures of Arlene and Audrey on the refrigerator, there were no photos or indication of any sort of life lived with Margaret or Delores.

At this point, Sue Ellen offered to show me all the badges Daniel had accumulated over his career. While there were 5 or 6 badges from his time at the Prison in Deer Lodge, there was not a single badge or bit of memorabilia to indicate any involvement with the California Patrol or being affiliated with any police departments in California. Sue Ellen kept a police uniform from his time as an assistant deputy sheriff in Red Lodge, which she wanted me to have which I reluctantly took. Seeing the items Daniel had kept and not seeing a single item from California confirmed my suspicions his (and Margaret's) narratives about his involvement with law enforcement in California had either been a complete fabrication or a gross overstatement. I believed he was a police groupie of sorts during his time in California, but that might also have been an attempt to keep one step ahead of any potential issues relating to the possible embezzlement charges from his time with the vending machine company or the many times he and his wife skipped out on rent by leaving in the dead of the night. Or worse…

I queried Sue Ellen about the girls (Arlene and Audrey) again and in as gentle a way as possible, asked why they hadn't been notified of Daniel's passing and why no mention in the obituary. I never received a cogent or complete answer, but kind of a wave of the hand saying things were very overwhelming when he passed. She again said she considered contacting me about Daniel's passing, but with everything happening, didn't. I hadn't been sure if she had been around when Marlon had talked to Daniel or if she had seen the letter I wrote. She said she found the letter and photo and had put it away for safe keeping. She commented that Daniel got rid of or destroyed things from the past that bothered him.

She was reluctant to ask about Dan and Margaret but eventually asked what I knew about his life with her. She told me at one point, possibly a year or so before Daniel passed, he wanted to talk about his past with Margaret.

He said he met her in the parking lot of a hospital she was working at in the Long Beach area. Sue Ellen sensed what he wanted to talk about wasn't anything she wanted to hear and walked away from the conversation. At this point she left the room and returned with several boxes of slides. She said I could have them. She said some were taken in Garden Grove when they lived in Southern California. This information immediately caught my attention. They lived in Garden Grove? That is where my parents moved from Long Beach a couple months after I was born. I relayed this fact to Sue Ellen, and she seemed perplexed and a tad troubled. She said she believed he destroyed many of the slides in there and there were none of Margaret. Sue Ellen had looked at them. There were mostly slides of Daniel, the house they lived in, and some taken up in the San Bernardino mountains. Yet again, I felt like the universe was spinning round me, with snippets of times long past jumping out into focus, then pulling back into the whirling vortex of memories engulfing me.

So now, the questions in my mind were:
- When did they arrive in Garden Grove?
- How long had they lived there before moving north?
- Did my parents know them?
- Did my parents socialize with them?
- Had I encountered them, not knowing who they were?

While coincidences may happen at certain points in time, this seemed beyond the possibility of mere coincidence. Another fact I had uncovered was now playing into this. While putting together a family tree on Ancestry.com, I had discovered Daniel's brother Donald had lived in Anaheim (adjacent to Garden Grove) during that time. Again, this seemed beyond coincidence now.

I asked Sue Ellen about Daniel's family. She said Daniel's oldest sister Kathleen was deceased, that his older sister Myrtle lives in Eastpointe, Michigan, and the family never knew what happened with Donald. And this also triggered a thought stemming from the obituary. *How* did Daniel know his brother was deceased, unless there was an ongoing relationship of some sort? She said she and Daniel went back to Detroit in 1980, visiting Myrtle and her family and visiting the locations Daniel grew up in. Sue Ellen shared

Chapter 16 – Sue Ellen

with me Daniel and Myrtle were two peas in a pod. She went on to say Myrtle was rather abrupt and prickly.

At some point while going through all the photos and things, Sue Ellen's daughter Karen came by. She was very friendly and outgoing. We agreed to go to dinner downtown where we'd also meet Sue Ellen's other daughter, Lisa (the Lisa that had signed for my registered letter back in 2007 and also read the eulogy), and their husbands. We went to a steakhouse and had a very enjoyable meal. By this time, I had become accustomed to being scrutinized, but thankfully nothing unpleasant transpired. We said our goodbyes and returned to our hotel.

The *activity* in the parking lot had intensified by the time we returned to the hotel. After sifting through the scans of all the pictures and mulling over the new questions they raised, I didn't sleep particularly well. Looking out the window of the bathroom I could see people going in and out of a dilapidated home behind the hotel. There was a couch and other indoor furniture strewn about outside, and it appeared Pendleton was as active after dark as my mind was.

Chapter 17 – Reassessment

After returning home, I shared copies of the pictures I had scanned with Delores, and her daughters. I also asked her daughters if they'd like one of Daniel's badges. Both said yes, and I sent one to each. In the meantime, I wanted to reach out to Myrtle, but Sue Ellen wasn't optimistic about the outcome. After researching it I discovered one of her sons lived a short distance away from her. Being aware that Myrtle was cantankerous I felt the best shot at making contact with the family would be through a younger family member that might be less tethered to whatever fantasy Daniel had created about himself. I sent a letter to her son, introducing myself and giving him my contact information. While out to dinner with friends in Palo Alto one night, my cell phone rang. Sue Ellen called me saying Myrtle had just called her. When Sue Ellen answered, Myrtle snapped, "Who the hell is this David?" Sue Ellen explained who I was, said she had met me, and kindly said I was nice and actually knew quite a bit about the family history Myrtle probably wasn't aware of. She suggested Myrtle should speak to me.

I waited and waited, but no call, email, or letter ever materialized. I continued to add as much as I could to Ancestry.com and researched Myrtle's family. She had eight children, and some had partial family trees. I also kept looking through the internet for any mention of clues for Danielle, but nothing was coming up.

When I realized I was not going to hear from Myrtle, I picked a Tuesday morning and dialed her number. The phone rang three times before a VERY gruff older woman bellowed, "HELLO!" While I knew I had reached Myrtle, I said, "May I speak to Myrtle?" She bellowed back, "Who is this and what do you want?" I introduced myself and said I'd like to speak to her. She made some grumbling noises and a some of the bluster seemed to drain from her voice as she muttered, "This isn't a good time. I'm doing laundry. I'm going on a trip."

I took a firmer tone and said, "Well, then when is a good time to call you back?"

Her voice took on a new more aggressive tone and snapped, "In a few weeks when I get home" and banged the phone down in my ear.

Chapter 17 – Reassessment

Sue Ellen had informed me she was planning to go to Texas to visit one of her sons. I marked the calendar.

When the requisite time had passed, I took a deep breath and dialed her number. This time a snarly man answered. I knew it was Myrtle's husband, Clyde. I politely asked if I could speak to Myrtle.

He snarled, "Who is this?"

I introduced myself. In the background I could hear Myrtle asking who it was, but it honestly sounded more like the trumpet sound they used for the teacher on the Peanut's TV specials. It was actually comical with him stammering with a few "Umm, uh, ummm..." and Myrtle obviously telling him to tell me she wasn't there, but from my end of the call, all I could hear was that muffled trumpet sound from the Peanuts cartoon specials.

He finally gathered his composure and said, "She's out doing laundry."

As I tried to ask for her to return my call, like his surly and rude wife, he banged the phone down on my ear. I knew I wouldn't be in communication with them again.

As fall continued my father Henry was complaining about an open sore on his foot. He had had a mild (*his assessment*) form of diabetes for many years. I prompted him to see a doctor, but he kept dismissing the idea. One weekend my sister called to tell us my father's leg was infected, and they were wheeling him into surgery. At first, the surgeons discussed amputating his foot, but as the surgery progressed the surgeons now wanted to amputate his leg to just below his knee. The infection turned out to be very aggressive and were unsure the amputation would work. No one was sure he'd make it, but miraculously, he did.

We had planned on having my father, sister, and her family come down for our annual holiday party, but now with the surgery and recovery, that wasn't an option. We agreed to go up there for Christmas but moved forward with having our holiday gathering as scheduled. Our parties have generally had anywhere from 40-80 people in attendance, so we extended an invite to Sue Ellen and Karen as well as to my new half-sisters and their families. I was surprised when they all agreed to attend, minus Arlene, who didn't respond to the invite. I had also extended an invite to Delores, but she immediately begged off saying her hypersensitivity to scents and perfumes prevented her from flying or taking long bus or train trips. But she said she appreciated the invite.

The Friday before the party, Sue Ellen and Karen flew in and checked into a hotel we recommended locally. We met for dinner at one our favorite restaurants and had a very enjoyable evening. I hadn't heard for sure if Audrey would be attending or not and kept checking social media. I saw they were in the Bay Area doing some sightseeing. Delores had emailed me saying she doubted Audrey would actually show up. Sue Ellen and Karen arrived early in the afternoon, and Karen buzzed about introducing herself to everyone in the room, while Sue Ellen sat downstairs taking in the view of San Francisco Bay.

Around 4:30 the doorbell rang, and I was stunned to see Audrey and her family standing there. I welcomed them and brought them in. They seemed nervous as they stepped into the very crowded entry hall, but Audrey seemed to freeze when she caught sight of Sue Ellen. Karen ran up and said hello. I couldn't hear what was said, but it was quick, and it didn't appear that Audrey had been cordial towards Karen. Karen later relayed that she said she remembered meeting her years ago and Audrey had frostily replied that it wasn't her she had met. Audrey did go downstairs and a brief exchange with Sue Ellen transpired. I wasn't nearby and only observed from a distance. Audrey and her family didn't stay terribly long and left shortly afterwards. It was obvious the visit had an adverse effect on Sue Ellen, but we all made it through without drinks being flung in faces, or objects thrown.

Chapter 18 – The Smallest Clue

As 2009 rolled into 2010, the biggest item on my mind was my older half-sister, Danielle. Was she alive? If she wasn't, when did she pass? Where did she pass? Had she been adopted herself, perhaps having no knowledge of Daniel being her father? I kept searching the Internet and did paid online searches every once in a while, hoping a larger database might reveal something a google query might miss. Delores and I kept in regular communication either with daily emails or often a 15-minute phone call.

I kept going through Ancestry.com entering searches and not coming up with any verifiable information. Towards the end of January, I noticed some of Myrtle's grandchildren had taken a swing at creating family trees. Most of them were useless with random incomplete lines (based on what I already knew), but I stumbled upon a very small tree. This tree was as incorrect as the others, *but* this one had Daniel and Sue Ellen listed, and most importantly, it listed them having a daughter, Danielle Lanyon. I knew Daniel and Sue Ellen did not have any children together, so this was the first mention of Danielle. And the last name of Lanyon. Had she been adopted? Does she even know who her birth father was?

I immediately did an Internet search and came up with absolutely nothing. But I knew there had to be something out there for that name to have found its way, granted erroneously, into this family tree. After a couple of days coming up with nothing, I did yet another paid search. What made this search interesting compared to previous ones is it contained only one hit of information. In my previous paid searches, I was always inundated with information, a lot of it inapplicable or superfluous, but this had just one item: a phone number in New Hampshire. By the time I had this information it was almost 10 p.m. on the West Coast. I printed the number out and planned to call first thing in the morning.

The next day when I felt it was late enough, I anxiously dialed the number only to get the annoying electronic sound followed by the automated voice saying that number was no longer in service. Under other circumstances I might have walked away from this information, but as this was the one and only clue I had been able to find after so much effort, I

Chapter 18 – The Smallest Clue

googled the phone number. I was not entirely surprised to see the number showed a rehabilitation facility in New Hampshire. I jotted down the name and address of the facility and then googled them.

I called the main number and a woman answered the phone in a breezy energetic voice. I asked if I could speak to Danielle Lanyon.

She replied, "Oh, she went home a while ago. You should call her at home."

I then went on to explain I thought I might be her half-brother and had been looking for her for quite a long time and there were no phone listings for her. Letting out a "Wow!" she then offered to give me Danielle's phone number.

In hindsight I probably should have taken it, but I immediately shouted, "YOU CAN'T DO THAT! There are privacy and HIPAA laws in place."

She sounded doubtful, so I said, "Go ask your supervisor."

She put me on hold and came back a few moments later saying, "Wow… you're right, I can't do that." There was a long pause then she brightened and said, "I could call her for you."

I was stunned, and then in a rush of words I started to relay what had now become the rather epic saga of Daniel and his winding life from Detroit.

The woman (whose name sadly escapes me) said, "I'm not sure she's lucid enough to understand all of that."

My mood deflated as I thought back to the scalding incident Delores had told me about, wondering if that had led to a life-long disability. I paused for a moment and then said, "Ask her if the names Andrews or Andrzejewski from Detroit mean anything to her. If they do, I might be a relative." I gave her my name and phone number and stared at the phone.

About 15 minutes later the phone rang. I picked it up, and the smallest voice I had ever heard on the other end gave me a very tentative hello. In an unsure tone she asked me what this had to do with Andrews and Detroit.

I asked her, "Was your father Daniel Andrews?"

She replied, "No. My father was Daniel Andrzejewski."

My heart skipped a beat and I said, "Well, I believe I am your half-brother."

After a pause she asked, "Who was your mother?"

I said, "Margaret."

She gasped and said, "I met Margaret."

I then said, "I was adopted…"

And she broke into tears and said, "I was, too!"

We talked for almost three hours non-stop and she told me a tale to make everything I had uncovered pale in comparison. The first thing Danni let me know was she didn't like the name Danielle and wanted to be called Danni. She explained Daniel was expecting a son with the plan being to name "him" Daniel Jr. When a daughter was born, he said he didn't care. Daniel's aunt Eleanor was the one who suggested Danielle, and that's the name they used.

Danni's Story

(As told by Danni)

Chapter 19 – Eleanor

1950

Eleanor raised me and was my "mom." She was actually my great-aunt, the sister of my grandfather, John Andrzejewski. Also living in the house were Eleanor's sister, also my great-aunt, Alexine, and her brother, my great-uncle, William. But Eleanor was the one who really raised me. She taught me things and corrected me if I did something wrong. She did all the cooking and cleaning. Alexine worked at a dry cleaner, but when she was home, she helped out a bit, but had ulcers on her legs and couldn't really do too much. William worked in a bar at night playing piano. He also played violin and gave me piano lessons.

Eleanor was about 5 feet tall, dark brown – almost black – hair with silver strands mixed in. Blue eyes with a dark olive complexion. She was large and weighed about 250 pounds. Not too many wrinkles, a small scar on her leg. She smiled all the time and laughed a lot. We went to church every Sunday.

Ours was one of the older houses in the neighborhood where I grew up: 8041 Dobel Street off of Van Dyke Avenue in Detroit. The house had six rooms and one bathroom. An upstairs with two bedrooms and a big attic. The outside was imitation brick with parts flaking off with big tall windows, with two panes, a top and a bottom. The house was furnished with hand-me-down furniture. The dining room had furniture from our great-grandparents, with two heavy carved wood cabinets, one larger and one smaller. The telephone and telephone book were kept on top. There was a huge wooden table – it had two leaves that were never used. There was a square archway that went into the living room.

Eleanor brought in laundry from the neighborhood and used sawed off broomsticks between the table and cabinet where she'd hang shirts, trousers, and skirts when they were ready, each stick labeled for which family the clothes belonged to. She would also hang longer or taller items on the wood frame of the archway and used an empty hanger to mark off which items belonged to which family.

Chapter 19 – Eleanor

The living room and dining room were wallpapered. They had the same type of wallpaper except the dining room had a rose-colored and silver print; the living room had the same print; it was silver and light grayish blue. There were battered hardwood floors with hand-me-down carpet remnants. Under the dining room table was a braided area rug.

Most of the artwork were pictures of me growing up. That was it for the living room. The dining room had an old-fashioned stand up radio and on top was a statue of the Virgin Mary with a candle.

The living room and dining room were side by side, and when you entered the front door, you entered the dining room. The kitchen was behind the dining room. The kitchen had pretty cupboards over the sink that had a wood frame with glass inset, and the bottom cupboards were solid wood, painted a beige with a pinkish tone. The kitchen walls were painted every few years. An uncle would paint it first a light green, and then a mustard color a few years later. The only thing on the wall was a calendar. On one wall was a closet door that held the shelves for a small pantry. To the right of the pantry was the kitchen stove, gas with a faux pink marble finish. There was a white enamel metal table with red decorative trim on the corners. Below the table was red wood with a small drawer that held the silverware. The legs were silver metal in a U-shape.

Off the kitchen to the right were two doorways. One was Eleanor's bedroom. There was a big cedar chest at the foot of the bed and a highboy dresser, and a vanity dresser with a big mirror. All of it hand-me-downs. Another door opened into a big walk-in closet with a light. To the right of the bedroom was a big bathroom with another room beyond it which was a big giant closet with shelves. The bathroom floor was tiled with small white octagon tiles and in the middle of the floor was a big black octagon with a white octagon in the middle. There was a bathtub with clawed feet, a sink, and a toilet.

Alexine, Eleanor's sister, slept in the living room with a rollaway bed and a nice cabinet in the living room where she kept her possessions. William slept upstairs. The stairs were off the kitchen and went up to four doors. The two center doors were to the two bedrooms, the two outer doors were to the closets. The attic also had a big window that overlooked the backyard, which also had a garage. The other upstairs bedroom was where Daniel, Mary and my crib were. There was also a full-sized basement. There was a coal furnace with pipes going in different directions that looked like an octopus wrapped in asbestos. There was a washing machine and two big metal tubs behind it, a wringer washer and a drain in the floor. If it was summer, she'd hang the clothes outside, if it was winter or raining, she'd hang them in the basement to dry before setting them up in the dining room to be picked up. There were two rooms in the basement: one was a fruit cellar where canned goods were stored. There was a space, the size of a room, but without a door that was dark. A table piled with papers and the meter for the gas was there. Next to that was the coal room, with a chute from outside for the delivery men to drop the coal into. I used to like to play with the new coal when it came in, but then Eleanor would have to give me a bath.

There was also a closed-in back porch. Old clothes, winter coats, and other things were stored there. There were steps down into the back yard. There was a porch in front running the width of the house with five wooden steps along with a big cement slab step down to the street.

Chapter 20 – Danni's Life with Eleanor

1950 (Continued)

One of my earliest memories was of my Mom telling me my parents, Daniel and Mary, had locked her in the basement. She heard me crying and she ran upstairs to try to get into the kitchen, but it was locked. She then went outside to the backyard and up to the back porch to the kitchen, which was also locked. She then went back down into the basement and picked an ax up, saying she'd break the door down if they didn't open it immediately. When she got in, she saw me on a towel either in the kitchen or bathroom, with this bright red burn on my legs and hips crying my head off. My aunt Eleanor called an ambulance. It arrived along with the fire and police department. They took me away to Holy Cross Hospital.

Daniel and Mary were removed from the house and charged with child endangerment. Neither of them would admit who burned me, but Daniel was informed he would be charged with murder if I didn't make it. Mary told the improbable story of one of them washing the floor with a scalding bucket of water and how I had gotten into it. As I was only six or eight weeks old, this was obviously untrue. I was in the hospital for a very long time but was eventually discharged.

Dr. Despelder would come by the house every day and burn the dead skin off with silver nitrate. Even though Eleanor had the windows closed, the neighbors could hear me screaming in pain whenever this happened. They knew what was happening and knew there was nothing they could do. The nurse that took care of me afterwards, Miss Mall, came to the house often to see how I was doing. When I was about three, my Mom asked me what I wanted for Christmas and I said I wanted an African American nurse doll, like Miss Mall. My Mom looked all over but was unable to find one. Miss Mall showed up one day with one and it meant so much to me! The year after I got the doll, I never saw her again. She just quit coming over.

The judge was going to make a decision on where I was going to be placed, adoption, foster care, or where, and he finally made the determination Eleanor would get full custody. The stipulation was Eleanor had to work from home and be a full-time caregiver. From that point on, things were very

Chapter 20 – Danni's Life with Eleanor

good in the house. Eleanor did everything and never complained. If I was sick, she'd bring me something to eat in bed, she never yelled, and we always had a wonderful Christmas.

1953

When I was about 3, my Mom (Eleanor) took me to Herman Keifer Sanitarium where they treated tuberculosis. She said my parents were there, and Mary had given it to Daniel. A friend drove us down there, and we stood in the parking lot while my Mom pointed to a window where a man was standing who waved. And we waved back. At another window a woman was standing there waving. Eleanor said they were my parents. It was in the winter, and there was snow on the ground. My Mom never discussed my parents, or why they weren't in the home, but standing there in the snow looking up at the windows, I felt an intense dislike for Mary. For whatever reason, I felt sorry for Daniel.

1954

In the summer when I was about four and a half, Mary showed up with her new husband, Boris Sanders.

Eleanor let her in, and Mary made all these overtures about, "Give mommy a hug and kiss" and "This is your new daddy" but I wondered, "Who are these people?" I didn't put it together that this was the woman I waved to at the sanitarium. I stood behind Eleanor and didn't want some stranger to hug me. I could tell Eleanor was tensing up.

Mary said, "Well, I just wanted to see my daughter."

Eleanor replied, "She isn't your daughter."

I wanted to go outside and somehow got my finger caught on the screen and Mary said, "See, God is punishing you for not giving your mother a kiss." I came back to my Mom (Eleanor), crying, and Mary said, "Well, we don't need you as we have a little boy at home to love" and they left.

Mary was about 5'8" and thin with dark brown, almost black, hair. Her hair was shoulder length and curly, almost like a perm. She had green eyes with a very pale complexion. She only wore a light red lipstick. She was wearing a woman's suit, with a white blouse with ruffles, and a pencil skirt.

Chapter 20 – Danni's Life with Eleanor

No high heels, but dress flats. Boris was a big man, easily over 6'2" and he wasn't fat, but stocky and rugged looking. He had blondish brown hair and an accent. Almost southern, but not quite. This was the first time I had actually seen the woman who gave birth to me up close and in person.

After they left, Eleanor said, "Don't worry about them, you don't have to live with them." In contrast, Mary's sister Mame and her husband Ralph came by every couple of years to visit. They were very nice. They were professional bowlers.

A few months later, it was early summer, and my Mom said, "Daniel and his girlfriend Margaret are coming over for dinner." She fixed spaghetti and meatballs. Around 3 or 4 in the afternoon my Mom saw them coming up the walk and opened the door. Daniel was probably 5'9" with medium brown hair in an almost a military cut, very thin. He wasn't dressed up and wore a short-sleeved shirt and slacks. Margaret was much shorter, petite, with a reddish-brown pixie haircut. It appeared to me she was wearing a nurse's uniform, minus the cap. It didn't seem like she was wearing any make-up, not even lipstick. Like the experience with Mary earlier, this was really the first time I saw my father up close and in person.

They said hello and Daniel turned right into the living room and headed for the tufted easy chair. Margaret and my Mom went into the kitchen. I followed Daniel into the living room, but he ignored me as if he didn't want me there. He was fidgeting and saying he thought bugs were crawling over him and biting him. He was rubbing his hair and twitching in the chair. After trying to get in his lap and getting the brush-off, I went into the kitchen with everyone else. As I walked in, I heard Margaret say, "He needs his medicine. I have to give it to him, and he'll be okay in a few minutes." She had a black doctor's bag with her. I peeked around the corner and saw her give him a shot of something and then she dropped everything back into the bag. After about five or ten minutes, he was better and let me sit in his lap as he patted my hair and gave me a hug.

We got up and went into the kitchen and ate. I sat with my Mom and Margaret sat with Daniel. They talked about the weather and general things and shortly after supper, they left. My Mom cleaned the dishes and put everything away and nothing more was said about it. I wished I knew my

Chapter 20 – Danni's Life with Eleanor

Dad better and wished he'd come back home. I didn't care for Margaret. She seemed bossy and too controlling.

Life went on as usual. I played with my friend Amy, and it was just a regular summer until August. Then my Mom received a call from Daniel saying they were leaving Detroit and wanted her to bring me to their apartment so we could say goodbye. It was a really nice summer day, and we took the bus to the downtown area of Detroit. We went to the apartment building. It was quite large, and we found the apartment. Margaret let us in, and Daniel was behind her. There was a long hallway that seemed to run the whole length of the apartment. The living room had quite a few big windows. The furniture didn't look brand new. It wasn't in the best section of town but wasn't in the worst. It was lower middle class. I'm looking around and Daniel and my Mom were talking. They didn't invite us to sit down, so we stood there talking. What appeared to be suitcases were stacked one on top of the other to the right of the couch. Margaret left the room and came back with two suitcases and gave one to Daniel. They both opened the cases, and instead of clothes, inside were disassembled guns and probably ammunition. They just said, "We have to take these with us to California for protection along the way." These weren't pistols: my impression was they were like the tommy guns like you'd see on TV shows about the mob. Margaret was very nervous, and Daniel seemed somewhat fidgety.

My Mom was holding my hand, and I could tell she was very tense and had not expected this. When she saw the guns, she said, "Well, it's getting near Danni's bedtime and we should leave." They said they were leaving for California and said they'd write when they got there. And we left. When we got outside, my Mom seemed displeased and said, "Well, it's a good thing we got out of there." It was never discussed after that. I was very confused and felt something very bad had happened and wasn't sure why they showed us the guns. The rest of the summer went on and we received a couple of letters from New Mexico from Daniel and Margaret. Each had $10 or $20 in it and said it was to get something I needed.

Then the phone calls started. They were always at 7:30 or 8:00 at night. Two or three, every week or every two weeks. Whoever it was on the other end was a man who said he was with the FBI and asked if we knew where

Chapter 20 – Danni's Life with Eleanor

Daniel was or anything about his whereabouts. They never asked about Margaret. My Aunt Alexine would answer the phone and tell them, "We don't know where he is or who he's with. Don't call here anymore, we don't have anything to do with him."

We finally received a letter from Daniel and Margaret saying they were in California. I'm not sure if they gave us their address or not. A couple of letters came from California with $5 or $10 in them, and another said Daniel regretted missing me growing up as a little girl and they wanted to come back and make it up to me. While at the time I thought these were from my dad, I now think these letters were from Margaret and were her idea. That Christmas a dress arrived. It was the right size. It had a red velveteen top and the skirt was white taffeta with red polka dots. The following year I got a big doll that I named Melissa. Then I never heard from them again.

1957

When I was almost seven, I started 1st grade. I'd walk across an empty lot to go home for lunch every day. The nuns said they observed a big black car with dark, tinted windows would slowly pull out and follow me home. Just when I went home for lunch. This went on for a couple of months. No one ever got out of the car though.

The following summer, late at night, somebody knocked at the door. Alexine answered the door, as she was sleeping in the living room. I heard her call out for my Mom. She talked to my Mom for a minute. She either knew who it was, or knew what it was about, and she pulled me into the kitchen and shut the door. I pushed the kitchen door open a bit and peeked out. I saw Eleanor open the door, and somebody punched her in the stomach. She doubled over and slammed the door and locked it. Catching her breath, she clutched her stomach. I was asking all sorts of questions, but they said not to worry about it and said whoever it was had left. No one ever came back, no more phone calls, no letters, nothing threatening.

1958

After the events of 1957 were subsiding, Uncle William had a stroke and was hemorrhaging through his nose. An ambulance came and took him to the

Chapter 20 – Danni's Life with Eleanor

hospital, and he returned home. Shortly after that, he had a massive stroke and died. At William's funeral, his daughter Geraldine and her husband Clarence and their four sons were there. They were offering hot chocolate and cookies downstairs, so I went down to have something. The boys went down and locked me in the lounge. I was screaming thinking no one was going to come get me. Finally, my Mom went down and got the door unlocked and started yelling at Geraldine, and Geraldine screamed that William loved me more than he did his own grandchildren.

I had my first communion at eight years old at the Holy Name of Jesus Catholic Church, and my mom had a special dress made for me, with Chantilly lace. The lady who made it was a laundry customer of my mom's. She was a dressmaker and took in alterations. Girls were required to wear a veil, and my mom got me white ankle socks and white patent leather shoes. I carried my Mom's rosary, real gold with clear crystals. It was probably my great-great-grandmother's and had come over from Germany. I also had a small prayer book with a mother-of-pearl cover and gold gilt on the edge of the pages with pictures and prayers.

1959

I always felt bad in school because kids would ask, "Where's your Dad?" or "How come your Mom is so old?" I felt ashamed and different. The nuns asked us to write a story about what our parents did for a living, and I wrote about my Mom. I referred to her as a "laundress" and talked about her washing and mending and said I didn't have a father. It was very embarrassing.

In the fall, Uncle Earl passed away. It was a cold rainy day. Leaves were falling on the ground, and Earl's wife and daughter were very distraught. His daughter was maybe three or four years older than I was. Uncle Earl was everybody's favorite, and everyone was feeling very bad. He was the last of the brothers, and it was an incredibly dismal day.

1960 – 1962

From ages 8 to 12 life was quiet. Nothing really exciting happened, except a tornado hit Detroit when I was either 9 or 10, but it didn't damage our home.

Chapter 20 – Danni's Life with Eleanor

My Mom tried to teach me to roller skate in front of the house, but I slipped and fell, and my skates went into her ribs, breaking a couple. But she continued to take in laundry and work. After that I got a two-wheel bicycle for Christmas. I finally learned to ride it without training wheels. All the kids were out riding in the evenings, and I was finally allowed to go around the block.

I'm terrified of bees, and one day a bee landed on me causing me to fall and crash my bike. I hit my head on a parked car and knocked myself out. This was a few doors down from where we lived, and my Mom took me and the bike home and put ice on my head. A while later there was a commotion down the street and my mom insisted, I go with her to see. A neighbor across the street had ridden her bike out into the street from between two parked cars, and she was struck. She only suffered a broken leg, but an ambulance showed up. My mom said, "See what can happen. I think we should sell your bike, and you can buy something else you like with the money from the bike." We sold the bike and I bought a three-foot, brown, stuffed monkey.

1962 – 1963

Around age 12, my Mom started getting sick. She couldn't take in as much laundry and she'd have to lay down because her leg was really bothering her. She wouldn't go to bed but would just sit non-stop at the kitchen table, moaning in pain, often not even conscious. Her leg just seemed to explode into one huge ulcer. And she had ulcers in her mouth the doctor would come to look at it and put ointment on them. I'd have to change the bandages, clean her wound, and tape it up. Alexine had her own ulcers to deal with. I'd swab my Mom's mouth. She never left the kitchen room table. About two months before she died, the skin on her arms just started coming off. I didn't know it at the time, but she was severely dehydrated.

I would cut the dead skin off, hoping new skin would come back in. Her mouth got worse, and I kept swabbing it and taking care of her wounds. She was afraid to go to the hospital as she felt Child Services would come take me away. I'd get her cleaned up before I went to school and the first thing I'd do when I came home was to clean her wounds again. Her pain and suffering became more and more intense, and I'd go outside and cover my

Chapter 20 – Danni's Life with Eleanor

ears, praying to God, thinking it was my fault she was suffering. That I wasn't good enough. I'd read prayers and pray, but she just kept getting worse and worse. And the ulcers were getting worse. I prayed so hard. I prayed for hours on end, but she didn't want to go to the hospital because of me.

One weekend I got up to dress her wounds, but I couldn't rouse her. She felt cold. I woke Alexine up and she called the ambulance. They said she passed away during the night, due to diabetes.

The EMTs removed Mom's body and I was told I had to arrange the funeral, pick out a casket, pick out a dress. I walked across the street to the funeral home and the funeral director helped me picked out a dress. I picked out a lovely casket, but was told the insurance wouldn't cover it, so he showed me a wooden casket with darker blue cloth covering the outside. My mom had a pink dress I picked out, but I kept hoping it was a mistake, and she'd get up. There were so many flowers you couldn't walk through the room. I scraped my money together with Aunt Alexine and we bought a blanket with baby's breath to cover her with a matching pillow. She looked lovely and she looked like she'd just get up and start going. She had to have gloves on because her hands looked so bad. So many people, who I didn't know, showed up, hugged me, and said how sorry they were. There were so many people!

Afterwards Alexine and I went back to the house. No one came over to visit or to see how things were going. We didn't have any money for coal to heat the house, so we shut the rooms and only heated the kitchen and bedroom. She'd light the pilot light on the gas stove and turn it up high and let the heat warm the rooms. It was a very hard, horrible winter. We didn't know if we'd have money for food. The only income was from social security. I was scared to be in the house after my Mom died. I felt like I had let her down, and she was going to haunt me.

Chapter 21 – Kathleen

1963

One of the visitors after Mom's funeral was Kathleen. Kathleen was my father's sister. I met her a few times before my Mom died. The first time I met her I was maybe five years old. She worked in burlesque. She brought a photo album that she showed my mom and Aunt Alexine. They turned the pages away from me, and I think both of them turned a bit white as they flipped through it. She had a flashy dress that had sparkles or sequins. She had clear plastic high-heeled shoes with a single wide strap over the toes. A slip-on, with something like a clear stem with rhinestones that caught the light. And the heels were VERY high. She had peroxide white-blonde hair and was wearing a LOT of make-up. Her eyebrows were drawn in with a LOT of eye shadow, rouge on her cheeks, and a very heavy base of make-up with bright red lips. I don't know if she was heading off to work or coming home from work.

After she left, my Mom and Aunt Alexine both said there were pictures of her half-dressed doing an act with a man. The gist was he told jokes and she was the butt of the jokes. The one picture that had them riled up was of the man taking a big drink of water and then spitting it all over her. They couldn't understand why she was proud of this.

I probably didn't see her again until my Mom's funeral. I saw her at the funeral, and she came over to the house after the viewing of the body. I was on the couch sleeping, as I was afraid to sleep in the bedroom, afraid my Mom was going to come back and do something bad to me because I let her die. She spent most of the time with me and sat with me and rubbed my back and tried to stop my crying. She was the only one who said anything nice or worried about me. No one else seemed to see the pain I was going through or acknowledge I was the one who had to pick out the casket and pick out the dress.

1964

A year after my mom died, in the spring, Kathleen called Aunt Alexine. She knew we were having a hard time without my Mom being there and said she

Chapter 21 – Kathleen

talked to her husband and they wanted us to move in with them. It was Kathleen, her husband Joe, and her daughter Nancy. Her older daughter Joyce was away at school. I said, "I want to move. I don't want another winter of being cold and afraid of sleeping in that bedroom." I was graduating 8th grade and didn't know where I was supposed to be going to school after that.

About two months before I graduated, the principal called me into her office. She explained she and my Mom had had discussions about me going to Adrian, Michigan, to attend the Adrian Boarding School. Everything would be paid for, I'd live there all year round, and when I graduated, I would be able to continue on to college with all the expenses covered. I told her, "No" and I think she was a bit shocked. My feeling was that after the time and expense the expectation would be that I'd become a nun and I didn't want to do that.

Aunt Alexine and I agreed to move in with Kathleen and Joe. The only things we took were the cedar chest, some nice dishes our great-grandmother had brought over from Germany, and our clothes. The cedar chest was packed with items my mom had made. There was my beautiful christening gown, some jewelry my mom had when she was younger, her diamond ring from when she was engaged, Mary's diamond engagement ring, and both her and Daniel's wedding bands. We left everything else behind.

Kathleen's house was very small. When we moved in the upstairs was in the process of being repainted, so I shared a bedroom downstairs with Nancy. Once the upstairs was painted, I had my own space. Not really a bedroom, there were three rooms but none of them had doors. If you looked up the stairs you could look directly into my bedroom. Aunt Alexine didn't have a bedroom. She slept in a kitchen chair next to the stove by the kitchen table. She always seemed to have a cigarette lit. Kathleen was nice, but Joe was a bit odd acting. Joe was a truck driver, delivering food to grocery stores. At this point in time, on Friday or Saturday night both of them worked at Cig's Bar. Joe would bartend and Kathleen worked as a waitress. She'd dress up, probably in one of the sparkly dresses she had worn when she was doing burlesque. Always with the big tall high heels.

Chapter 21 – Kathleen

Joe would get really drunk. He was never without a beer or a cigarette. He'd say stupid things trying to egg on Kathleen, Nancy, or me on into a fight. Once they got into such a bad fight Kathleen, Nancy, and I moved into a motel. One time after the motel incident, they got into another fight that was always escalating, so Kathleen moved out of the house with me and Nancy and moved into the house of a 60-something woman I had never met, Mavis. Mavis had a chihuahua: it was either trying to bite me or hump my leg. We stayed with her for three or four days and didn't see much of her. Mavis was always angry at us saying it was probably our fault Kathleen and Joe were fighting, and it was too much stress. We finally went back to Joe.

As Alexine and I moved into Kathleen's, I was about to start 9th grade at Grant Junior High. Grant Junior High covered grades 7 through 9.

1965

School ended that summer and things were fairly quiet and normal. I graduated to the 10th grade and tried to enroll at Osborne High School. But they said I couldn't enroll because I was a minor and had no legal guardian or parents. I explained I lived with my Aunt Kathleen and Aunt Alexine, but they said they didn't have legal custody, and the school couldn't take the legal responsibility. I felt horrible I couldn't continue with school. I came home and explained what happened to Kathleen, and she said I would need to get a job. Nancy also said she had had enough of school and wasn't going to continue as well. We weren't 16 yet, as you needed to be 16 to get a work permit. But only a school can issue a work permit and I could not attend school. I was a Catch-22.

As summer was coming to an end, Aunt Kathleen pulled me aside and said, "Mary is coming over and wants you to live with her. You can go for a weekend and see how you like it." Other than the one-time Mary and her husband came to the house, we had no other contact or communications. But the way she said it translated to me as "You're going to go there and stay there." I didn't feel like I was welcome at Aunt Kathleen's any longer. That day Mary showed up later in the afternoon. Mary said, "I want to make up for all the lost years." I took enough clothes for the weekend and went with Mary. We went to a newer one-story ranch house with three bedrooms, a

Chapter 21 – Kathleen

large living room, large dining room, fairly big kitchen, a big bathroom, and a combination mudroom / washer dryer. Living in the house along with Mary was her husband Boris, his daughter Peggy and son Boris Jr. from a previous marriage, and their son Ron, who was six years younger than me.

Boris Jr. was about my age and Peggy was about a year and a half older than I. The kids treated me nice enough, but I felt as though I was in a military barracks. As an example, I couldn't shave my legs until Boris Sr. and Mary had viewed them and agreed it was necessary. When bath time came, one tub of water was drawn, Boris Sr. and Mary took their baths first (separately), then Boris Jr. went next, but the same tub of water was used for Ron, then Peggy, and then I was the last one to use the same bathwater, which was dirty and cold by the time my turn came. After a while I wised up and would wait until Mary and Boris Sr. were asleep, then I'd creep into the bathroom, drain the water, clean the tub out, and as quietly as possible slowly fill it up with warm clean water and take my bath.

Mary and Boris Sr. had one bedroom, the two boys, Boris Jr. and Ron shared another, and Peggy and I shared the third bedroom. Peggy and Boris Jr. and I got along okay, but Ron was a snitch. Mary cut the boys' hair and Boris Sr's. She gave a buzz cut to all of them. Mary also cut her own hair, more of a trim. She never allowed Peggy or me to get ours cut professionally.

Boris Sr. was on workman's compensation and had worked in a papermill. He said he hurt his back. He went back to work for short periods of time and wore a big back brace. When he got home, he'd take the back brace off, and do whatever he wanted, including hunting, or doing things around the house. Mary worked as a secretary at a company that sold swimming pools, and she was also a CPA and ran a tax business out of the house. She also sold Avon cosmetics and had a long list of customers.

Now I was living with my actual mother, I could enroll in school and went to Jefferson High School. After about three or four months, they decided to move. One of Mary's tax clients was an elderly woman whose son had just died in Vietnam and whose husband had recently passed. When this woman passed away, she left her house and everything in it to Mary. Mary and Boris Sr. sold their house and with the money they remodeled this woman's house, which had fallen into disrepair. They did a complete remodel.

Peggy and I were required to clean the entire house, take the laundry to the laundromat, and do the ironing. The house had to be spotless, and we even had to take a vacuum down into the basement and vacuum the support beams. Cleaning had to be done before we could do homework. We had no new clothes and we had to share or had to wear hand-me-downs from Boris Sr.'s family, who were all bigger people. It wasn't fun going to school in some middle-aged woman's dresses. Boris Sr. and Boris Jr. would go on expensive hunting expeditions where they were guaranteed to get a hunting trophy. The dining room was full of the stuffed animal heads.

Due to the antibiotics I was given because of the scalding incident, my adult teeth never came in correctly. By this time, they were almost black and falling out, including a front tooth which broke. Mary and Boris Sr. spent money on the other kids going to the dentist, but not on me. One afternoon a teacher asked me to stay after school. She said she and a bunch of other teachers had gotten together and pooled their money to get my teeth fixed. I was happy they were willing to do that, but I was also embarrassed. I was so mortified; I refused their very kind offer. I was also angry at Mary and Boris Sr. because they had money and said they'd get around to it, but never did. I never told Mary or Boris Sr. about the teacher's offer, knowing they'd blame me.

Boris Sr. worked only a few hours a day and would be home by the time we got home from school. He'd chase everyone around like a game, but the others would fall away, and he'd chase me into his and Mary's bedroom. He'd throw me down on the bed, on my back and say he was tickling me, and he'd flop on me, pinning me down and start dry humping me. He'd do this with the door open with the kids in the house. This would go on for five or six minutes, then I'd squirm, and he'd finally get off and I'd run out of the room. This would happen once or twice a week. This went on for about nine or ten months.

Chapter 21 – Kathleen

1966

Now that I was living with my mother, my legal guardian, I could attend school again. Peggy and I weren't allowed to go to dances or social events. Peggy finally got a boyfriend at school. He came to the house and got Mary and Boris Sr.'s approval. There was a prom coming up, and Peggy wanted me to go with her and her boyfriend. I didn't want to go because no one had asked me. Peggy found a guy from the school who I'd never seen before. Peggy's boyfriend picked her up, but I walked to the school. Peggy and her boyfriend came up to me and introduced me to the guy. He was short, had dark very greasy hair pushed back from his face, and black horn-rimmed glasses. He had on an ill-fitting suit, he had severe acne, but his personality was the turn off. We went to dance a waltz, and he pulled me in real tight and was very grabby and tried to kiss me. After the second dance, he said he needed to go bathroom. I said I did as well, but instead I left and went home. I never said anything to Peggy or anyone else. Peggy asked me what happened when she got home, and I told her he was a creep and a jerk. That was the first and the last blind date they tried to arrange.

This was spring of 1966, two weeks before school was out. Nancy called and asked if I'd like to spend Memorial Day weekend with her in the old house with her, Kathleen, Joe, and Aunt Alexine. I asked Mary and Boris, and they said they'd drive me down. At that point I realized I did not want to come back. I knew I couldn't take my cedar chest or any of my belongings. I grabbed a few clothes but didn't have much time to plan or pack. Mary drove me to Kathleen's. Even though it had been bad with Kathleen, it was so much better with her than with Mary and Boris. It was like going from hell to heaven. When Sunday night came and I was supposed to go back, I called Mary and told her I wasn't coming back.

She said, "What do you mean you're not coming back? I'm your mother!"

I told her, "No, you're not. You're just someone who gave birth to me."

She said, "What are you going to do? You can't go to school there."

Mary then asked to speak to Aunt Kathleen. I couldn't hear what they were saying, but I heard Aunt Kathleen say, "She's lived here before, she can live here again and stay as long as she wants to."

Chapter 21 – Kathleen

During summer recess, Nancy and I found jobs in downtown Detroit. Our first jobs were in K-Mart. Aunt Kathleen was working in Infants and got us the job. I worked full time in the shoe department, and Nancy was working part-time in the men's department. I really hated the shoe department. I was told with the first snowfall we'd get lots of overtime. It became a madhouse with everyone trying to get boots and shoes. The store was open from 9 a.m. to 9 p.m. We would normally work an 8-hour day, but during this time, we were doing 12-hour days. My job ended up with me going to the front of the store and gathering all the returns. I'd bring them back and then have to match them up. One shoe from a pair might be in one basket, while its mate might be in another. I'd rematch them and reattach them with a plastic gun and price tag.

We also sold shoes for weddings, and the brides would wear white shoes (generally) but if the bridesmaid needed a specific color, we'd either dye them with the dyes we had, or we'd mix the dye custom based on a chart we had in the back. After being stuck in the back a couple of months, I asked to be put back out on the floor. Aunt Kathleen worked in the department next to shoes and was trying to micro-manage me. She was buddy-buddy with the shoe department manager and snooping on me. After a few months of this, I finally had enough and quit. Nancy quit at the same time as she wanted more hours but was only getting part-time shifts.

While I was working at K-Mart, I started going to the dentist to get my teeth fixed. I went to the dentist for almost a year. The cost was about $1,500. My teeth were so bad he couldn't save the top ones and had to put a plate in, and he did what he could to save the bottom ones. I was making $65 a week with $50 going to the dentist, so I only had $15 to give Kathleen, even though she wanted $20. When he put the plate in, my mouth was swollen and sore, but I was happy I could finally smile. Kathleen laughed, pointed at my mouth, and said I looked like a horse. When the last payment was due for the dentist, I borrowed $100 from a friend of Aunt Alexine's that I paid back when I got my tax refund.

Chapter 21 – Kathleen

1967

My next job downtown was at the S. S. Kresge Five-and-Dime Store. I worked in cosmetics, a little section where there were glass cases with makeup, and I'd pull things out of the case to look at it, then close it, and put it back in the case. The customers could look but couldn't touch. I worked there for about three months. Then I was promoted upstairs and I'd balance out the registers and get the money ready for the Brink's truck each day. Kenneth Weiss was the first guy I had real feelings for. He was two or three years older than I. He worked in the camera department. He was a photographer and used to do news-style photography. He started asking me out or come over to watch TV, and he took me Christmas shopping for his mother, whom I had never met. Then I found out he had been dating another girl for years and was engaged. Someone at work told me Kenneth was engaged, and I was devastated. He kept asking to see me, and I'd say okay. It was him and a younger brother, and he decided it was his duty to enlist.

Later on, I got a job at Hughes, Hatcher, and Suffrin Department Store. They sold higher end apparel and would tailor everything there if you needed alterations. I worked in the lady's ready-to-wear department. This was more money and more enjoyable than K-Mart. There *were* prostitutes who would come in. One of the women had open sores all over her body and I was told not to let her try any of the clothes on. She did buy things and paid in cash. It was a nice store, but not in a good part of town. One man, who was obviously a pimp, would call into one lady with the instructions that the clothes should not look like a whore's, but something classy. He'd spend a minimum of a $1,000, if not more, for each order.

1970

I worked there for three years. Aunt Kathleen had left Joe again, and her daughter Joyce was back at home. She worked as a keypunch operator, and Nancy was working downtown at Fanny Farmer's Candy. Despite being robbed at gunpoint once, she still kept the job at Fanny's. And any candy she didn't sell at the end of the day she could bring home or throw away. All four of us had an apartment together in Highland Park. Aunt Kathleen slept

Chapter 21 – Kathleen

on the couch in the living room, Joyce had her own bedroom, and Nancy and I shared a room. Joyce got me a bed for Christmas. We all lived there for about a year. Then Aunt Kathleen moved back in with Joe. Then Nancy started dating Larry Goldman and moved in with Aunt Kathleen and Joe until she married Larry. After a brief honeymoon before he shipped out to Vietnam, Nancy went back with Aunt Kathleen and Joe.

When Larry came home after a year in Vietnam, he was stationed in Fort Stewart, Hinesville, Georgia, almost on the Florida border. Nancy bought a brand-new trailer as Larry didn't want to live on base.

Then Joyce got a boyfriend and found out she was pregnant. They were going to take over my bedroom and turn it into a nursery and she redid her bedroom. I was left out in the cold. I couldn't afford my own place, so I moved in with Aunt Kathleen and Joe once again.

The distance to my job was becoming stressful. Over an hour each way. Once night the bus stopped in front of the burlesque place Kathleen used to work, and a big African American guy came up to me and put his arm around mine and said, "You're coming home with me tonight."

I said, "No, I'm not, I don't even know you."

His grip kept getting tighter, when suddenly (what I assumed was) a student from the M.I.T. campus was nearby says, "Sorry, I'm late" and grabbed me by the other arm. I didn't know either of them, but the second guy seemed much nicer, I felt safer with the new guy.

I started reading fashion magazines and started refining and redefining my look. I went from a frumpy, dumpy someone with bad teeth to someone who was dressing well and was getting a bit of style. I think this annoyed Aunt Kathleen. She was aging, I was younger, had boyfriends, and even though Aunt Kathleen was still with Joe, she seemed to resent me. One night when Kathleen was still working at K-Mart, Joe asked me to give him a bath because Kathleen couldn't do that anymore. He said she was too old. He hollered at me from the bathroom into my bedroom. He was naked in the bathroom, and I said, "No, I don't do that sort of thing" and I knew it was time to get out of there.

Then one night there was a knock at the door. I said, "Who is it?"
A man said, "It's Kenneth, Kenneth Weiss."

Chapter 21 – Kathleen

I asked, "What do you want?"

He said, "I want you to marry me."

I asked what happened with the other woman and he said he hadn't been with her for a long time, but my mind was made up and I didn't open the door.

Nancy called and said she knew I didn't have anything going on in Michigan, and there were jobs in Hinesville, and she said I could live with her and Larry. The rent would be low and there would be guys to meet and I could get away from Aunt Kathleen and Joe. So, I said, okay.

The guy who moved me was Larry's friend Ronald, nicknamed Phi (pronounced (Pie), and he was a teacher. Phi was tall, maybe 6'3" with a regular build, dark brown hair, nice looking with a nice personality. Aunt Kathleen went down with us to visit, but I had a feeling Aunt Kathleen was interested in Phi and wanted to get to know him better.

Chapter 22 – Martin

1970 (Continued)

Nancy and Larry owned a brand-new trailer in an older trailer park, somewhat packed in. No trees, no landscaping. A lot of military people lived here. Nancy was pregnant with her first child, maybe three or four months along. The room I had was really nice with wallpaper with thin red squiggly lines, and about 1/3 of the way up from the floor had wood paneling. The ceiling had white acoustic tiles. I also had a half bathroom in my room with a sink and toilet. I got settled, and Nancy and Larry said I should rest for a couple of days and get acclimated. We were near the main section of Hinesville, which was very small. I went out looking for a job and I applied to Terry, the owner of the Terry's Café. I was hired as a waitress. I worked with another girl, Marcy, whose husband was also in the military. We would trade off working the day or evening shifts.

While I was working at the café, a young man came in fairly regularly and we got to talking. He was in his fatigues and worked on the base. He introduced himself and moved over, so I sat down, and we started talking. His name was Martin Lanyon, and he was from New Hampshire. Martin was about 6', he had thick brown hair with reddish highlights, and really intense blue eyes. He had a very nice personality and was very gentle and protective of me. One evening Martin invited me to a get together at one of the officer's homes on base. There were four couples, including us, and two single guys. The women all ended up going into the kitchen sitting around the table with one of the guys, who we figured out was gay. The men stayed in the living room for a while. The single guys left. The remaining couples had a few drinks and some nibbles and then we left. I went home and Martin went back to base. I had a nice time, everyone seemed very nice, and Martin continued to come into the café to see me.

If you worked the early shift, you'd get a free lunch and if you worked the evening shift, you'd get dinner. The cook was a lovely African American woman, whose daughter would come in and help washing dishes. I would usually eat my meal back in the kitchen and chat with them while they cooked or washed the dishes. About a week and a half later, Terry pulled me aside

Chapter 22 – Martin

and said I couldn't do that any longer. He said, "They're black, you're white" and insinuated they were an inferior race and I shouldn't fraternize. I told him it was my lunch break and I would eat with whomever I wanted to. He said I couldn't do that, so I quit on the spot.

I went back to Nancy's and told her what had happened, and she supported my decision. She said I'd find something else. Martin started coming over to the trailer because I didn't have another job. The couple who had the party on base had another gathering about two weeks later with the same people invited. This time instead of going off into the kitchen with the women, or Martin separating with the guys, we sat together in the living room and Martin proposed. I said yes, even though I had only known him for three weeks. I said yes so quickly because Nancy was married and having a baby, Joyce was married and having a baby, Aunt Kathleen didn't want me, and I did think I was in love with him. I just wanted to belong to someone, to have a family, MY FAMILY.

The next day Martin planned we would go to get our blood work done and get a marriage license. He also wanted to call his Mom and Dad, which he did from a payphone. I was standing somewhat inside the phone booth and I could hear his Mother, who had a VERY LOUD VOICE, say "DO YOU HAVE TO GET MARRIED? IS SHE PREGNANT? HOW FAR ALONG IS SHE?" I ended up talking to her for a little bit, but her demeanor rubbed me the wrong way. For lack of a better word, she sounded like an uneducated hick. I didn't talk to his father. We got our blood work done and the marriage license. The clerk said there was a week-long waiting period. We told him we had planned to get married that weekend, so he very kindly backdated the license so we could get married then.

Within the course of a week after deciding to get married, Martin and I moved in together. We went out looking for a place to live. We found a trailer in a trailer park, which wasn't as nice as Nancy's. It had a double wide extended living room with a pull-out extension that was out all the time. It had a kitchen / dining room combination, which was only separated by a counter. It came furnished. All of the appliances, the sink, even the toilet and tub, were turquoise. It had two bedrooms, and a place to park your car. This park was strictly for rent to military families, as opposed to owning your trailer at Nancy's.

We made plans to get married. I didn't have a fancy dress but wore the nicest dress I had brought from Michigan. Nancy was the matron of honor. Larry gave me away. The three couples who were at the parties we were at and the guy we suspected was gay were at the wedding too. Martin's sister Joann and her husband Vern came from New Hampshire. Even though it was February, it must have been 90 degrees in the shade, and Joann had on a heavy winter coat and heavy winter boots. She couldn't take her coat off, as she had started her period and it had bled through and she broke the upper part of her false teeth in half by biting into a hard piece of candy. To top that off, Greyhound had lost their luggage.

Joann and Vern wanted to stay a week, so Joann wanted to drive around until we found a Sears or JC Penney so she could buy some outfits until Greyhound could figure out what happened to their luggage. We went to a Sears store in Savannah, and Joann found a couple of outfits but couldn't find a dress she wanted to wear to the wedding. I offered to lend her one of my dresses. She weighed about 20 lbs. more than I did, but I had some looser fitting dresses, and she fit into the one I selected. She was so embarrassed her top denture had cracked, and she didn't know any dentists in the area, so Martin offered to glue the dentures together. After they were glued together, she put them in, and started feeling ill and getting a bit high from the glue. Despite that, she didn't want to go without her teeth in, so she kept wearing them.

The day of the wedding came, and Nancy and Larry took us to a chapel on the base. Martin was supposed to bring me some flowers to carry down the aisle, but he forgot the flowers. I just kind of folded my hands together, walked down the aisle, and we were married in five minutes. After the wedding, I'm riding with Joann, Vern and Martin, and we stopped at a flower shop and he got me a bouquet of carnations, which I put in a vase when we got home. Everyone came back to the trailer, Nancy had baked a nice sheet cake, everyone made sandwiches, we had sodas, and Martin bought a decorative, collector's style ceramic stagecoach, that held whiskey. You pull out the section where the luggage would have gone, and that's where you

Chapter 22 – Martin

drew the whiskey from. It was a morning wedding, and everyone stayed until about 5:30, lasting about 6 hours.

    Later in the evening, one of the couples who were at the party, who we thought had gone home, returned a couple of hours later. One of the single guys who didn't make it to the wedding showed up later and had given Martin two tabs of acid as a wedding gift. He said for Martin to take one and one was for me. When Martin offered this to me, I said, "NO WAY," so Martin offered them to a couple who had left and had just returned. The man seemed like he had already taken something and asked all of us to come back to the base to see where they lived. He had apparently also invited everyone else who was at the wedding. He went into the house and took both hits of acid. He ran into the backyard, getting caught up in the clothesline with clothes on it, and he was freaking out saying something from outer space was after him. At first it seemed kind of funny, but all the guys eventually calmed him down and pulled him back into the house. His wife was upset and hysterical, and we calmed her down. After this experience, no one ever saw them or socialized with them again.

    Martin only had three days of leave for the wedding and honeymoon. But he was called back to the base sooner. Apparently, there was a bad cockroach problem, but I had never seen any, and really knew nothing about them. Martin brought home an insecticide to deal with this on his lunchtime and left. Vern read the instructions and sprayed the entire place. Joann, Vern and I sat around in the living room saying "Well, I don't think there's any cockroaches. I haven't seen one." Suddenly, they were coming out of what seemed like everywhere and were swarming all over the place. Joann and I ran out of the place leaving Vern with the dying cockroaches. Joann and I were not going to go back in until there weren't any cockroaches in there. Vern started sweeping up the dead cockroaches and wiping the counters and surfaces down. Hours later we went back inside, and Martin came home, and we told him what happened.

    We only lived in the trailer for about a month. The landlord was going to increase the rent, but hadn't addressed any of the problems inside, so we eventually found a small house to rent. It was just outside the back of the base and somewhat in the country. There were two or three lots between us and the people who owned the house. A retired military man and his wife who hired a maid who wore a traditional maid's uniform. The house had originally been a chicken coop, but they had added onto it and fixed it up. They put a big air conditioner and a small gas heater on the floor. We had a kitchen/dining room combination with a half wall separating that from the living room. There was a doorway in the living room leading into the only bedroom. In the back of the bedroom was the only bathroom. Very tiny. It was furnished. We lived there from the end of March until about August 1970, when Martin was discharged. Upon being discharged, Martin had a job lined up at Campbell's Envelope and Stationery in New Hampshire where he wanted to return.

In the beginning of April, I found out I was pregnant with my first child. The OB/GYN kept taking my blood every couple of days. I kept asking what was wrong. My blood type was B-, and my child was going to be A+ and the nurses kept asking if I had any miscarriages or abortions previously. But they kept checking my blood work and checking the baby. By August, the doctor said it was safe for me to fly up to New Hampshire with Martin. Martin was excited about having a child and was also looking forward to returning to the job at the Campbell's Envelope & Stationary where he had four years in already.

When we had moved into the small house, we acquired a pet rabbit. We asked if there were any shots the rabbit would require in order fly and they said he would probably need to travel in the luggage compartment. Being the animal lover that I am, we put him in a duffel bag that we kept between our legs. At some point during the flight, when it was my turn to hold the duffel bag, it got away and the bag started hopping down the aisle. The flight attendant picked it up by the handle and dryly said, "Your bag seems to have gotten away from you."

Chapter 23 – New Hampshire
1970 (Continued)

In August, we landed in Boston, and Martin's brother-in-law Ted picked us up. Four and a half hours later we arrived in North Stratford, New Hampshire, where Martin's parents lived. The plan was to stay with them until we got settled. Martin's parents had a big older white farmhouse, but it was in dire need of a paintjob and repairs. They had a big barn across the road with a fair amount of land. They had been dairy farmers and then sold the livestock to neighboring businesses. They were no longer working the farm, but both had jobs at Campbell's Envelope & Stationery. They had added onto the living room with a cement slab with a tile floor and a big picture window that looked out on the highway. One step up was the laundry room with a small office where Martin's mother would keep track of each and every expense.

We arrived around 5 p.m., and Martin's parents were sitting in front of the TV in their rocking chairs, with an open can of beer by them, and both of them obviously well on their way to being quite drunk. Martin's mother curled her lip and said, "Well, if you want anything to eat there's some lunch meat in the refrigerator and you can make yourself a sandwich." We scrounged around for something to eat and then went to bed. All our belongings, such as they were, had been shipped up and were now stacked up in the bedroom. I just laid in bed with my back to Martin and just quietly sobbed all night. I knew life with his parents was going to be unpleasant.

We lived there until the end of October. Some friends of Martin's were moving into a new home and were vacating a nice apartment in nearby Groveton. The apartment was quite nice. You could walk into the kitchen or living room, but most people went into the kitchen first. It was on the first floor, with a porch. You walked into the kitchen, and at the back and to the right was the bathroom. Before the bathroom there was another door with access to a shed where we kept kerosene to heat the apartment. It would usually take four large glass jugs to heat the place for the night. There were two bedrooms you could access off the living room. The rent was only $12 a week, but we had to pay the utilities (gas, electric, phone), and for kerosene

Chapter 23 – New Hampshire

to heat the house. It was not a furnished apartment, so Martin took out a loan, which his parents co-signed, and we bought furniture for the apartment.

We bought a full bedroom set, a new kitchen set (with a leaf to extend it) and six metal chairs with padded seats and backs. A new refrigerator, a new living room set with a couch that opened up into a bed, an armchair, a matching rocking chair, a coffee table with matching end tables, and lamps for the end tables. Each room had an overhead light fixture. Martin's Mom hosted a baby shower and gave me a bassinet, but everything else we needed to get on our own.

One tradition that started immediately after we arrived was every Sunday all the family members gathered at Martin's parents' house. His folks were well into their beers by the time everyone arrived. At this point, Martin would usually only have one beer. His parents would go through a case of beer a day often with his father passing out and his mother just going off to bed. Everyone else drank right along, but Joann and Vern didn't drink as much, and they'd leave early.

On December 12, 1970, I went into labor with my daughter April. I was in labor for 26 hours. The doctor was going to give me one more hour or they were going to do a caesarean section, but I started to dilate. As it was, I wasn't dilating enough so they put me under, and the doctors performed an episiotomy. I was out for a day, and the nurses brought April to me to feed her. Every time I fed her; she would throw up. She was just under 6 pounds, and the other babies in the ward weren't doing that. They explained she had colic. I was in the hospital for five days, but on the fourth night they said April was losing weight and they'd have to keep us until she started to gain weight. She finally gained the ¾ of a pound she had lost, and they let me go home.

1971

We settled into life. April had the second bedroom. She couldn't sleep in the bassinet due to colic, so we'd got a smaller carrier, which we put inside the bassinet, and she slept really well. The colic was really bad the first couple of months, but by the third month she finally got over that and was sleeping through the night.

Martin was a really good husband during the first two years. He'd often get up in the middle of the night to change and feed her and let me sleep. Then I got pregnant with my second child and Martin changed. He seemed very happy about this, but he started hanging around his old friends from before the service. They were older, unmarried, they drank a lot, and he'd hang out with them and started drinking more, partying more, and he wouldn't come home. One night he showed up at 1 a.m. I was pregnant and knew he got out of work at 3 p.m. that day. I snapped, "Where the fuck have you been?" I hadn't done anything like that before and then continued on by calling him a pig fucker, and he pushed me very hard into the TV. The TV had a screen cover and it broke with the TV almost falling over. He then pushed me down into a chair and went to bed.

The next morning, he didn't apologize and only said I shouldn't have called him those names that made him so mad. I said, "Why couldn't you have called me that you were going to be late? You knew I had supper waiting. I was worried about you." I didn't want to press the issue so he wouldn't hit me again. I didn't know it at the time, but that was also the start of his drug use. I later found out he was smoking pot as well as using cocaine. There very well may have been other substances, but I wasn't aware of all of them. I found out when a couple of his friends he worked with turned out to be dealing as well. They came by the house to sell drugs to him. I was in the dining room, and they had the stuff on the table, letting him pick out whatever he wanted. I just looked and didn't say too much. I didn't know what the dealers would do, or what Martin would do, so I just left and went into another room.

His erratic behavior continued for several months, and I finally reached out to Martin's family for assistance. I told them something was obviously bothering him and needed help. Instead of supporting me or offering help, they berated me saying I was a party-pooper, I was from the city and thought that I was acting "better" than anyone else. They said they thought I thought I was better looking than everyone else and I had no business questioning Martin if he hit me or did whatever else he wanted to do. One night when I

Chapter 23 – New Hampshire

was eight months pregnant, we were outside, and it was winter. He was mad at me, and he hit me really hard in the arm, knocking me down and he was going to leave me there. I couldn't get up. I was almost 8 months pregnant and couldn't get up off the ground, but he finally offered me his arm and helped me up. But he didn't say anything and didn't apologize.

1972

In May 1972, Douglas was born. Martin handed cigars out to everyone: he *hadn't* done that with April. When Douglas was born, he had a bright red rash that ran up from his diaper. I was in the hospital for 6-7 days. I showed the doctor the rash, and it started covering his arm, neck, and face. They said it was probably just diaper rash. We took him to another pediatrician who put him into another hospital. Douglas was in isolation. It turned out I had had a yeast infection prior to giving birth. The doctor had given me a douche to deal with it, and I questioned if this would be harmful to my child. He said it wouldn't. It turned out when Douglas was born some of the infection had gotten into his belly button from the placenta and he had to be isolated for about three weeks.

Martin seemed to feel bad but wasn't outwardly bothered. I was heartbroken, worried that if anything happened, I would be responsible. We finally got to bring Douglas home in August. Douglas could only wear a diaper, loosely draped around him, not snug or pinned, and we had a heater on at all times. We had diapers draped on the sides and over the crib, so if his diaper fell off anything would be caught before hitting the wall or floor. This went on for about two months. The pediatrician said due to the rash and almost dying, his immune system wasn't that great, and he would probably be more susceptible to every illness that went around.

I also noticed April started to exhibit the same rash, so I took her to the doctor, and he gave me a cream to treat it. The rash cleared up in April and Douglas, so Douglas could wear regular diapers and clothes. In December, Douglas came down with pneumonia really bad. He was barely responding. I called the doctor's office, and they instructed me to bring him in immediately, even though it was the weekend. The doctor gave Douglas a shot and said, "If you don't see any improvement in 24 hours, you'll need to take him to the hospital."

We brought him home, gave him his medicine, and about 20 hours later he was responding and acting better. But up until age six, he would pick up every bug that went around be it a cold, flu, or whatever. After that he started to gain weight, was active, and wasn't coming down as often with illnesses.

When Douglas was about one and a half, and April was about three, I went back to work. I worked at Style's Drug Store in Groveton. We did a little of everything including working the soda fountain, taking phone company payments, taking people's prescriptions, order and fill the magazine rack and cards, and ring up sales. I usually worked 8 a.m. to 4 p.m.

A woman I knew had just had a baby and was going to be a stay-at-home mom, so she watched the kids at her house. The downside of this was she didn't want any noise while her baby was asleep and she would have April and Douglas sleep as well, so by the time I got home they were wound up and ready to be up all night. I eventually found another sitter after a couple of months. The husband was a friend of Martin's in high school, and his wife ran a daycare out of their home. She watched about 10 children and was very good with kids. She watched them for a couple of years, but then decided she wanted to go back to a regular work. Thankfully, her aunt agreed to take over the daycare, and she was possibly the best day care provider the kids ever had.

1976

After a few years in the apartment, several things came to a head: April wasn't doing as well in school as she should have. Part this was due to the school being very large where kids weren't getting individual attention, and older kids were bullying the younger ones at an ever-increasing rate. There was no supervision on the playground, and I felt it was getting to be a bit dangerous. Also, the owners of the apartment were older and weren't wild about kids running around or making noise. So, we started looking for houses for sale, so we could have our own house, and the kids could have a backyard and not worry about disturbing our landlords. We finally found a house for $10,000 in Groveton, which was a very good price.

Chapter 23 – New Hampshire

It was an older house with green slate siding, sort of like shingles. It sat on an acre of land. It was small with two bedrooms downstairs and an attic with insulation and windows, but no sheet rock and an unfinished floor. You needed a step ladder to get up into it. The kids took one bedroom, we had the other. There was an eat-in kitchen and one bathroom. The bedroom we took didn't have a closet, but was larger, while the kids' room was much smaller but had a large walk-in closet adjacent. It's possible the walk-in closet was actually used as a bedroom at one point. It had a window, similar to one you'd find over a kitchen sink. It had linoleum and a light fixture, but we used it as a closet.

1977 – PART I

The kids got to be too big to be in one bedroom, so Martin and his father put a drop stairway with a railing and divided the attic in half and put sheet rock up and linoleum on the floors. We moved the kid's toys and furniture up to the attic. This was when Martin started drinking a lot more and was getting more violent. The kids weren't happy in school, Martin and I were fighting, and there were always worries about money. Martin was spending money going out drinking, buying drugs, and just carousing. After a while, we sold the house and its furnishings, minus the kid's things. There wasn't much equity afterwards, and we moved back in with Martin's parents, for what we hoped would be a short period of time.

Chapter 24 – Bad to Really Bad
1977 – PART II

The highlight of the moving back to Martin's parents' house was that our kids could enroll in Stratford School in North Stratford. Both kids did much better, but April really excelled. She made lots of friends, became more social, and her grades shot right up. Douglas, on the other hand, was prone to daydreaming and was not hitting his full potential. The downside was we were living with Martin's parents, whose drinking was getting worse. Martin would try to keep up and his drinking also got worse. There were arguments between his parents, arguments between Martin and me, and arguments between Martin and his parents. One day the arguments got so bad and they were screaming and screeching so loudly, I couldn't even understand what they were trying to say.

One night, Martin's parents got exceptionally drunk, beyond their usual amount. All of us, Martin, myself, April, and Douglas had barricaded ourselves into our bedroom. Martin's father, who had been an assistant deputy brought a loaded gun out of his bedroom and wanted to kill someone. He kept roaring around the house saying, "I'm going to kill you, you bastard," but finally collapsed in the living room and gave up.

A couple of months after this incident, Martin quit his job in the mill and went to work for Metropolitan Life Insurance but had to attend school for six or eight weeks in Rhode Island. Martin would only come home on the weekends and leave late Sunday afternoon to get back there. One Sunday afternoon after he had, left the kids were outside playing. Martin's father was up and staggering about drunk. Martin's father cornered me in the kitchen and said, "I love you more than just a daughter in law." And he wanted to know if I could love him back. I said, "No, I'm married to your son, you're married, and you're just my father-in-law, and it's out of the question." And he just stood there with a dumbfounded look of shock on his face. I scurried to the bedroom, locking the door until I heard the kids come in. The final argument wasn't over everyone's drinking, or Martin's father approaching me, but over a dog. We had a dog, and Martin's parents just didn't like it. They accused the dog of being too big, of going in the house (which it

Chapter 24 – Bad to Really Bad

didn't), and of chasing Martin's mother around the clothesline. But it didn't. We got rid of the dog. So once again Martin packed up everything we owned, called his sister Joann and her new husband Dan, and we moved in with them. They lived in Groveton.

This move lasted about two and a half months. This was during the summer break. If we stayed, we'd need to reregister the kids in the Groveton School, which we really didn't want to do. We started looking and found a duplex to rent in Stratford. I didn't want to rent it, but Martin did. He wanted to get out of Joann and Dan's, and the kids could stay in their school. But the rent was about $300-$400 a month. Martin wasn't doing well with selling the insurance, and I heard later on he would take their deposits for life insurance and not turn in the form and pocket the money. We got behind on the rent and with utilities. The living room had this huge rock fireplace that you could actually walk into. When you didn't have the fireplace going, cold air surged through the apartment, which made the house even colder. We asked the landlord and bought some wood from him as the only heating for the house was the fireplace. We'd all had to sleep in the living room on the couch when it was opened up.

1978

Martin kept saying he was calling clients on the phone upstairs. But I went upstairs and listened, and I could hear Martin snoring. I said, "Shouldn't you be calling clients?" and we got into another massive fight. We were getting behind in paying our bills, and I asked our landlords if I could work in his convenience store after my regular job and weekends. They didn't pay me a salary but took it off what we owed for rent. In the meantime, a woman Martin knew through her parents had an apartment above the grocery store they were moving out of. So, we moved into that apartment. Our former landlords took us to court, saying we stole their wood. Martin had been going to throw away the receipt for the sale of the wood, but I kept it. They went on and on, but I had worked enough to make up the differences in the rent and I produced the receipt. The judge threw the case out. What a relief!

Prior to this, I had quit my job in Groveton as the commute was just too long. I then got a job in Colebrook in a sewing factory, Manchester

Chapter 24 – Bad to Really Bad

Manufacturing. I set pockets on coats, which they sewed for Sears. I wasn't the greatest pocket-setter, but I was promoted to a supervisor position of final inspections. That included clipping the price tag on the coat with a plastic gun, putting on the buttons, snipping all loose threads, making sure the linings were put in correctly, and adding an inspector tag. If the coats were dirty, they'd put masking tape on it and it would go to the cleaning department, all of it piecework. I was salaried, which didn't include overtime, but I was sick one day, and my pay wasn't docked.

1979 – 1984

I worked at Manchester Manufacturing for about five years. Business started falling off and they lost their contract with Sears. I was demoted with three other women from supervisor positions to inspectors, doing piecemeal work. I worked for about a year doing this.

By this time, Martin had lost his job selling insurance but was able to collect a meagre amount of unemployment. Martin eventually got a job at Tillotson's Rubber Company. They made rubber gloves.

1986 – 1989

I talked to Martin and suggested we should go to marriage counseling. He agreed. The local counselor was a Catholic priest, who was very open-minded and progressive. Under certain circumstance, he was not averse to abortion or divorce. We went to see him together, and then started seeing him separately. Martin saw him a couple of times by himself, and Father Tim got to the source of the trouble and said Martin was the cause of our problems and needed to change. Father Tim said I wasn't going to change, and Martin would need to. Martin told me everything was my fault, and I was the one who needed to change. Martin quit going, and I couldn't see going if Martin wasn't going.

Once again, I went back to his parents and sister, and they laughed me out of the house. It was all my fault; I didn't know how to have a good time. The same old song and dance. I had no one to talk to or go to.

Manchester Manufacturing just started going under. After talking to other people who worked at Tillotson's, and hearing what they did and what

Chapter 24 – Bad to Really Bad

they were paid versus what I was being paid, I applied there. I was 36, and the plant manager said I was the oldest person he had ever hired. He said, "This is a job for 18- to 20-year-olds, not a 36-year-old woman."

At that point, I was determined to prove him wrong. There were 67 racks of glove conveyers that went around, like the cleat on a bulldozer track. When it goes on the bottom half of the machine, it goes through the chemical tanks then comes up and around and goes through an oven run by steam-powered heat, which cures and dries the gloves. I'd pull 1,500 racks of gloves per day, and on each rack were 52 gloves. Which made 78,000 gloves. There were separate tubs for the good and bad gloves. They powdered the tubs, and even with blowers, you looked like the Pillsbury Doughboy, covered in cornstarch. Each shift was 12 hours.

At the beginning, I worked the same shift as Martin until I learned how to pull the gloves on my own. Our shift would start at 7 a.m., but Martin would start drinking at 6 a.m., he'd drink during work, and then stop at the mini mart on the way home to get more beer and continue drinking until he went to bed. This wasn't a once-in-a-while thing, it became standard each and every day. I'd ask him to let me drive on the way to work, but he'd get nasty and violent and say he could "fucking" drive. He already had one DUI.

Not only was I beat up physically, but there was mental abuse. When April turned 14, she'd try to break up fights and pull him off of me, he'd turn on her and beat both of us. He'd become like a caged animal. Douglas would leave when Martin got into one of these moods. One day on a day off, the kids weren't around, we got into another argument and he started to choke me to the point I was about to black out. I had fingerprints around my neck for a few days afterwards. After choking me, he pushed me hard, down to the floor.

A few months after the choking incident he came to the dinner table with a strange look. It only took moving a certain way or just asking what his day was like, and he'd lose it. On this night, he slapped and beat me until his anger either dissipated, or I got away from him. It was like Dr. Jekyll and Mr. Hyde. After this incident he slept with a loaded gun on his side of the bed by his headboard for the next week.

Chapter 24 – Bad to Really Bad

April called him a loser one night at the dinner table, and he pulled her out of the chair and drove her head right into the wall and kept banging it. I tried to pull him off, and it was impossible. It was like he had superhuman strength. Douglas would usually leave and go over to friends or lock himself into his bedroom. This became a regular event every couple of weeks. It would always get much worse if April or I tried to intervene when he went after the other one. After he was done and calmed down, there were no apologies or empathy. It was always our fault. I went again to his parents and sister and they weren't interested. They thought it was all my fault.

One day in early spring 1987, we got into a big fight, and he packed everything up and left. He said he was sick of me and the kids and wanted to do what he wanted to do. He went back to live with his parents yet again, but they turned him down. An hour later he came home and knocked on the door. He was crying at the door, saying how sorry he was and how his parents told him he had a wife and children and a responsibility so he couldn't leave. The kids were saying I should give him another chance. Maybe he meant it this time, so I let him in.

He was better for a while, maybe a month and a half. Then it started all over again. The same routine. Name calling, physical attacks, Douglas leaving, April being attacked. I was giving him the cold shoulder and he said, "You'll never leave me. If you try to leave, I'll have my friends lie and say you were sleeping with them, then I'll get the kids and leave you with nothing." I had no friends. Every time I tried to make a friend, Martin would become obnoxious and rude and drive them away.

Around June of 1987, I had a hysterectomy. I was hemorrhaging and the doctors couldn't stop it. While I was in the hospital, Martin beat up April, giving her black eyes. She took the car and stayed with her cousin Mary, who lived about 10-15 minutes away. They came to visit me in the hospital, and I asked what happened? She said she got hurt playing basketball with Mary. I told her that wasn't what happened. She then told me the truth that her and Martin got into a bad argument and he beat her. Martin came to visit me in the hospital after she left and came down with his mother and father and said he didn't know where April was. I asked what happened, and he said, "She took the car. She probably stole it." I asked, "Why would she do that?"

Chapter 24 – Bad to Really Bad

Martin said, "Well, she's a punk." Martin's parents just stood there. Their mouths were kind of hanging open. I thought I was safe in the hospital arguing with him. What was he going to do? Beat me up in the hospital? I said, "You beat her up. She has two black eyes. She took the car to get away from you. I know where she is and she's safe." Martin's face got red, his parents looked shocked, but Martin didn't say anything. Eventually he said, "I hope she comes home so I can apologize to her." I was so disgusted with the three of them I said, "I'm tired and need to sleep." And they left.

Three weeks later his parents moved to Arizona and we went back to their house to live. We were now living in his parents' house. April said something that I said wasn't very nice, and April got furious and punched me in the stomach really hard, just a few weeks after having the hysterectomy. While this argument unfolded, Douglas was standing behind me. He moved in front of me and grabbed April by the shoulders to try and hold her still, she broke free, jumped up in the air, grabbed his glasses off his face. She threw the glasses into the brick wall, shattering them. Douglas couldn't see anything without his glasses. I started yelling at April. I was out of work for six weeks due to the hysterectomy and was only getting minimal disability. I knew Martin wasn't going to provide any money, so I told April she was going to have to get a part-time job over the summer and pay to replace Douglas's glasses. Thankfully Douglas had just gotten contact lens, and his girlfriend Nicki heard what happened and got him some new glasses and new contacts. April never said she was sorry, never paid him back, and she denies it ever happened.

Chapter 25 – Alex

At work, I finally learned how to pull the gloves without Martin. After I learned how to pull gloves on my own, I switched shifts. We would put our names on a list when a machine and shift became open, and after a certain amount of time, the plant manager would discuss with the shift manager who was best for the job. They'd weigh your abilities and speed along with days missed and try to match the best person to the individual machine and task at hand. It also went by seniority. I was given the bid for the fourth shift, which was Thursday, Friday, Saturday and every other Sunday, 7 p.m. to 7 a.m. Martin didn't seem to care one way or another, and I was making more working the nightshift and the bonuses were a bit higher, based on how many racks of gloves you pulled in the twelve hours.

Alex was a machine tender, he added chemicals to the different tanks; if machines broke down or malfunctioned, he would be the one to fix and repair them. If it was too hard or difficult, then they'd have to call in the company electrician. Most of the time Alex fixed things himself. I knew him by name from him working various shifts on occasion, but we didn't actually know each other.

Alex was always very serious and business like. He actually intimidated me more than the plant foreman. Alex wore glasses, had a long beard and ponytail, and had a very strict no-nonsense demeanor. When I got on the fourth shift, he was my machine tender. He added the chemicals and he'd fix my machine, and little by little, we got to talking more and more. It turned out he wasn't the strict, intimidating person I had presumed him to be. He was very kind, gentle, and had a very good sense of humor. One day he was smirking about his German shepherd, Star. He'd obviously leave her alone while he went to work, and often she'd misbehave to show her displeasure at being left alone. He had a coat he loved, an antique from Canada made by Hudson Bay, and when he got home, he discovered Star had destroyed the coat. While not pleased, he chained Star up and went for a long drive to cool down. Upon hearing this, I got an entirely new perspective on who Alex was, and it opened my eyes to what a marriage to someone could actually be. The examples I had in front of me were my marriage to Martin, his parents'

Chapter 25 – Alex

marriage, and his sister's marriages. All of them were toxic, and for the first time, I could envision a better life.

Martin wouldn't let me have the car, or April insisted on having the car, so I'd ride to work with Barb and Ted. They had been living together for years. Barb and Ted were both using and selling drugs, with Ted doing time for possession. Unlike Martin, Barb and Ted were very kind to me, and no pressures to do or sell drugs. They understood what a hard time I was having as they knew Martin.

Barb and Ted lived maybe a mile away, and when Martin was going into one of his fits, I could call them anytime, even if it was late, they'd come over and Ted would distract Martin with a card game and Barb would spend time with me. This would distract Martin and diffuse the situation. Despite the drug use, they were good people and were good workers. One night I was talking to Barb and the subject came up about who we wished we could have for a husband or mate. Barb figured she'd stay with Ted as they'd been together for so long, and she asked who I'd pick and I said, "I'd pick Alex Smith. If he's so nice to animals and people at work, I'd choose Alex." So, I became more interested in Alex, but I don't think he knew it.

1990

This was near the end of the school year, and Douglas and April were seniors. (I had held April back in first grade due to a variety of issues, one being she was very bashful and shy and had reading disabilities. The teacher said they could promote her and push her through, but I opted to hold her back, so she'd have a better foundation.) Douglas enlisted in the Marines during his junior year and was set to join them two weeks after graduation to start basic training in South Carolina. April was already moving out little by little. She was going to move in with her boyfriend Steve in Groveton. That left me with Martin.

One afternoon before April moved out, she was going to be the Maid of Honor at her best friend's wedding. April had gone to be fitted for her dress, and they had wedding things to attend to. Douglas's girlfriend Nancy came by, and April and Nancy went out. I was left alone with Martin getting supper ready. I was in the very narrow galley kitchen with a big farm window behind

Chapter 25 – Alex

me, going almost from the floor to ceiling, four big panes on the top and four on the bottom, shut. Martin got into one of his fits, and I was frying pork chops on the stove and the grease was popping.

He's screaming about why the kids weren't home yet, and he got super angry and said, "You know, it would be so easy to just push you through that window."

I picked up the scalding frying pan and I said, "C'mon, make my day! Push me through the window and see what you're going to get." I had had enough. No more hitting, no more mental abuse. I wasn't going to take anything from him any longer. Martin had the common sense to back off.

I started making no-bake chocolate oatmeal cookies. I had laid it out in a pan like fudge, a solid 9x11 and brought them into work for Alex. He ate the whole thing and got sick that night. By this time, Alex had started to show some interest in me. I started bringing more things in and we got to talking more and more. Things with Martin started getting even worse. The frying pan incident hadn't sat well with him or me, and things were just escalating to such a point, I made up my mind to leave him.

Alex knew Martin and knew his reputation, which wasn't good. We decided we loved each other and wanted to be together. I didn't want to just spring the news on my kids. April had met Alex as she worked in the factory during summers and liked him. April would drop me off at wherever Alex was waiting, and she'd go visit friends and then come pick me up, so Martin wouldn't wonder where I was. Then I introduced Alex to Douglas. Douglas didn't like Alex at all. He said he was going to beat the crap out of him.

A friend of Martin's moved in with us about a month before I left. He was a co-worker named Mark. Mark was into drugs and used to beat his girlfriend. Mark moved into the bedroom I shared with Martin, and they unceremoniously took all my clothes and dumped them into a small spare bedroom. I suspected there was more going on than just "buddies" rooming together. There was a woman who worked at the factory named Laura. She was gay and had a child from a previous relationship. She wouldn't tell anyone who the father was. Her parents kicked her out, so I figured if there was room for Mark, there was room for Laura. I also didn't want to see her baby left out in the cold. Plus, there is safety in numbers.

Chapter 25 – Alex

Between Martin openly being with Mark, with my things dumped all over the place, finding Martin going through my purse looking for money, as he had spent all his on alcohol and drugs, I had had enough! One day when I was at home, Martin was at work, the kids were in school, and Laura and Mark were sitting in front of the TV smoking dope, I called Alex. I said, "Are you ready for me? Because I'm coming, ready or not." I then called Barb and said, "I'm leaving Martin. Can you help me move the last of my things?" which were just boxes of clothes and mementos. She agreed, no questions asked. Barb came to Alex's, left her car, and took his truck over to load things up with. Mark and Laura didn't even look up.

Around the end of February to the beginning of March, Alex and I had discussed the possibilities of moving in together. I had now known Alex for five years. Alex suggested we wait a bit so he could get his house together. Alex had built the home himself ten years previously and had lived in it as the sole occupant for the last seven years. The house didn't have running water but had a hand-pump in the kitchen sink and an attached shed that functioned as a shed and outhouse. The bathtub was in the kitchen, so water heated on the stove could be carried upstairs and put into a bucket with a showerhead on the bottom, creating a gravity shower. Over the years anything Alex thought might be of use for a project or repair, he'd take and stockpiled it in the house. So, in March, Alex took nine loads to the dump in Colebrook, just before it closed for good. He also started making miscellaneous repairs, trying to make it as livable as possible.

On the day of the move, Barb brought me and my belongings to Alex's. Barb took her car and left, and Alex and I started to unload stuff. I felt like a 10,000-pound weight had been lifted from me. The sense of relief was overwhelming for both of us. There was a learning curve to learn the hand-pump and how the house worked, but it felt like the first home I had since my mom passed. Alex and I spent the night relaxing.

The day I moved in, we received so many phone calls that we took the phone off the hook. The next day when I got to work, they said there was a call for me. The phone was next to the foreman's office and even he could hear the kids screaming. They were saying, "You're the mom, you're supposed to stay home and be there when we come home to visit." So, I'm

Chapter 25 – Alex

not supposed to have a boyfriend or live with anyone, but just be alone by myself and wait for them? The foreman told them the phone was for work only, and if they were going to call and harass me their calls wouldn't be put through. They didn't call at work anymore.

Within a week of moving out, I went to the bank where Martin and I had co-signed for a car loan that was taken out a couple of years previously. I spoke to the bank president and informed him I was not living with Martin any longer and no longer had possession of the car. I said I knew Martin was late on payments, but he's planning to move to Arizona, I told him if he wanted to get the car back, he should reclaim it now before Martin moved. He sort of laughed it off and said, "Well, maybe he'll come up with the payments."

I called Douglas at Martin's and asked him to meet me and say goodbye before he left for the Marines, but he made excuses, said goodbye, and hung up. I didn't even know where to write to him. About a month after Douglas left for basic training, I received a letter from him. He said no one had written to him so far and was hoping I would write. He said he was lonely and basic training was very hard. I contacted April and asked why she hadn't written, and she said she didn't have an address. She promised she'd write him that night. April became friendlier and would come over to visit. We'd barbecue or something. She didn't like how I was living, but figured it was my life. Douglas had sent a notice that he was graduating from Paris Island. He said he also sent a notice to Martin, but Douglas wasn't sure if Martin would show up.

Alex and I put our money together and drove to Paris Island to watch Douglas graduate. It was a very large and impressive ceremony. Douglas was given an award for Sharpshooting. After the ceremony, they were allowed to take us to certain points on the base. He showed us his barracks and a Burger King. Recruits weren't allowed into the Burger King until they graduated, so we took him to Burger King. He ate so much it was like he hadn't eaten in weeks. Martin never showed up. We got Douglas breakfast at the airport before we left, and again, it was an endless breakfast.

After we landed and as we were leaving the airport, as I approached the automated sliding doors, and thinking there the push/pull doors, I yanked

Chapter 25 – Alex

on the door and pulled it right off its track! As quietly as you can lay down a heavy glass door, we laid the door by the wall and very quickly drove home.

With the kids gone and me no longer there, I heard from people at work that Martin was going to give his notice, and that he and his "buddy" Mark were moving to Arizona. I knew that would make a divorce costlier and more difficult.

I went to a lawyer to see if he would represent me in a divorce. His secretary said, "Do you have any minor children or own property together?" I told her no. She said we could do the divorce ourselves, and they had a book they could sell me that showed me all the steps, and I bought it. It laid out everything from A to Z and pointed out what should be asked of the judge, etc.

It took about a month to go through the book. The forms had to be typed written, so I had to find someone who had a typewriter and could do this for me. I found a typist in the next town over. It cost more for her to type the forms than the fees for the actual divorce. All together the total costs were about $650. All the paperwork was notarized and needed to be served. I called the secretary and asked how the paperwork should be served and she said, "The sheriff can do that." I knew the sheriff, so we dropped the paperwork off with him to serve Martin. He had transported a prisoner to jail and the route back was right past Martin's, so he served him. Martin was incensed and so were the kids. They didn't understand why the sheriff had to be involved, why things were notarized, and why there was a court date.

The court date was the end of July or beginning of August 1990. Martin had been served in the beginning of July, but by then Martin had moved to Arizona. He didn't show up for work and April had gone by the house, and it was empty. I went to the court date and figured Martin wouldn't show up. It was in the judge's private chambers with the sheriff, who was there to keep the peace, in case Martin did show up. The judge asked you, "Even though the kids were over 18 and not in college, if they needed financial help, would he be able to?" I replied I would never ask Martin for any kind of assistance and I would take care of whatever the kids might need. The judge said, "What do you want of this marriage? Are you going to ask for alimony?"

Chapter 25 – Alex

The only things I wanted were a food chopper, the mixer, and silverware and plates I had paid for and already had. I requested that Martin make the car payments as he was in possession of the car. I informed him Martin was already delinquent. He just shook his head, and the Sheriff started to say he knew that Martin was not a good or a kind person. The judge said, "I'll grant the divorce in your favor!" and it was over. The final decree stated Martin would make up the back payments and all future payments on the car, he would pay any fines or late charges imposed by the bank, and he would keep insurance current on the car.

A couple months after the final decree, I received a notice in the mail the bank was suing me in regard to payments not being made on the car. It was small claims court. I went to court alone and had to sit and wait for the bank representative to show up. The court should have called a mistrial due to the bank not showing, but the court clerk called the bank and allowed them time to arrive.

Once the woman from the bank arrived, the judge took us into his private chambers. This was a different judge from the one who did the divorce. He asked for the divorce decree, read it all the way through, and told the bank representative that per the decree Martin was responsible any and all charges. The bank representative then said, "The bank is asking for $1,000 because we all know what a deadbeat her husband is. We know she's working and has earning power and could afford to make these payments."

The judge said, "Maybe you and Martin could work this out?"

At that point I flew into a rage and I threw the divorce papers in his face and said, "What the fuck difference does a divorce make? It doesn't mean shit? Why bother? I could have saved myself $650 dollars and put it to good use."

He said, "You better watch your mouth, or you can be held for contempt of court. I'm going to let you two ladies work it out. What can you afford to pay the bank each week?"

I said, "$25" and the woman from the bank looked like she was going to blow a gasket. She opened her mouth, then shut it.

Chapter 26 – The Accident
1990 – 1992

Now the divorce was final, and all the financial entanglements settled, I settled into a life I had always wanted and never had. Alex and I worked the same shifts, we took our breaks together, and spent all our time together. We got paid on Thursday nights, and we'd have breakfast the next morning and wait for the bank to open, then go do our grocery shopping and errands together. It was our routine. We took two trips out West. The first was a three-week trip in 1990 right after Labor Day. We drove west to Colorado. Included in the trip were stops in Arizona, New Mexico, Utah, Montana, Wyoming, and Idaho. This was a leisurely trip with no set schedule. We spent a few days in Cortez, Colorado. We had friends there and even thought it would be a nice place to retire to. We got back in the beginning of October.

For the next two years, we settled in for what would be the best years of our lives. April went out to Arizona for a week in the summer of 1991 to visit her father, her grandparents, and Martin's sister Margaret. Martin was hardly there. Margaret took her around and showed her things so April wouldn't be sitting around waiting for Martin and Mark to get home. While April was there, she nosed around a bit and found a cache of mushy love letters Mark had written to Martin. Each apartment had its own backyard section, divided with a white picket fence. Once day, April noticed Martin's face looked like someone had taken a hammer to it. When she asked, he said, "I got drunk and fell on the fence". Later April found out Martin and Mark had gotten very drunk, and Mark had beaten Martin.

Shortly after April returned home, Martin let her know Mark had lost his job at the train station. Money had gone missing from the ticket station, and they more-or-less accused Mark. As a result, they lost their fancy apartment. Martin was doing landscaping work. Martin also let April know they took a very nice vacation once she had left. Despite this, April always looked up to her father but held me responsible for everything that had gone wrong.

After the trip, April started to see Martin more for who he actually was, and things improved between us. In the meantime, her boyfriend, whom she

Chapter 26 – The Accident

had moved in with, wasn't doing as well. He'd go out, not tell her where he was, and come back at all hours. About three to four months after the Arizona trip, sometime in fall, she came down with Graves' disease and moved in with us. She started losing her hair and lost a lot of weight. Her nerves were frayed, and she had dark circles under her eyes. Her doctor sent her to Dartmouth for three days of tests. After she was diagnosed with Graves' disease, we were there for a couple more days so they could start the treatments.

April stayed with us for about two months while she recovered and eventually got back together with her boyfriend and moved back in with him. Douglas had been deployed to the Middle East, Somalia, Israel, Saudi Arabia, Kuwait, and he even called collect from Spain. We talked for over half an hour and the charge was only $28.

At the beginning of 1992, April broke up again with her boyfriend for keeps and got her own apartment in Colebrook. We helped her with groceries, car repairs, and other things she couldn't swing on her own. April was doing better, and our relationship was doing well too.

The second trip we took was a few weeks before Memorial Day in 1992. This was basically the same loop as the previous trip, but with various different side trips. This trip was about three weeks as well. We made it down to the Grand Canyon and Bryce Canyon.

We had been back home a couple of weeks when Douglas came home for leave. The plan was that he would stay with April in her apartment, which was about 15 minutes away from us. Before he came home, he had bought a brand-new Chevrolet Geo Tracker from a dealership in Berlin, New Hampshire. He had insurance through a North Carolina company, but I paid the registration and inspection fees so he could drive it the second he got back. He was coming over every day for a barbecue or supper, but he was spending most of his time with his girlfriend. Towards the end of Douglas's leave, Alex got a call from his cousin. His cousin was going on a Mercy Ship and wanted to give Alex a wood burning stove, which had belonged to Alex's grandmother. Alex went up to Connecticut to get the stove, and I stayed home so I could spend some more time with Douglas before he went back

Chapter 26 – The Accident

from leave. We also had a small puppy then at home in a cage, so I had to be around to feed her.

Douglas had had a couple of beers at April's earlier in the afternoon and April said, "Douglas, do you want me to take Mom home to feed the puppy? You've had a couple, maybe I should drive so you don't get in trouble?"

And Douglas said, "No, I'm fine. I'll drive her home."

He wanted to show off his new car to me. The Geo Tracker had a short wheelbase, with a high center of gravity, and a convertible canvas top. We were heading down Marshall Hill Road, which was paved until you hit the crest, and then it was dirt. About 50 feet past where the paving ended, there was a culvert creating a sizable bump in the road that has never been addressed. Douglas and I got into an argument about me going to court over the car Martin took to Arizona. He asked me why I didn't win, and I said the judge said it was between me and the woman from the bank. Douglas asked why they couldn't get the money from Martin and I told him they said Martin was a deadbeat and that I was working, lived in town, and they knew they could get the money from me, and my name was on the car loan.

Douglas got mad and said, "WHY DID THEY CALL HIM A DEAD-BEAT?"

"It's true. It's what he is," I said and gave him examples about not making payments, him taking the car out of state, never contacting the bank, and just keep driving the car. At this point, we got off the asphalt, hit a bump, and the car rolled into a telephone pole. I was unconscious. Douglas either got out or was thrown out of the car and ran to a neighbor and asked them to call an ambulance. They took me to the Colebrook Hospital. Alex was still in Connecticut.

After I was out of the hospital, they told me they had to open my stomach and check for internal bleeding before they could move me to Dartmouth. Alex got home sometime after 10 p.m., and the phone was ringing. Alex's aunt was on the phone and told him to get down to the Colebrook hospital right away. Alex went in and could hardly recognize me. April came down and almost passed out when she saw me.

Douglas was in another room with a broken collarbone and torn ligaments in his leg but was otherwise okay. April stormed into his room and

Chapter 26 – The Accident

screamed at him. She told him, "THIS IS ALL YOUR FAULT! IF YOU LET ME DRIVE, THIS ACCIDENT WOULD NOT HAVE HAPPENED! WE DON'T KNOW IF MOM IS GOING TO LIVE OR DIE! IT'S ALL YOUR FAULT!!!"

Alex went in and told Douglas no one was blaming him for the accident. It was an accident, and no one was holding anything against him.

Chapter 27 – Alex's Story

(As told by Alex)

I was born in Connecticut to parents who were from New Hampshire. We had relatives here and spent a lot of time visiting them in New Hampshir3e. As a little kid we used to visit a dairy farm where my mother was raised in Stratham, New Hampshire. I was enthralled with the dairy farm and that was my dream and goal growing up: being a farmer. On my 18th birthday I headed north because Connecticut had nothing to offer. I studied for two years at the University of New Hampshire. I studied forestry a year, and then I transferred to milk production management for another year. I left UNH and started working in various dairy farms for about six years. At that point I thought I was better off working in a sawmill as I was interested in that, and it also paid better. That went on for a couple of years. This was around southern New Hampshire, but I always wanted to live in the Colebrook area. There were originally 250 acres that belonged to my family. When my grandfather passed 1934 the property was in flux with no clear ownership and in 1987, I got clear ownership of the property in exchange for paying off my grandmother's nursing home bills. I moved to Colebrook in 1978 and started working at Tillotson's Rubber Company. Tillotson's was the only job in the Colebrook I could find.

My first job there was working the production line, pulling balloons for about a year. They shut down the balloon falling apart. My foreman thought I had more going for me than working on the production line, so he trained me to be a machine tender. There would be two machine tenders per shift with 11 machines, so one tender would do five and the other would do six. Normally, I would have five machines and also provide backup when someone took their 20-minute break.

I was living in Jefferson when I first started. That was 55 miles away and I was getting tired of the long commute, especially in the winter. There had been a house on the land that was still in flux with ownership designation, but it had burnt to the ground just prior to my moving to Colebrook. I decided I was going to build a little camp on the lot where the house was

Chapter 27 – Alex's Story

until I could build a real house. This cost $750 to build utilizing wood from Tillotson's dump. It was going to be a temporary place to live.

I went to the New Hampshire Folk Festival in 1979 and met my future wife, Samantha. I knew her for about six months, and she had a daughter from a previous relationship. We got married in 1980, and they moved in with me. It was obvious things weren't going to work out from the beginning. But it took three years to reach that conclusion that it wasn't going to work. I came home from work one day. Samantha was gone and so was everything in the house. It was obvious she had this planned for a while. It took two years of legal battles to finalize the divorce. That set me back a bit in terms of building a house.

I met Danni on the various shifts that we'd be on and got know her over a period of four and a half years. I knew her husband and knew what a rotten home life she had. Martin was not a nice person. I knew she had to get out of there. I really wanted her to move out and get her own place, just for a while, so the kids wouldn't resent me. She finally hit the breaking point, so our mutual friend, Barb and her boyfriend Willie, who were trying to push us together, went down and got Danni and all her belongings and brought them to my place. We had a very good first couple of years, then the car accident changed everything. An event like this could easily have driven us apart, but it pulled us together stronger than ever.

When I got to Colebrook hospital, I could hardly recognize Danni. She had two black eyes, her face was swollen up, she was severely bruised on the right side of her body. She was black and blue. She had a compound fracture with her arm, but just had a temporary splint on it. The doctors sat April and me down in the waiting room, trying to prepare us for the worst. In their efforts to try and calm us down, they were actually making things much worse. They needed to stabilize her before they transferred her to Dartmouth. Dartmouth is about 4 hours away.

I went home to get some sleep and headed down to Dartmouth around 7 a.m. I got there and realized I had no control over anything. I wasn't a relative and had no legal say so, but I did not want to leave the decision making up to April. When she was in Dartmouth, teams of doctors would come in and talk to her and observe her, but they wouldn't talk to me. I was

Chapter 27 – Alex's Story

in the main hall one day and ran into a medical student in that group and explained my situation. She set me up with a doctor, a reconstructive surgeon, to come talk to me and he was very helpful and told me I needed to get power of attorney. I went to an office in Dartmouth, and it went quickly and easily. After that I could question people and was listed as the person to call and talk to and was the one to make decisions.

Danni's condition was worse than we imagined. She had a broken neck; a compound fracture of her right arm, which resulted in two plates and 12 pins; and the nerves were severed in her right eye – when they opened it manually it was only the white. They had to manually center it, and they wanted to wait some time to see how it might recover on its own. They had to put a silicon sling in the eyelid and connect it to Danni's eyebrow muscle, so she could control it with that. She had a blood clot on the brain, and they tried to dissolve it with medication, but it didn't work, so they had to do surgery and remove it: otherwise she would die. Once they had performed the surgery to remove the blood clot, they put on a halo neck brace that she needed to wear for quite a while.

Danni was in ICU for three weeks, and I honestly had no idea if she was going to make it or not. Towards the end of the three weeks in ICU, I finally started to get the feeling things were going to improve. They moved her into a step-down room, which was half-way between the ICU and a regular room. Danni had regular nurses, rather than assistants, and the level of care and responsiveness was much better. It seemed like there was always a nurse around. She was in the step-down room for about a week, and then she went into a regular room. Danni ended up staying there for five and half weeks. There was permanent brain damage, which resulted in needing speech therapy as well as physical therapy along with occupational therapy.

Once she was in intensive care, I went back to the bank who had won the settlement over the car and told the woman, "Danni is in critical condition, I don't know if or when she can ever pay the judgement," turned and left. Things were 100% better after receiving power of attorney. All medical conversations now involved me. I took the five and a half weeks off from work, and then took an extended leave for almost a year. Thankfully, they kept my job for me. I was travelling back and forth from Colebrook to

Chapter 27 – Alex's Story

Dartmouth and back, as we had a fairly large menagerie of animals including horses, cows, cats and dogs that needed to be cared for.

Prior to the accident Danni was planning to open a new bank account at a different bank to reestablish her credit. Between what she had saved and her paycheck that week she had about $450 in her purse. Her purse went missing in the accident, but one of the ENT's found it and brought it home with her. A few days afterwards she called me and said I could come up and get it. As was expected, the money was no longer in the purse. Between the accident and taking the time off from work, we had no money coming. I went back to the factory and talked to the manager. He gave me a check for $200. They had a benefit club at work, so if you're out for more than 10 days, they'd give you a check. They also went around the company, and everyone donated. I can't recall the exact amount, but it certainly helped out. After that money was gone, my mother helped out.

After the five and a half weeks I went home. Up until this point, Danni's medical insurance was covering everything. Once discharged, Dartmouth referred her to a rehab facility in Vermont, but the insurance wouldn't cover it. The rehab the insurer would cover wasn't comprehensive enough, so basically the advanced rehab Dartmouth wanted you to receive wasn't available. Douglas's insurance company was in North Carolina. We talked with them once, and they said they would send a check to tide us over until everything was figured out. The check was for $2,000. When we received it, we looked on the back and in very tiny print it said, "In Full and Final Settlement." We found a lawyer out of the phone book. The lawyer was in Concord, and he said do not sign the check and to send it back to the company. Douglas received a similar check, and Douglas' commanding officer said the same thing. Douglas' commanding officer called the insurance company and told them not to send any more checks like this, or they'd have the Marines to deal with.

The lawyer felt we'd have a good chance at a successful lawsuit against Chevrolet and the Geo Tracker, as it had such a poor track record for accidents. It had a short wheelbase and a high center of gravity. Two lawsuits were started, one against the insurance company and one against Chevrolet. Part of the discovery process entailed us buying the Geo Tracker and putting

Chapter 27 – Alex's Story

it in storage, so we would have it as evidence. Over the course of a year, our lawyer would give us $1,000 here or $2,000 there. In the end, one of the lawyers involved had a conflict of interest with Chevrolet, so that lawsuit was dropped. We eventually secured a settlement of $100,000 from the insurance company, but by the time the lawyer took his 25%, the hospital took about 50% and once the costs of the Geo Tracker and storage were factored in, we ended up owing the law firm money. They said they'd take the Geo Tracker and call it even. Now I wish I had taken their offer in the first place!

Prior to the accident when Douglas had been visiting, he was seeing a local girl. We both liked her. She was the one that drove April to the hospital. Douglas was in the Colebrook Hospital and was discharged after two or three days. Either just before the accident or just afterwards, he went to a cousin's high school graduation party in Lancaster. He met a girl named Wilma who was graduating at the same time. Two weeks into Danni's stay in ICU he showed up – after not hearing a peep from him – with Wilma in tow. He introduced her as the woman he was going to marry. He didn't ask how Danni was, it was all about he had a fiancée. They stayed for about half an hour and only talked about their upcoming nuptials. A couple of weeks after the visit, we heard that they had a wedding at Wilma's parents' home. Towards the end of Danni's stay at Dartmouth, Douglas and Wilma came to visit one more time as Douglas was shipping out again. They walked in and said they were married; she had a diamond ring and he had a wedding band. They stayed for about half an hour. They complained that very few showed up to the wedding and were unhappy with the number of gifts they got. Douglas left first, and Wilma hung back and then said, "Do you have $50 I could borrow so I can fly down with Douglas, otherwise I'll have to wait until I get paid next week?" We explained we had no money coming in, and she shot us an incredulous glance, said goodbye, and left.

About a week and a half before Danni was discharged, April was going to come and spend the weekend in Danni's room with her before her discharge the following Wednesday. About a week before the discharge, I was on my way home and stopped in Lancaster at the McDonald's to eat. April's then-boyfriend worked there. During the conversation I let him know

Chapter 27 – Alex's Story

that when Danni was going to be discharged, she'd be coming home with me, not April. He immediately called April and informed her.

April called Danni at Dartmouth and said, "Who are you coming home with? Him or me?"

Danni said, "Well, I'm going home with Alex."

She then said, "Then you can rot in hell!" and hung up!

Chapter 28 – Danni's Story Continued
1992

After being discharged from the hospital, I went home with Alex. I asked the nurses if I could go back to work in a month or six weeks. They had said it was up to the doctor to answer. I thought maybe going back to work wasn't going to happen. Just sitting up at the table wore me out. I couldn't finish a bowl of soup. I was drinking and going to the bathroom non-stop. I got the idea that Gatorade would be a good idea and was drinking massive amounts. The nerves to my pituitary gland had been severed and this resulted in me continuously being thirsty and needing to urinate. Within a year's time I gained 100 lbs. I had a cast on my arm from my fingers past my elbow, I couldn't see, because my left eye was my bad eye, and my right eye was out of commission. Alex's mother sent some money to get glasses. At this point, light was almost unbearable and even though my main glasses had the transitions that got darker outside, it was still too bright, so I had to get a prescription pair of darker glasses.

I wore the halo neck brace for three months. Along with the halo itself, there was a large part of the brace went all the way down to my waist, very heavy, and a sheepskin vest underneath the metal vest to protect the body. This was incredibly warm during the summer months. The doctor said that if one more vertebra had broken in my neck, I'd have been a quadriplegic. One time there was a crocheted Afghan on my bed, and I'm not sure how, but it got tangled up in the halo. Alex was outside talking to a friend and I had to find my way out the door with this Afghan hanging in front of my face. I also managed to get it stuck in the refrigerator one time. We had antlers around the house, and I managed to get stuck in a pair. I couldn't move, and Alex had to finally free me. He removed the antlers from the walls after that.

About the third night after I was discharged from the hospital, April came over with a big pan of lasagna. We had a nice talk, and it was like she trying to make up for being nasty earlier on the phone. She only stayed for a few minutes and then left.

Chapter 28 – Danni's Story Continued

The halo was attached in four spots on my head, and the contact points needed to be cleaned at least twice a day. After about three months, I went to the hospital for a checkup and the doctors wanted to do an X-ray and said it was time for the halo come off. In the meantime, between drinking the Gatorade and the weight gain, the vest had gotten very tight. While the vest was adjustable, it was up to the doctors to adjust it, not me. They had me standing up on the floor, with nothing around to support me, two doctors on each side of me, with their tools undoing things and unscrewing things. The way it would normally work would be one screw/contact point over each eyebrow, but due to the severity of the head injury, they had two almost side-by-side over my left eye, as well as a screw behind each ear. They got the top of the halo off, and there's blood running in my eye, once they removed the screws it was bleeding. They then took the vest off. It was one piece and had to be lifted off over my head. My knees started to buckle, and it felt like was going to pass out. Both doctors grabbed me under my arms and said, "We've never lost anyone on the floor yet." They removed the fleece vest and put a band aid on my head and told Alex to keep the area clean. They then gave me a more standard-issue neck brace. I was told to wear that it 24/7 for about three months. After those three months were over, they said I'd need to wear the brace if I went anywhere, or if I felt discomfort in my neck to wear it until it felt better.

About six months later Wilma's mother threw her a baby shower, and we received an invitation. I attended with April. April bought a very expensive and nice car seat and both our names were on the gift. I was very nervous getting ready for the event. Wilma's parents lived in Lancaster (about 36 miles away) in an older house, but very well kept up. When I walked in there were maybe a dozen people, with Wilma's mother center stage showing me all the things they had bought for the baby. It looked like the infant's department in a large department store. I felt she was bragging about everything she had done, and I was fighting back tears, feeling as though I wasn't a very good mother. She could tell I was upset and asked what was wrong. I explained that I felt like the poor church mouse. She said rather dismissively, "Oh, don't worry, you have to pick these things up when they're on sale." I kept my mouth shut and was happy for Wilma and

Chapter 28 – Danni's Story Continued

Douglas. We stayed maybe 45 minutes to an hour. We waited until all the gifts were opened. Neither Douglas nor Wilma asked how I was doing. They simply said, "Hi" and greeted us like they would a neighbor from down the street. April didn't care for Wilma's mother, her husband, or Wilma. The separation between April and Douglas was getting wider.

Douglas had been able to get leave for Thanksgiving in 1992, and we had a small Thanksgiving meal at April's apartment. Her parents had a larger gathering earlier in the day, but for dinner it was me, Alex, April, Wilma and Douglas.

At one point during the evening April was cleaning, Wilma kind of nudged me off into a corner. She then said, "Douglas felt really bad because you didn't show up at the wedding, and my mother wanted to have the ceremony in your hospital room." Wilma got a distasteful look on her face and said, "I've never been married before and wanted a proper wedding."

I said, "Well, I'm sorry. Do you realize I was in intensive care? There was no way I could come to your wedding. I didn't know if I was going to live or die. I didn't even know you were getting married on that day or at any other time!"

Wilma shrugged and said, "Well, Douglas can't get over it."

April called the week before Christmas saying that Douglas and Wilma were going to stay with her for Christmas. Douglas had a four-day leave, and they'd be heading out the day after Christmas. I was happy to see Douglas but wasn't thrilled about seeing Wilma. Wilma would throw out snide remarks, and then turn around and say, "Just kidding." She would be mean and say hurtful things, and then try to brush it off as a joke.

We arrived at April's place Christmas Eve for dinner, and Wilma and Douglas were there. Wilma had made stockings with everyone's name on it, all filled with tiny wrapped gifts. As we sat down Douglas said, "What happened is water under the bridge. I want us to all start over and be a family" and gave Alex a big hug and Alex hugged him back. We settled in for a nice meal. April was doing dishes and Wilma got me aside once again. She said, "Douglas can never forgive you for leaving him and his sister behind and running off with Alex. Douglas wanted a mother, and I'm not going to be his mother. If he wants that, he'll have to come back to you."

Chapter 28 – Danni's Story Continued

She went on to say Douglas would compare the way I did things to the way Wilma did them, and he preferred the way I did them. Before I could even respond, April or someone came into the room, she shot me a smile and walked away. I was so hurt; I couldn't have even responded even if I wanted to.

1993

As 1993 started, I realized I was going to be permanently disabled, but I also figured it would be something where I'd go to the doctor once or twice a year. I thought there was nothing that they could really do for me. We settled into what was now the new normal. Things were fairly routine.

Alex went back to work in April. They held his job open and were also very understanding that he might have to leave at a moment's notice if he received a call from me. It didn't happen often, but it was a worry that was there. They offered Alex a supervisory position over a shift, but he just couldn't accept knowing there would be times he might have to leave. And there were times he had to.

Alex related, "One time after I went back to work, Danni became obsessed with the wood burning stove. She was constantly opening the door and looking in it. She was putting things in it all the time and actually ended up burning a pair of my boots. The house would fill up with smoke, and she'd be sitting there just staring at the fire."

At a regular check in April or May and the doctor discovered some strange lumps and bumps on the side of my stomach. Before they had taken Me to Dartmouth after the accident, they had to open me up to look for internal bleeding, then after being at Dartmouth, they put the halo with the vest on. What no one knew was the incision from Colebrook had opened, and a few months after removing the halo and vest, they discovered I needed hernia surgery. We drove down to Dartmouth and I was there for about a week. When I came home there were two drains on either side that had to be emptied and measured. The drains were in for a month, possibly more.

Chapter 28 – Danni's Story Continued

1994

April got married January 1. She was a beautiful bride, and the gown she selected was THE gown. She looked like a princess. It fit her perfectly. Douglas was going to give her away but wasn't sure if he would make it or not, so Alex was ready to stand in if needed. Douglas did make it. He wore his military dress blues, with white gloves, and a sword by his side. The pastor that married April and John was John's second uncle through marriage. The ceremony was very nice, and the church was already full of flowers from Christmas. First Alex and I and then John's parents went to the altar and lit a candle. The reception was held at a hall April had rented not too far from the church. There was no alcohol served, per the hall's rules. The food was a potluck with many wonderful things to choose from. John's aunt, also named Danni, DJ'd. The reception ended early, everyone went home, and April and John headed off on their honeymoon. That night April bought a pregnancy kit and discovered she was pregnant. Her son was born in September that year.

Shortly after the wedding, Alex noticed I had this weird rash on my hip, thigh and running down my calf, and the back of my arm and it almost looked like chicken pox. The rash was on my right side, the side that was injured in the accident. If a scab caught on something, it would hurt, but otherwise it didn't bother me. In March we went to the regular doctor in Dartmouth. At first, he thought it was shingles, and took pictures of it. He sent me to dermatology, and they took biopsies and took more pictures and after seeing every department, it went undiagnosed. They could never figure out what it was, and after a year it started to recede and finally cleared up.

After being diagnosed with diabetes insipidus from the accident, someone at the hospital made me aware of a newsletter dedicated to this topic. I read the newsletter and it was $10 to subscribe. I wrote them a note saying I'd like to subscribe but just didn't have the money for it. I told them it was good that they were printing this and putting it out there, letting people know they weren't alone and that others had this too. It's not well known, and less than two million people have it in the US. The newsletter printed my reply and a woman read my letter and said she'd pay for the subscription

Chapter 28 – Danni's Story Continued

for me if I wanted it. She had a daughter who was born a month before my accident who also had disabilities and challenges.

Early that summer I had my first eye surgery, to bring my right eye back to where it should be. The ophthalmologists had wanted to give me time to see if my eye would correct itself, but it didn't. Sometimes it would be up, or all over the place. The ophthalmologist – who was also the surgeon – asked if I'd be able to get used to double or triple vision with the eye. There was no depth perception left. If something was moving, I'd have trouble knowing what was moving and what wasn't. She said some manage with it, others don't. I asked if they took the eye out if it could help someone else who couldn't see. She said there wasn't anything worth saving for anyone else. I agreed to have the eye surgery.

After the surgery, my eye stayed in place, but I had double or triple vision with it. The cornea is open all the time, and the eye lid won't close all the way. There's a slight crack, so I need to use a special eye lubricant all the time, as it dries out easily. It also doesn't make its own tears. They put a patch on my eye and eye drops with an antibiotic to avoid getting an infection. After five days, I had a follow-up and the doctor said I didn't need to see them again. While not what it was before the accident, it was better after the surgery.

Things reached a certain normalcy. We'd go on moose rides, where we'd drive about 45 minutes to an hour away north to swampy land that moose like. We'd do this at dusk and one night we counted 28, mostly bull moose with the full antlers. These were individual moose, in different spots, not a herd.

Shortly after Labor Day, we had enough money that we took a trip out west. We went to Colorado, Montana, Utah, Wyoming, Idaho, and we slept in campgrounds, sleeping in the truck in a rest area, and sometimes stayed in motels. We went to different shops, and we stopped at one in Colorado. They would get merchandise from all over: Western saddles, old boots, hats, older Indian jewelry with turquoise and silver. We found a really lovely wedding vase. The wedding vase had two spouts and is glazed on the inside, and the outside is porous and painted in lovely Indian designs. The Navajo tradition is that the husband and wife drink from their respective spouts at the same time, and then the vase is put on display in a place of honor. If the couple separates, or one dies, then the vase is to be destroyed. We found one we thought that was exceptionally beautiful and bought it for Douglas and Wilma and wrote the story of the vase. Their first child was coming up on two years, and we found a figurine of an Indian woman sitting on the ground with a loom in front of her. Her hands were on the loom and she had started to weave a blanket or rug and had balls of yarn beside her. We thought that would be nice for her.

We had always heard Wilma's Mom had done this or that for the kids, and frankly, I was a bit jealous. We thought these items would be something truly unique and would have a deeper meaning for Douglas, Wilma, and their daughter. Also, Douglas and April are part Indian (French Abenaki Indian), so a bit of significance.

Fall came and went, and we had a nice Thanksgiving with April and her husband. And then Christmas came. For Christmas we wrapped the gifts for Douglas and his family, who were living in North Carolina at that time, and sent them off in plenty of time to get there before Christmas. Christmas eve, in the evening, I get a phone call from Douglas. He sounded upset.

Douglas said, "Mom, you know the gifts you sent us? We're going to have to send them back."

I could hear Wilma muttering something in the back, but it was unintelligible.

Douglas said, "We're sending the gifts back."

I asked, "Why? Did they get broken?"

He then said, "Because they were made by heathens, and it's against our religion to accept them."

I started crying, I was upset, and these weren't cheap trinkets. They were handmade and very nice and not inexpensive.

I said, "Douglas, you are part Indian. I've gotten gifts in the past that maybe didn't fit or were something I didn't like, but I appreciated the thought and effort."

He then said, "Aren't you afraid you're going to go to hell, Alex and you, by living in sin? Don't you want to be in heaven with Wilma and me when you die?"

Chapter 28 – Danni's Story Continued

I said, "How can you be so sure and full of yourself that you and Wilma are going to heaven? Maybe you'll find out you're not good enough to get into heaven? Douglas, as of this Christmas I will no longer send any Christmas gifts to you and Wilma and the only thing we send to your daughter will be a savings bond or gift certificate." I then said, "Goodbye" and hung up the phone. Within a week the gifts showed up, before New Year's Eve.

I shared the story with April, and she dismissively said, "He's just a dink."

1995 – 1996

Things were quiet after the Christmas fiasco: I didn't want to keep the gifts we had purchased and were rejected. It hurt too much looking at them. I wrote a thank you letter to the woman thanking her for the newsletter subscription, and I called her on the phone. I explained the situation with the gifts we had given to Douglas and said I couldn't think of nicer people and asked her if she'd like the gifts and she said yes. Since then every year we've exchanged Christmas cards and talk on the phone occasionally, but we've never met face-to-face. She is now an advocate for handicapped people.

A couple of weeks before Memorial Day, we took our final trip and vacation out West visiting Colorado, New Mexico, Utah, Idaho, and Montana. Monument Valley and the Grand Teton National Park were both outstanding and very memorable.

That summer my eye had centered enough that they wanted to do the silicon sling that would be hooked to my eyebrow muscles and forehead, allowing me to open and close my eye. The surgery went well.

Things went fairly well, and nothing was amiss until 1997.

1997

During a routine office visit for bloodwork, the doctors discovered that I was severely anemic. My primary care doctor wanted to include the Oncology Department. They were concerned I might have leukemia. They did a spinal tap, taking marrow from the base of my spine, which hurt, but they were able to rule out leukemia. Their next course of action was a blood transfusion to try and jump-start treatment. The anemia actually got worse. Then they were going to put me on iron medicine, but it made me very sick. I'd have to go into Oncology and have iron infusions. It was the same place they were doing chemotherapy, and each infusion would take about four hours. The chairs had individual TVs, they served us lunch, and had handmade quilts to make everyone comfortable. I had to go every week for about three months. They never could figure out what the cause of the anemia was. After each infusion, I felt fine, but the day after that I'd feel sick as a dog. They started giving me Ativan, which really helped. Towards the end of the infusions my blood started going back to where it should be and has stayed there.

The rest of the year things were fine.

1999

Things were going fairly smoothly, the only things that took place were cataract surgeries on both eyes, done at different times. Both surgeries went fine.

2000

After having two sons, April and John separated and divorced in 2000.

2004

Subsequent operation on each eye and different times. Thankfully, both of those worked out fine.

2005

Alex was at work one evening on the night shift, and I lost my balance and fell sideways into the wood stove, which was on full blast. I was wearing a chenille bathrobe, which caught fire as I knocked the pipe that ran to the chimney. But I was able to use a hot pad and put the pipe back before too much smoke entered the house. We kept a pan of water on the stove so the air wouldn't get too dry and used that to put the fire out on the robe. Thankfully there wasn't a serious burn. But what a scare I had!

Chapter 28 – Danni's Story Continued

Later in 2005, the doctor ordered an endoscopy and a colonoscopy. I wasn't feeling well and had lost about 50 lbs. within two months. After gaining 100 pounds, losing 50 pounds in two months was scary. I went in for the endoscopy, and they found out I had H Pylori (Helicobacter pylori), which is a type of bacteria. These germs can enter your body and live in your digestive tract. After many years, they can cause ulcers. For some people, an infection can lead to stomach cancer. I took antibiotics for about two weeks, however they made me sicker than the bacteria they were trying to cure. It did get things under control though. The colonoscopy, which took place later, was uneventful and everything was fine.

In August, it was one of April's son's birthday. It was her, her kids, and us. We arrived a bit late at April's home, but we knew right away that April was in a foul mood. April was busy in the kitchen, didn't say hello, just acted like we weren't even there. We sat down at the table with her and the boys. Previously, April had told me that Martin's sister, Sue, who we liked a lot, had been diagnosed with cancer. She had also told us that Sue's daughter Katie had been diagnosed as well. As we were having cake and ice cream, and I asked how Sue was doing.

April went into a major hissy fit. She said, "How the fuck do you think she's doing? She has cancer! Get the fuck out of my house, bitch, and don't ever come back!"

We gave the birthday boy his birthday present and explained that we couldn't come back. The boys had a shocked look on their face because I was their nana. But we left anyway

In November, April called to invite us for Thanksgiving. She had a nasty tone of voice.

I asked, "Do you want us there, or is it the boys want us there?"

And April said, "I don't give a fuck if you come back or not. The boys are giving me a hard time because of how I treated you at the birthday party."

I said, "Well, we won't be coming for Thanksgiving then." I asked her to put the boys on the phone and I explained why we couldn't be there for Thanksgiving. They understood why we couldn't be there, but they didn't sound happy about it.

Chapter 28 – Danni's Story Continued

Just before Christmas, April's best friend Barbara Ann called me up. Barbara Ann said, "April wanted me to call and apologize for the way she acted and that she felt really bad afterwards and it's bothered her since it happened. She wants you to be Mom and daughter again."

I said, "Why didn't April call herself?"

Barbara Ann said, "April was embarrassed, and she felt really bad for what she did and was sorry."

I didn't feel that April had requested her to call, but that Barbara Ann took it upon herself to try and make things better. I waited a couple of weeks and as it got closer to Christmas, I called April. I told her friend had called and apologized for her, and she didn't really reply. She very nicely invited Alex and I for Christmas. I said we'd go, and we went. Christmas went very well, no arguments, the boys were happy, and everything was fine.

Chapter 29 – Precursor to the Big Surgery
2006

Friends of April's owned a timeshare in the Bahamas. One of the sisters couldn't go, so there was an extra plane ticket and bedroom, so she went with them. She needed a babysitter. Alex and I talked it over, and I stayed with the boys for a week and babysat. The dinners were already prepared, and I just needed to warm them up in the microwave. One night we were watching TV and the phone was ringing and I picked up the remote control and was cussing that no one was there, while the boys kept smirking and laughing. They finally said, "Nana, that's the remote control, here's the phone." I was embarrassed! We had a good laugh over Nana's lack of electronic expertise!

The night April came home, she just barely got in the door maybe 10 p.m. and car pulled up. Someone was leaning on the horn. She ran outside to see whoever it was. It was a bunch of guys in a car and they wanted her to go to bar drinking with them. She said, "I'll only be gone for a little while. I'm going to go and have a couple of drinks."

She came home a bit after 1 a.m. after the bars closed. They were making all sorts of racket. I was surprised the boys didn't wake up. She was drunk and I should have kept my mouth shut but said, "You've been gone a whole week couldn't you have stayed home a night?"

She sort of mumbled, "I wish I never had you for a mother."

I was very hurt. I had stayed, cleaned the house, the boys were taken care of, and had pushed myself fairly hard to make sure everything was taken care of.

That night after everyone had gone to bed, I got up around 4 a.m. and had severe chest pains and couldn't breathe. I was burning up and felt like I was dying. I woke April up and told her I was really sick. I said, "I don't know what's wrong with me, but something serious is going on." It was snowing out, and she gave me two Tylenols and told me to rest in the easy chair. I was feeling worse. I saw there were lights on across the way at her friend Barbara Ann's so I called and asked her if she thought I should call Alex to take me to Dartmouth or wait until he picked me up the next day.

Chapter 29 – Precursor to the Big Surgery

The pains were so intense, I just didn't know what was wrong. Barbara Ann said she thought I should call Alex and have him take me to Dartmouth. I didn't want to call Alex, because the snow was coming down heavily and he was also working that weekend.

April woke up and started yelling at me. She said, "Don't call Alex because he's going to get into an accident, and I'll take you to the local hospital in Vermont."

I said, "I can't go to the hospital in Vermont. I have medical history in New Hampshire, and they don't like to pay for anything out of state."

April said, "Well, then, I'm going back to bed."

I went back to the recliner feeling worse. Alex got off work about 7 a.m., and I called him around 8 or 9. Alex came and got me. It was about an hour and 45 minutes to get to April's in the weather. I was very sick by this point. Alex asked if I wanted to go to Dartmouth or the hospital in Colebrook. I just wanted to go to Colebrook because it was closer, and Alex could go home and get some rest. The doctor at Colebrook had been a student of my primary care doctor at Dartmouth. He examined me and admitted me right away. He said I had very severe case of pneumonia. Also, the scoliosis I developed in my childhood was progressively getting worse. The scoliosis and the pneumonia were putting pressure on my heart and lungs. I was in the hospital for at least ten days, on oxygen and an IV of antibiotics. The doctor said, "If I were you, I'd ask your doctor to see if there's anything that can be done about the scoliosis. If you were to get pneumonia or a really bad cold, it could be fatal." Alex said once I was out, we were going to see my primary doctor, and get his opinion on the scoliosis.

We had a routine check-up scheduled in about three months, and Colebrook had sent all the medical records to my primary doctor at Dartmouth once I was discharged. I told the doctor what had happened, and he had read the reports. He said it was pretty serious, and what the other doctor had said was true, and I should see the spinal orthopedic doctors at Dartmouth. A referral was set up and a month or two later I went to see them. The first doctor I saw took my vitals and after a primary examination said, "I wouldn't do this surgery. It's very severe and dangerous and your age is against you." He suggested that if I do any surgery that I should go to New

Chapter 29 – Precursor to the Big Surgery

York. I explained I didn't know anyone in New York, didn't have the money and that I wanted to be closer to home. Then the doctor who would do the surgery, if possible, came in. Dr. "X" came in and examined me, and they took X-rays. They found my spine was curving in two different directions, with the top being the worst. He said he could do the surgery, but he would need assistance. There was another surgeon who was a pediatric spinal surgeon, Dr. "M" that he wanted to be involved.

First, I had to go through several tests over the course of a year. They punctured an artery to test for blood gases. Once a month they'd give me breathing tests to see if I could withstand several hours of anesthesia. They asked me if I minded if the interns and residents could watch the surgery. I told them if they could learn anything they could observe. The year passed and I was ready for surgery.

Chapter 30 – The Surgery
2007

For the first surgery they removed a disc and a rib to make room for the rods and hardware that would go in its place. They ground the disc and rib, along with cadaver bones and "cemented" everything in place. They put another halo on my head, hooking the halo to the top of the bed and with straps from the ankles, seeing how far they could straighten my spine. This first operation took maybe six hours, but they kept me in the hospital for a week before they began the second, major operation.

To put all the rods in took 18 hours. Along with the two main surgeons, there was also a general internal surgeon to put all the vital organs back and make sure everything was in place. They kept me there for two or three weeks after the surgery, maybe a month total with the first surgery included. Two days after surgery they got me out of bed and had me using a walker. There were couches and chairs along the hallway. I kept walking and walking.

The nurses and RNAs started timing me and were commenting, "Why are you walking so much? You've walked more than you need to."

And I said, "Every step I take is one step closer to going home."

After the month ended, I went to a rehabilitation center. The hospital selected the facility, which was in Concord, New Hampshire. My diabetes insipidus had gotten worse because the rehabilitation facility had ignored the list of medications I had been on, and this caused me to urinate frequently. I had a commode next to my bed, but if I got off the bed without ringing for the nurse, a light would go on in the station and they'd come in and get upset. One night I had to go really bad. I had rung for the nurse, but no one came. I waited and waited and knew I was going to go in the bed if I didn't do something, so I got out of bed by myself. And I fell flat on my back on the cement floor. By law in New Hampshire if you fall in a medical facility, the immediate caregiver in the family is to be immediately notified. They never contacted Alex. They came in and started yelling at me for not waiting for the nurse, picked me up, put me back in bed, never asking if I hurt myself. The next night the nurse's aide came in and said, "I don't want you ringing that bell until after we have our meeting for shift change. I'm sick and tired

Chapter 30 – The Surgery

of cleaning your shitty ass." What was she talking about? I had never once soiled myself.

The head doctor at the clinic refused to give me my medicine for the diabetes insipidus saying, "It's just a figment of your imagination. No one has this. Only overwrought women make this up." Along with the medication for the diabetes they changed my pain medications threw everything into turmoil. I was there for five days. And it was five days of sheer hell!

I decided there and then I wanted to go home. I told the nurse I was going to call Alex to come and take me home. The nurses came in, pulled the phone apart, and put the pieces behind a highboy dresser I couldn't even reach. I told the nurses if they wouldn't let me call anyone, I was just going to walk out the door.

One of the nurses said, "Fine, go head and go. Who cares what happens to you anyway?"

But the head nurse said, "No, she'd die if she went out there, and I don't want that responsibility on me."

I watched and I could see there was only one nurse I didn't recognize at the nursing station and took the walker by my bed. This nurse was very nice, and she called a friend of Alex's and told him to drive around and find Alex and tell him to come pick me up right away. I thanked the nurse and asked her if she was going to get in trouble.

She said, "I'm always in trouble, and you needed help."

Alex got there, and I had to see the administrator. He said, "It might take two or three days to get an ambulance to take her home."

Alex said, "I have a car outside and am going to take her now."

The administrator then said, "Well, we were going to throw her out anyway because she's not complying to our rules." According to their rules I needed three hours of strenuous exercise, but I was very sick at this point in the recovery, but they wanted a blood test before I left.

A nurse from the hospital came over to take the blood test and said, "Oh, my goodness. She's dehydrated." He gave us his card and phone number saying if we ever needed testimony about them and their neglect.

Chapter 30 – The Surgery

By the time Alex drove me to Dartmouth, I was incoherent and was taken to emergency. It turned out I had an infection in my back that no one had caught. I was in Dartmouth for another three weeks. They sat me down in the emergency room, and there was a puddle on the floor, almost a quart of liquid from the infection. They took me into surgery and removed almost another quart of infectious liquid. They tried to grow a sample in the lab, so they could see what it was, but due to the antibiotics I had been on, it wouldn't grow. They finally figured it out and gave me an IV. This particular infection – whose name escapes me – can live for up to five years if they don't get it.

After I got better at Dartmouth, I still couldn't go home. This time they sent me to a facility in Lancaster. I stayed there for several months. They were very good, but they kept switching rooms and one night one of my roommates died. They left her there for the night and never closed the curtain. They finally sent me home, but I was still having recovery issues, so they sent me to a rehabilitation place in Stewartstown. I was there for almost a year. They had me walking up and down steps and doing other types of physical therapy. They were very nice and followed Dartmouth's directions to the letter. They were very prompt on getting my medication to me on time.

When I had been here for about eight months, one night I told the nurses I didn't want to be alone in my bedroom. I felt like something bad was going to happen that night. They let me stay in a room that the patients used during the day for arts and crafts and at night it was the nurses' lounge. They had a big recliner in there and put me in it and made me comfortable. This was early in the evening. Around 11 p.m. or so they tried to wake me up, but they couldn't. My fingers were turning blue, and I wasn't breathing very well. They called an ambulance and took me to Colebrook Hospital which was about 12 minutes away. In Colebrook, they got me breathing again and called Dartmouth, but they said they couldn't take me, so they got a helicopter transport and took me to Maine Medical Center in Portland, Maine.

They called Alex at 3 a.m. and said I had respiratory failure and told him I was being transported to Portland. Alex got there just as they were putting

Chapter 30 – The Surgery

me in the helicopter. The Ambulance drivers gave him directions on how to get to the hospital.

I was in intensive care. I'd wake up and then go back out. I had a breathing tube down my throat. I was trying to ask for Alex, and they gave me a piece of paper, but that didn't work. Then they gave me a chalk board slate and I still couldn't read what I wrote. I didn't have my glasses and would fall back into unconsciousness.

Alex showed up the next morning and I wrote "Where are my glasses?" on the slate, and Alex went back to the nursing home and picked up a pair of glasses that were on my bureau, but they weren't my glasses. He went back and found mine and was able to bring them back the next day.

Finally, they got the breathing tube out, the doctor who was taking care of me asked how I was feeling, and I said, "It's a good day. I haven't died yet."

The doctor was furious and said, "Don't you know you almost died! You have to be very careful saying things like that!"

I asked what was wrong with me? He said I was A Fib and had congestive heart failure. I was in intensive care for about a week and was in a private room. They were giving me the dosage via IV and I couldn't go home until the dosage was right.

They didn't know how long my brain had been without oxygen, so I had to undergo the same type and levels of physical therapy, occupational and speech therapy that I had undergone in Dartmouth before they would discharge me.

Alex called April to let her know I was there. She called me and threw a screaming fit on the telephone. It happened that a nurse was in the room and could hear April yelling and hollering at me. I said, "I have to go" and hung up. They banned April from having calls put through to my room, as she got me so upset.

Upon release from the hospital in Portland, I returned to the nursing home for another three months. I was finally able to come home. During the times Alex would visit, I'd walk him to the elevator, and we'd both say we loved each other, even after the door closed until we couldn't hear each

Chapter 30 – The Surgery

other any longer. The nurses got a kick out of this and they'd say, "I love you" as I'd walk back to my room. They thought it was cute.

2008

It was very hard to adjust to home life after being in the hospitals and nursing homes for almost a year. Alex did everything for me but getting used to a different routine was hard on both of us. Things started getting easier, but I still had doctors' appointments in Dartmouth and had to see a heart specialist along with everything else. Things finally settled into a regular routine, and I felt I was back home again.

Out of all the time I was in the hospital or nursing care, I kept expecting to see a bill for my hospital stay or rehabilitation stays, but never did. I was aware that Dartmouth was a teaching facility and being one of oldest patients to have the back surgery. It was in a large surgery with several students observing, so I suspect it was written off as a teaching experience.

On a follow-up visit with Dr. "X" we had first gone to dermatology, as the rash/skin condition, while it had faded, had never gone away. While in dermatology they had taken photos of the rash. When we got to Dr. "X" he demanded I take my clothes off so he could photograph the rash. Alex explained that with the head injury, it was a major undertaking to have me remove my clothes and that photographs had already been taken. Dr. "X" became enraged and then thrust the hospital walker in front of me and demanded I walk. Between being flustered and thrown off by his aggression, and trying to maneuver a different walker, I wasn't able to respond or process everything as he was getting angrier and angrier. Dr. "M" was going to join this consolation, and when she started to walk in, Dr. "X" slammed the door in her face, narrowly missing hitting her in the nose. With that Alex got angry, and we stormed out.

We never went back to Dr. "X" or saw Dr. "M" again. We're not sure if they compared notes, or if Dr. "X" presented the last meeting in a different light, but we never dealt with either of them ever again. About a year later, when I was seeing my regular doctor, I asked if Dr. "X" and Dr. "M" were still there. I was informed that Dr. "X" had returned to India and Dr. "M" was elsewhere.

Chapter 30 – The Surgery

The summer of 2008, in August, I got an infection in my right leg. It swelled up and fluid was oozing out from the knee down. Alex took me to Dartmouth to Emergency in the middle of the night, and they immediately admitted me. Dr. "J" saw me, and she took care of me for the duration of my stay. They had me on an IV and my leg elevated fairly high. They wanted me to use a bedpan, but I couldn't, so I could only go when I had a nurse there to assist. I was there for about 5 days, and they figured I might have lost about 60lbs. of fluid during the visit. I was released to go home and took a follow up course of antibiotics.

2009

A year later to the day, I was back in Emergency at Dartmouth and once again got Dr. "J" for the exact same thing. Same leg, same symptoms, and the exact same treatment. The same amount of time. It was like a carbon copy. They said it was caused by a bacterium that lives on everyone's body, and most people aren't affected. For whatever reason, my resistance was low, I might have had a bug bite or scratch, but was told it could come back at another point in time, or not return at all

.

Chapter 31 – Discovery
2010

In late February, I received a call from a woman from the last nursing home I was in. I sort of recognized her voice and she said, "I'm calling you because someone from California is trying to get a hold of you. Because of confidentiality laws, I couldn't give them your number. They left their number, and I think you should call them back. I think you'll be pleasantly surprised and happy."

I instantly replied, "I don't know anyone in California. It's probably a scam artist or fast-talking salesperson looking to get something I don't have or sell me something I don't need."

She replied, "You're going to be happy you called. Write the number down. You'll be very happy you did."

I said, "I'll think about it" but was thinking, "What a crock of crap." But she had also mentioned something about Andrews or Andrzejewski and Detroit, which made me wonder.

She said goodbye and implored me to call and said, "It's really to your benefit to make this call."

I said thank you and hung up. I sat there for a couple of minutes with the phone number in my hand. At first, I wasn't going to call. Why should I call someone I don't know? But my curiosity started eating at me. So, I called out of sheer curiosity.

The phone was picked up on what seemed like the first ring. A man on the other end introduced himself as David Roundsley.

I asked, "What is this about? Andrews? Andrzejewski?"

He said, "Was your father Daniel Andrews?"

I replied, "No." After a bit of a pause I said, "My father was Daniel Andrzejewski."

He paused a second and said, "I believe I'm your half-brother."

I asked, "Who was your mother?"

He replied, "Margaret."

I let out a slight gasp and said, "I met Margaret."

Chapter 31 – Discovery

He went to explain that he had been adopted and I broke into tears and said, "I was adopted too." We must have talked for the next two or three hours…

Journey of a Lifetime

Words & Music by David B. Roundsley

A chance decision, a coin-toss of the moment
A roll of the dice, and a chance
The edge of the abyss, a hit without a miss,
The perfect circumstance

Across lifetimes, time, and space
Sifting through the history, looking for a trace
Against the odds the clock ticking away
A sense of urgency, with no delay

> The first step of a journey of a lifetime
> Not knowing where it would lead to
> The reasons or the rhymes, traveling through times
> That finally led me to you

Unanswered questions, lurking in the shadows
Would vanish, but never fade away
Small reminders, a constant feeling
To follow the path and stay…

Separate lives, lived undiscovered
So many secrets were uncovered
Mysteries to explore, and transcend
The best conclusion of a journey's end

> The first step of the journey of a lifetime
> Not knowing where it would lead to
> The reasons or the rhymes, traveling through times
> That finally led me to you

Reprinted by permission – Syndrome Sounds / ASCAP
From Munich Syndrome's 8th album, Electro Pop 2 (Deluxe Edition)

# The Search – Part II

Chapter 32 – 2010

After spending over three hours on the phone listening to Danni's harrowing and Dickensian tale, I immediately called Delores and let my half-sisters know I had found her. Along with the excitement, and to a degree, some relief Danni was still with us, everyone was very excited to talk to her. Arlene immediately put forth she should call and cited her "online" training as a reason to call.

Both Audrey and Delores both felt Arlene *shouldn't* be the first to talk to Danni.

As I had gotten to know Arlene a bit more, she was taking courses at an online educational business that was about to lose accreditation. As she had attempted to do armchair analysis on me (in a rather ham-fisted manner), the consensus was we didn't feel it would be good for Danni to be exposed to this until we had a better relationship established.

Audrey volunteered to call Danni, and I told her I would arrange it. After the first call I had with Danni, we then began to speak every day, often for an hour or longer. Despite the hardships she had suffered, there was an instant bond and connection that we both felt from the very beginning. Audrey called her that night. I called Danni the next morning, excited to hear how the call went. A different tone came into her voice. One I hadn't heard before. She was hesitant and basically said the call was *uncomfortable*, they made small talk, but there hadn't been any flow, and the call hadn't lasted very long. I was very disappointed hearing this. I dropped a note to Audrey asking how it went, and she was rather vague and really didn't comment on it.

A short time after that, Delores and Danni spoke, and that call went better. But it didn't seem to develop into a deeper friendship, which was what I was hoping for from all of them. From this point on, Delores would often ask about Danni and make the occasional call, but everything felt like it was held at arm's length. Arlene on the other hand never mentioned Danni again, never asking to try and contact her. But most troubling, to me, was Audrey. She never asked about Danni or made any further efforts at contact.

Chapter 32 – 2010

While this bothered me, it wasn't my place to comment on it and it was Audrey's decision if she didn't want to pursue communications.

While this was going on, I was also taking extended courses in web design and multi-media. My finals finished on May 25th. At the beginning of May, Sue Ellen let us know her 70th birthday was approaching, and we were invited to her birthday party. We left Monday, June 1st, and went to Seattle to spend some time with my family, and then on Friday the 4th, we drove east and down to Pendleton. After our last stay, we found a much nicer place to stay, a Hampton Inn, and arrived early in the afternoon. There were some gatherings and parties taking place that day, before the actual party on Saturday. We were both rather exhausted after the drive and laid down. My cell phone went off the second we closed our eyes, and it was Sue Ellen asking if we had arrived and when were we going to make it out to the house.

We roused ourselves and headed over. Despite the long drives getting up to Washington and then over to Oregon, there was much less tension heading into Pendleton compared to our first visit. Lisa and Karen were buzzing about the kitchen pulling food and drinks together. Karen had super high energy and seemed to be doing 12 things at one time, while keeping a lively conversation going. We hung out in the kitchen and chatted with everyone as the afternoon rolled on into evening. Again, if memory serves, there was a barbecue that evening with the extended family. The weather was wonderful, and everyone was very cordial. There was a ton of food, all of it excellent. We finally said our goodbyes before it got too late and crashed into a very deep sleep.

Saturday was the big day, and it was BIG. I had no idea how many people were actually there, but it felt like a small army. While we had some idea as to the size of Sue Ellen's family from looking at the family trees on Ancestry.com and knew most of them have been in the same general region for generations, we were a bit surprised and a tad overwhelmed by the amount of activity buzzing around us. Everyone was very friendly and quite cordial, but as the day wore on, various people would come up, lower their voice, cast a wary glance about and whisper, "Daniel wasn't really the law and order guy he pretended to be, was he?"

And I'd reply, "Not by a long shot!"

One woman walked by, stopped, and almost did a spit-take looking at me. She paused and said, "Well, isn't that a blast from the past?" (This was Sue Ellen's sister.)

I understood this was due to my resemblance to my birth father, which while I understood, isn't something I took as a compliment, naturally.

One thing struck me early on was how isolating Daniel had been with Sue Ellen and her family. Around us were these lively conversations about vacations and holidays past where everyone had gotten together, and there were plans and talk of upcoming events. There was genuine affection and warmth as people talked about trips, vacations, and events in the past and upcoming ones. And I noticed Sue Ellen sitting there, almost like she was on her own private island with a lot of this not seeming to resonate. It's redundant for me to say how badly I felt, and do feel, for all the people Daniel seems to have come into contact with and upended their lives, but I could really see the cause and effect of his selfishness in that very moment. While Sue Ellen's daughters were there and rallying about, I could see the time Daniel had robbed all of them of and the distance he had put between them and just felt incredibly sad.

Everyone pulled together, and it was a very large and lovely gathering. While (as with most things in this journey) I wasn't 100% sure what the outcome of our going would be, we were really happy we could attend and that they were kind enough to include us in such a wonderful event.

As it was, we needed to leave first thing Sunday, as in less than two weeks we were scheduled to leave for Detroit. While previously, Detroit wouldn't have been a blip on our radar, obviously with the things I had uncovered, and in hearing Danni's tales of growing up, it suddenly was. Dave had an opportunity to do a three-day Symantec training just outside of Detroit. We left Wednesday, June 16th, and were there through Sunday. While Dave was at training during the day, with the aid of our GPS and the addresses Danni had provided, I set out see where the Andrzejewski family had lived for several generations.

We stayed in a suburb of Detroit, Southfield, a few miles west of the actual town. When we went to check in at the Hawthorne Suites, there was an unusual number of cars in the parking lot and the check-in area was more

Chapter 32 – 2010

crowded than one would expect. Several people were trying to extend their stay or book a room. It appeared that fairly large families were trying to get more than five or six people into some of the rooms, and the office staff weren't pleased.

After getting checked in, we went out to find a restaurant and settled on Bacco Ristorante. Once we were seated, our server, Anthony, who was very openly gay, tripped onto the fact that Dave and I were a couple and proceeded to tell us enthusiastically about Drag Bingo and other gay-themed events in the area. He asked where we were from. We told him San Francisco, and he almost squealed, "I LOVE San Francisco. Why would you come here?"

I was under no illusions about the state Detroit was in when we went there, but I was truly caught off guard as I ventured towards the area where Danni had been born and grown up. At the time, there was a *lot* of sensory data coming in, and I wasn't processing it in real time. But there was a definite disconnect between what I was seeing and what I was able to process. As I drove along, I could tell something was amiss, but couldn't put my finger on it. Along with there being absolutely no foot traffic or traffic in general I realized there weren't any food, liquor, or convenience stores. As I went along, I started noticing signs instructing drivers "DO NOT ENTER THIS STREET" but driving past, they just appeared to be benign streets. The streets had sidewalks, and paving, but no visible housing or buildings. It was like they had laid the streets out with the plan for either housing or businesses, but never got around to the building part. I discovered many of these areas DID have housing, but due to them being abandoned, many had just been knocked down and destroyed.

Despite there not being a sign of any people, as I continued on, I could see an individual off in the distance walking in the same direction I was driving. As I got closer, I could tell it was an elderly African American woman walking with what I thought was a walker. As I got closer, I realized she didn't have a walker, but instead she had two golf clubs. They were fairway wood clubs, and she would stop every few feet and wave the right club in front of her, like she was keeping a threat at bay. I couldn't see anyone else and frankly couldn't figure out where she had come from nor where she was going to.

I continued on, and the landscape began to feel even more surreal. It was almost like one of those movies where it was the end of the world and there's not a single soul left in the world. I kept driving and then had a mild feeling of panic, that other than following the directions of the GPS, I had no real sense of where I was, what was actually around me. *If* there was any sort of trouble, I wasn't sure where I'd go or how I would be able to deal with it.

I continued on until I got to the address Danni gave me. There were no longer any buildings on this part of the street. In its place were weeds over three feet tall. The area looked like some type of radioactive bomb had gone off, leaving plants and a few scattered buildings, but wiping out all humanity. The next stop on my trip was Mt. Olivet Cemetery. Mt. Olivet was almost as shocking as anything I had encountered. In this sea of abandoned buildings and overgrown lots, there was this immaculately maintained cemetery. It was almost like it had an invisible force field around it that had protected it from whatever carnage had befallen the surrounding area.

I drove in and went up the long driveway to the office. I went in and thought I detected mild surprise from the office staff that someone had come in. I explained I was looking for the Andrzejewski / Andrews area. They very kindly looked through their records and gave me a map to the location they were located in. I took the map and some other literature they had out and set out for that part of the cemetery. A very peaceful serenity engulfed me. I spotted a few cars of people obviously visiting graves as well as several utility vehicles with gardeners or maintenance people working in various sections.

I finally arrived at the area I was directed to and made my way towards it. I was worried at first, as there were no larger monuments. In this section, it was a simple stone plaque in the ground, and in many parts, no plaques at all. Also, the crabgrass, while freshly mowed, had grown over many of the markers and it was clear it had been years since anyone had visited or attempted any sort of personal maintenance. Despite having no tools with me, I was able to clear some of the thick overgrown grass and eventually found the area I was looking for. Several of the people who were interred

Chapter 32 – 2010

here did not have markers, but with the map I knew I was in the right place. I called Danni from the spot and described where I was and what I was seeing.

What was dismaying for both myself and Danni was Daniel's sister Myrtle lived less than mile away, as did many of her children and extended family. It was clear this place was not visited or maintained by them. I spent a fair amount of time there after Danni and I finished talking. I was thinking about the past and the people buried here.

When we were at Sue Ellen's, I told her about the trip to Detroit. I mentioned I might knock on Myrtle's door, despite her hostile and rude response when I called at the end of last year. She told me Myrtle wouldn't be there. She'd be in Texas again, visiting one of her sons. In some ways, this reduced any tension I might have had about what would probably have been a contentious meeting.

When I finished, I plugged in Myrtle's address and drove over to her house. I knew she had lived in the area for quite some time and wasn't expecting much. I wasn't surprised. The house seemed kind of dumpy and a bit more run down compared to the houses on either side. Directly behind her was a school yard, which afforded me the chance to walk over to the school and walk up and look at the house from the back. Some houses exude a bit of personality from the inhabitants, and this one seemed resigned and unhappy. I went back round to the front to where my rental car was parked and noticed a car pulling into the driveway. I sat back and observed an overweight man in his 50s get out and walk up to the door. I assumed this was Clyde Jr. whom I had sent the letter to the previous year. As he didn't have the manners to reply to my letter back then, I didn't expect there would be much of an interaction now and chose to leave. I had his address as well and drove by his home. He was a few streets down on the other side off the main street. I was rather taken aback at the number of bumper stickers on the vehicles out front and signs all over the front of the house. It had the miraculous effect of transforming a stand-alone home into looking and feeling like a mobile home. Absolutely nothing about the home beckoned anyone to knock on the door. The vibe was "DO NOT ENTER."

Chapter 32 – 2010

I decided to drive around a bit and get a feel for their neighborhood, shops, and area while there. I found a shopping center not far away and decided to go in and see what life there was like as they most likely shopped there. The overriding feeling was that of walking into an older black and white movie. While it didn't feel unsafe or bad, it all had a rather defeated and deflated feel. People listlessly walked through the aisles tossing items into their shopping carts. I didn't see people smiling at one another, or friends greeting one another. From the people going through the motions behind the counter, to the people blankly standing in line, it was a place whose best days were well behind it. More exhausted than I should have been with such a short journey, I went back to the hotel.

The rest of our stay found me staying at the hotel doing research. Our last night in the area, June 19, we went to Bastone in Royal Oak. We had a very nice meal and called it an early night. Prior to going to Detroit, we had touched base with Lloyd (my birth mother's brother) and Janine as they had indicated they would be staying at their farm in Fife Lake. Lloyd had left a very specific set of instructions to get up to the farm, as well as the precise time we should arrive. We had reviewed the directions, but plugged the address into our GPS, which altered the route. We headed out and made our way north. Just a bit past the city of Flint, my cell phone went off. It was Lloyd. He wanted to know where we were. Not giving it much thought, I gave him our location. He became upset and stated vigorously, "I GAVE YOU DIRECTIONS. YOU WERE SUPPOSED TO FOLLOW THEM. DO YOU HAVE THEM?" I did have them, but they were in my computer bag in the trunk, so I signaled Dave to pull over *on the freeway* while I retrieved the directions and my computer. I had the phone wedged in my ear with my shoulder as I called my computer up to recall the directions. Between Lloyd's displeasure on the phone, cars whizzing past at very high speeds, it was challenging to get the information. I was finally able to retrieve his directions and reassured him we would be arriving at the specified time.

As it was, we had already gone a bit far afield going by the GPS directions, which had never let us down yet. We had always been rather shocked at how precise our arrival times always synced up with the ETA the GPS provided at the start of any given trip. We continued on, but there was a

Chapter 32 – 2010

slight knot in my stomach. Despite NOT taking the specific turns and detours Lloyd had laid out, we pulled into the front of the farm within a five-minute window of the ETA Lloyd had set out. When we explained we had relied solely on the guidance of our GPS, he seemed a bit deflated that our little box had a better way of getting there than his tried-and-true directions.

Thankfully, whatever tensions that were present in our phone conversations had evaporated. Lloyd and Janine showed us around the farm that he had inherited from his parents. They both explained that the family had always come up here in the summers, and they had maintained that schedule even after Lloyd and Janine had moved to Oklahoma to teach. All the décor, books, and artwork dated back to those days. It was a cozy and homey place, and it was easy to envision Lloyd and Margaret as small children spending their summers here.

After showing us around the farm, we checked into the Chateau Chantal Winery. A lovely place whose claim to fame was a sumptuous breakfast buffet. We met for dinner at the Boathouse, out on the Mission Peninsula. The next day Lloyd and Janine drove us around, giving us a guided tour of the area, stopping at various wineries. One of the more memorable was the Boskydel Winery. It was run by Bernie Rink. Lloyd had given us a heads up that Bernie was a bit on the crusty side and didn't like it if people went in and didn't do a tasting. He mentioned it was on the *rough side*, but had Lloyd not known where we were going, we'd have sailed right past it. From the looks of it, it could have been an old car repair shop or handyman staging area. I didn't notice any signs advertising it, and as we parked, an older man standing out front struck me as being the personification of what Bernie Rink would look like based on Lloyd's description. Dave & I walked in, with Lloyd and Janine trailing behind us. It was a very funky tasting room that kind of reminded me of Knott's Berry Farm in Buena Park, California. VERY rustic. Bernie asked what we wanted, and we asked to taste a couple of different wines.

Lloyd and Janine said they'd pass on tasting (hadn't he told us Bernie gets cranky if people don't taste?) and Bernie grunted, "Good. It saves my dishpan hands."

We liked what we tasted, and Dave asked to buy a couple of bottles and pulled out his credit card.

Bernie grunted, "We only do cash" which didn't come as a big surprise.

Bernie was the librarian at the Northwestern Michigan College and the first person to believe there was a future for wine grapes in the region. He planted French hybrids, thinking they would withstand the cold better. Others planted the common varietals and found they prospered. The area is host to everything from Chardonnay to Cabernet, and it turned out there wasn't much interest in Vignoles, so Bernie has now passed, and the sons have put his place up for sale.

As we left, Lloyd pointed out this or that place, and casually pointed to the right and said, "That's Ciccone Vineyards, Madonna's father's place." As I was going to say I'd be interested in checking it out and before I could open my mouth, Lloyd punched it saying, "It's crap" and sped past. (I think I caught a glimpse of it.) Another very memorable winery they took us to was 2 Lads. Not only were wines wonderful, but the (very) modern architecture of the tasting room with a sweeping view of the lake made it a most enjoyable visit. (They also ship to California and have a great rosé!)

Over the course of several lunches and dinners we discussed in detail some of the things I had uncovered about Margaret. There was a point at one dinner where some of the details of Margaret's life seemed to upset Janine, and she left the table. One item Lloyd seemed unclear about was if Margaret knew *he* was adopted. He initially said it was never discussed (per our original conversation in 2007), but after time he seemed to "recall" a time when he and Margaret discussed their both being adopted. He said there was a weekend at the lake he now recalled where they had a warm conversation about this. From what I had heard from multiple friends of Margaret's, I firmly believe Margaret never knew Lloyd was adopted and that she felt she was adopted solely to provide assistance and help to the household. Also referencing our initial conversations, I do not believe the weekend at the lake ever transpired. By that point in time Lloyd was married with young children and Margaret was already living away doing nursing rotations.

Chapter 32 – 2010

In Traverse City, we stayed at an absolutely gorgeous restored Victorian, The Wellington Inn. Lloyd and Janine very kindly treated us to our first night there, and we stayed an additional night. It was the epitome of comfort and was a delight to wander around and explore. The top floor had been a full-sized ballroom in a past life, and while the dance floor was still there, they had converted a small part to a kitchenette, snack, and wine area the guests could utilize. Our first morning there, before breakfast, we decided to head out and explore the neighborhood. There were other equally well-maintained Victorians and some really amazing gardens. We stopped to admire one garden as a woman was watering on the other end of the yard. She spotted us and asked if we were staying at the Wellington. We told her we were, and she invited us to use the chairs on her covered porch if we wanted to just sit and relax in her garden.

While driving around that day I noticed stands in front of some homes stacked with mason jars. Lloyd commented that it reminded him they needed some jam and they pulled up in front of one of these stands. Not a soul around, there were six or more jars and a coffee can. Lloyd fished in his pocket for some money, threw it in the can, took the jar, and we drove off. I marveled at the honesty involved. I commented that if someone were to try that out where we lived in California, not only would there be no money in the coffee can, the odds would be good that the can, the jars, and probably the table would be gone by the time you went out to check.

Another restaurant we ate at and explored was at the old mental hospital, which they were about one-third of the way through redeveloping into housing, shops and dining. It turned out my mother (Margaret) had done a rotation of her training as a nurse there back in the early 1950's. We ate at Trattoria Stella one night and had a delightful meal. While not fully redeveloped, they had what appeared to be very stylish condos on the upper floors, and shops and restaurants on the lower and subterranean levels. The Village at Grand Traverse Commons was really lovely, and you could see the full potential as they were rolling out the redevelopment.

We came out during a balmy afternoon and had cider at Left Foot Charlie. It was most enjoyable and relaxing. Left Foot Charlie also makes an amazing Pinot Blanc. For our final day there, Lloyd and Janine drove us out to a semi-remote area, Eagle View, for a picnic. At the site was a finished patio / deck area, with lovely views stretching out. They brought an amazing selection of cheeses, things to nibble, and (of course) some utterly amazing wines. It was an absolutely wonderful weekend, and also nice to see the areas Margaret and Lloyd had grown up in and getting more family history, the history of the area, and a feel for what was, as well as what is.

Chapter 33 – New Hampshire

As 2010 rolled into 2011, I talked with Danni and Alex (if he was home when I called) daily and got more details and information about her life.

At the same time Delores was giving me a lot of details about her life as well. She said she never felt loved or wanted by either of her parents and was always the 'black sheep' of the family. She told me her tales of woe and abuse with her choices of husbands and mates. I realized fairly early on Delores did not make good choices where mates were concerned. At the time we first met, she was in the process of divorcing her current husband, John, for either the second or third time. A lot of what she shared didn't add up. When we invited her to our Christmas party, she said she couldn't fly or take a bus as she's very allergic to perfumes, creams, scents and odors. She said traveling with people who even used a scented soap made her ill. Yet, she would go on at length about her (soon-to-be) ex-husband not bathing for days, never brushing his teeth regularly, tracking dirt and even animal waste into the house, and not changing underwear for significant lengths of time. Just listening to the litany of uncleanliness was making me a bit ill, and I was several hundred miles away.

Also, at the time I met Delores, she was in the process of reclaiming her living space, repainting, and refurbishing it. She confessed to an addiction to the outlet stores like Ross and was continually adding to her house. As she was a Leo, she was partial to lions and items that had lions on them. She relayed how John had hurt her feelings deeply by commenting on some pretty young woman, saying, "She's got such a nice slim figure, and really pert tits, not like you." She was all but certain he was either having an affair with this woman, or John wanted one to start, so he was being as nasty as possible, so she'd take the lead in finding him a new place. Which she did. I didn't comment but found it odd her putting so much time and effort finding nice things to make his place livable. The separation didn't last long. Within a month or two John was back home. While Delores seemed to welcome that, she shared she thought either this woman had shot John down, or it never even got off the ground enough to be shot down.

Chapter 33 – New Hampshire

Frankly, from what she described; I was having a hard time imagining ANYONE giving him the time of day or getting within 5 feet of him. She never commented on his overall appearance, but I didn't get the impression he was a looker. I'm not sure if they made it all the way through the divorce process, but she seemed happy he was back. At first. Little by little, she had small complaints that kept escalating. But it also seemed like her 'normal' state, so I never questioned her or how their lives were going.

One thing I picked up with Delores, both on our phone calls and when we met her, was she'd present herself as somewhat prudish, very religious and righteous, but if something angered her, every foul word anyone could muster would fly out in a fit of rage, then she'd suddenly revert back to her general demeanor. Despite Delores' proclamations that Audrey was her favorite and most dependable daughter, Audrey had shared events when Delores had become enraged with her for whatever reasons. I do think Delores meant it when she said Audrey was her favorite, but I also believe Audrey when she said Delores unleashed her rage on her as well. Delores also mentioned on more than one occasion that Arlene was "the movie star" and the looker of the two.

On February 21st, Dave and I bought tickets to fly back East to meet Danni and Alex. This was something we had discussed for a while. In fact, after I had found Danni, I had floated the idea of Audrey flying out with us to meet her. She demurred. We flew to Logan Airport, Boston, April 1st on Virgin America. We were able to snag an upgrade to first class. We rented a car at the airport and drove to Manchester-Bedford, New Hampshire. We weren't really sure about the distances, and thought stopping halfway would be wise, after a long flight.

We called Danni and Alex to let them know we had arrived safely and would see them the following day. We stayed at the Hampton Inn & Suites and had a quick dinner at Carabba's Italian Grill. There was still evidence of snow about, so being able to take off more refreshed wasn't a bad call. We stopped for lunch at Monroe's Family Restaurant in Twin Mountain. When we arrived in Colebrook, we checked into the Northern Comfort Motel, which had a rustic log-cabin feel. It was very comfortable, but the one thing

Chapter 33 – New Hampshire

we noticed the first night was the office turned off the wi-fi when they went to bed.

After getting settled, we let Alex and Danni know which room we were in and they said they'd head over. A short while later a pickup truck pulled up. A man got out that could have easily been mistaken for either the guitarist or bass player with ZZ Top. He had a very long beard. He went around to the passenger door and helped a significantly shorter woman out. After getting her safely out, he got her situated with a walker. I stepped out to say hello. I'm not sure what they were expecting, but after a moment of sizing each other up, big hugs were exchanged by everyone.

One thing that surprised me was how young Danni looked. She had sent a picture of her and Alex taken the previous summer, but in it she had her hair up, with a stick in it, that was not dissimilar to the hairdo of Pebbles on the Flintstones, wearing dark glasses, and sitting in a wheelchair. She had pale blonde hair and luminous skin that belied her 61 years. We brought them into our room, which was rather large and had a large table we could all sit around. As we had talked almost every day since I first found her, the only things to update were our trip out and the drive up to Colebrook. We finally decided to go for an early dinner and ate at Howard's Restaurant (which closed around 2013). It was very homey, and the food had an appetizing selection of traditional American fare.

From talking to both Danni and Alex over the year, we knew they loved books and reading as much as we did. There was a bookstore in Maine they went to occasionally, so we decided to make a day trip out of the next day. They met us at the motel, and I drove. I will say I was incredibly nervous and cautious driving there. Aware of what Danni had endured in the previous car accident, I was particularly aware and cautious going and coming back. We had GPS, but the road was very curvy and there were mounds of snow about. Thankfully, we made it to Pa's Tradin' Company, located in Oxford, Maine without incident. A large space offering books, antiques, and all sorts of interesting items. Danni didn't venture too far into the space and sat on the seat of her walker most of the time. While Alex and Dave browsed, I happened to be looking at something closer to the register and door. The people behind the counter looked over at Danni warmly, and

Chapter 33 – New Hampshire

lowering their voice they asked, "How's she doing? She looks like she's struggling a bit more." I introduced myself as Danni's brother, and they commented that they used to come in more often, but they hadn't seen Danni and Alex for a while.

They found a few items, as did Dave. Before heading out there, Dave had searched for places to eat and had found a French restaurant, Maurice Restaurant Francais. Danni had a slightly worried look on her face as we went in, but once we were seated, we had a very lovely dinner, and the staff couldn't have been nicer or more welcoming. Driving home was a bit stressful for me, as it was getting dark, and the main route, by my standards, was rather rural. I didn't want to be caught by a snow drift or surprised by a deer darting out in front of me. Thankfully, we made it back without incident. We said our goodnights and made plans for the following day.

The next day, we shopped at The Old Appletree, and had lunch and dinner at the Spa Restaurant & Outback Pub in Stewartstown. We also drove out to see the new place Alex was building. Neither Danni nor Alex wanted us to come out to where they were currently living, but their new place was just across the road. There was quite a bit of snow on the ground, but the house was up. Inside was still unfinished for the most part. There were frames where walls would be, the kitchen counters weren't installed yet, and it was a bit challenging to picture where everything would eventually be laid out.

We had a long and emotional goodbye that evening, and we drove back to Boston on April 5th, stopping for breakfast at the Tilt'n Diner in Tilton. We grabbed lunch at the Legal Sea Bar near Logan Airport and had dinner at Remy's Sports Bar. It was a wonderful visit and we were very glad we were able to get out there to meet them in person.

Chapter 34 – 2011 Onward

The remainder of 2011 was mostly quiet. We stayed busy going to a wide array of concerts, attending my continuing education classes, continually sifting through public records and family trees on Ancestry.com, and checking DNA matches on the two DNA sites we were registered with. After our trip out to see Danni and Alex, I updated Sue Ellen and she said she'd like to give Danni and Alex a call. That led to fairly regular calls, and Sue Ellen's daughter Karen would get on the phone as well if she was over when Sue Ellen and Danni were talking.

Delores continued to call often, but on the days she didn't, she'd send detail-rich emails. She talked about her upbringing, her parents separating, and how neither parent seemed to want her. This was a common theme she would return to again and again. I noticed she could take offense at the slightest thing anyone said and tried to be mindful of what I said to her, and how I said it. She talked about all her children. Her oldest was developmentally disabled, and as time went by, his ability to take care of himself became more of a challenge. Delores had found a shared housing where they'd watch over him and take care him. As this transition took place, she commented her son was becoming more forgetful and it seemed almost like he would forget Delores herself, which caused her a lot of pain. Her second oldest had fallen into drugs, and as a result, a life of crime. He was currently serving a very long stretch in the same prison system Daniel had once worked in. She wasn't sure if he'd be in for life or not. She did try to make the trip down to visit him when she could.

Her relationship with her oldest daughter was strained and nearly non-existent at this time. She went into great detail about the developmental and emotional issues she, and the family, dealt with when she was growing up. The one child she seemed to have a good relationship with was her youngest son. He lived a few doors down from her, and she adored and doted on him. But she was also a bit hurt that he seemed to connect with and idolize his father (the soon-to-be-divorced-but-ricochet-back-yoyo spouse), and not with her.

Chapter 34 – 2011 Onward

In August, we made a trip north to take Dave's Mom to her sister's in Oregon and continued on to visit my adoptive family in Washington.

Another change that was now on the horizon was Delores's oldest daughter, Arlene, and family were going to relocate. There were options on the table, but ultimately, they were able to relocate to the general area where Audrey was living. Arlene made mention of finally meeting in person. I sent an email to Audrey and asked if she could facilitate a time and a place for all of us to meet around the holidays. The plan was we were going to spend Christmas with my father Henry, as we didn't know if it would be his last Christmas or not. What I noticed was, Audrey would respond to my emails, but completely ignored the part about Arlene or trying to meet up. Arlene was also rather quiet as the holidays were fast approaching. I didn't have Arlene's new address, so we sent a Christmas card to her at her old address (figuring if they were relocated it would be forwarded) and sent one to Audrey.

By the time we had arrived for the holidays in central Washington, I had not heard from either Arlene or Audrey. Two days before Christmas, Arlene texted me with a blunt "So, when are we meeting?" A bit dismayed and peeved Audrey and Arlene had obviously not discussed this, I replied to her and Audrey that we were now in central Washington (about an hour and a half away from Seattle) and we'd love to have them all over for dinner. We told them Christmas Eve, the day after Christmas, or the day after that were all good. Anticipating a very full house, we went to the local grocery store and got a massive prime rib and the accoutrements for a large meal. And even though I had never heard back from either sister earlier, we had gifts for all of them and their families in anticipation of finally all getting together.

Christmas Eve came and went and nary a peep. Christmas Day was also quiet. On the day after Christmas, I saw a Facebook post with both Audrey and Arlene and their kids all ice skating. The day before we were leaving, Arlene texted we should meet her at a restaurant about two miles from the airport the afternoon we were flying home. I explained to her that with the heavy holiday traffic, I wasn't comfortable carting all our stuff to a restaurant and then trying to make our flight, and potentially getting caught in the security lines or missing our fully booked flight. I suggested as an alternative,

Chapter 34 – 2011 Onward

she meet us as the airport. There were a couple of fairly decent places we could meet at after we had checked our luggage. We had met friends in the area this way before and it was quite pleasant.

She replied rather curtly with a, "Next time."

When we got home, I found the card we had sent to Audrey with "Return to Sender" written on the front. I emailed her and she brushed it aside saying, "Oh, our postman does that from time to time. He just sends stuff back." I didn't believe that for a second. So, I took the card with the "Return to Sender" envelope and re-sent it in a new envelope, which didn't come back. What I also noticed was neither of my sisters had bothered to send a Christmas card to us. Thankfully, we were able to return the gifts we had purchased for the planned Christmas visit.

As January 2012 rolled around, Arlene unfriended both me and Dave. I commented on this to Delores, and she said Arlene was offended that Dave had tagged her as a sister. (They don't have sister-in-law or in-law designations on Facebook) I also didn't hear anything more from Audrey. When her birthday came around in February, I wished her a Happy Birthday on Facebook, but heard nothing further from her.

As the year wore on, I hadn't heard anything more from Audrey. It didn't feel like there was much of a relationship at this point.

Delores inquired in a roundabout way, and I explained the whole Christmas debacle and complete lack of effort on her daughter's part, and nothing more was ever said about it.

What *was* interesting were the public records, data, and items I was finding. Also, with the slide trays of photos that were taken in Garden Grove Sue Ellen had given me, I had a starting point for a more focused search. I called and asked Sue Ellen more about Garden Grove, and she said, "Oh yes, Daniel lived in Garden Grove for a few years on Pinto Drive" and gave me the address. I googled the address and saw the home was about a mile away from where my adoptive parents had moved to shortly after I was born. I had only held the slides up to the light when Sue Ellen first gave them to me. Now I pulled them out and put them into the projector and scrutinized them more closely. She had cautioned me that there wouldn't be any slides of my mother in there and there weren't.

Chapter 34 – 2011 Onward

In continuing my research, I *also* found several addresses Daniel's brother, Donald, had lived at less than two miles from Daniel (as well as myself). I didn't believe the proximity to each other or myself was a coincidence.

Daniel and Margaret moved to the address on Pinto Drive around 1956, and the next address I had for them was also listed in Garden Grove. It was a townhouse not far from the library. But the numbers didn't sync. I wasn't sure if the original buildings had been knocked down to make way for (somewhat) newer townhomes or not? Upon further investigation, I found they had moved from Garden Grove to an apartment in *Buena Park* (the directory had mistakenly tagged the address in the wrong city). Again, this was all within a stone's throw of where I grew up and the areas that I used to frequent both with my family and with friends, or even by myself.

So, my research showed Daniel and Margaret lived at an apartment house at 1637 E 3rd Street in Long Beach after arriving in California. Could this have been the apartment house Daniel supposedly did maintenance on? In yet another "coincidence" the address in Long Beach was just a few blocks from where my adoptive parents were living when began the adoption process. Shortly after my birth, their next home and address was 13202 Pinto Drive in Garden Grove. At the time they lived there, the house was charcoal grey with a pink accents and pink garage door and white rock on the roof. There were newly planted junipers and big stretch of lawn around this corner house. One of the photos in the slide tray showed a family in what was an address across the street the Kings. Their address was listed as 11861 Mustang Road. Pinto Drive was on the corner of an "L" intersection with Mustang Road. Margaret and Daniel lived in Garden Grove until 1962. I'm not sure what led to the need to downsize, but their next address was a small apartment at 7270 8th Street in Buena Park, #49. This was the apartment they were living in when Daniel convinced Margaret they were being watched by espionage agents but was most likely where Daniel wanted to skip out due to pending embezzlement charges from the vending machine company he was working at. They lived at this address until 1964. This was when they fled to Big Bear Lake.

In reviewing the letters from Lloyd and conversations we had while we were in Michigan, it was while they were at Big Bear Lake the last call was made to Margaret's parents. Saying she was in trouble and needed the *money* for a plane ticket home, they had called their church who in turn contacted an affiliated church in the Big Bear area. The minister had gone to the cabin to ask about helping them. Daniel was angry, waved a gun in his face. and told him to "fuck off."

The next period of time remains a bit hazy, but with voter registration records, they were listed as having "General Delivery" in Cedarpines Park, California, in the Riverside area about ten miles northwest of San Bernardino. This was a period where both Daniel and Margaret said Daniel had become a volunteer deputy sheriff. But there wasn't a shred of evidence in all of Daniel's belongings to support this claim. What was even more curious was a manuscript Daniel had started that was about this time.

Chapter 35 – Sam

This is a story Daniel told his last wife and documented in a handwritten notebook.

(As written by Daniel)

It was late spring; I was driving along a mountain road nearing a small village in the San Bernardino National Forest. The traffic was very sparse, so I drove rather slowly, enjoying the weather, when I looked to left and saw very large dog on the hillside. I stopped the car and sat there looking at the dog. He appeared to be looking at me also. I got out of the car, and the dog did not attempt to run or move. The dog appeared to be a German Shepherd, but he was much larger than any German Shepherd I had ever seen. I whistled and called to the dog, but he just stood there looking at me. Traffic began to increase, so I got back in car and drove away, but I could not forget the dog.

I drove this road every day, and I could not get this dog out of my mind, yet I had not thought about dogs or any other animals. I found myself looking every day for the dog, and I began looking around the small mountain village hoping I would again see him. As time went on, I still could not forget that dog. On several occasions, I did catch glimpses of him in the town and just outside of town. One day as I was driving, a school bus was parked waiting for the children, and I saw the dog on the bus. I stopped my car and walked up to the bus, and sure enough this dog was sitting by the driver. I introduced myself and began asking the driver about the dog. The driver did not own the dog, but he did know the dog's name was "Sam."

He began to tell me about Sam, he said that Sam was there every morning to ride the bus and all the kids knew Sam. They may have not known their own name, but they knew Sam. The driver did not know who

Chapter 35 – Sam

owned Sam but said he would try to find out for me. We talked for a few more minutes and I started petting Sam, he was very friendly and eager for the attention. Several weeks went by and I met the school bus driver in the grocery store. He said he did not find out about Sam, that perhaps some of the kids might know. I thanked him and went home, all my thoughts were concentrated on Sam. I knew I wanted that dog and was determined to find out who owned him.

I began my search by asking the various kids I would meet in town, and none of them seemed to know who owned Sam. I also checked at the post office because I saw Sam there a few times, but the people at the post office did not offer much help either. One day in August, I met two older boys in town, so as usual I asked them about Sam. Yes, they knew Sam and the man they thought owned him, Mr. Rice. After I got what information I could about Mr. Rice, I went to his house and as luck would have it, he was not home. Repeatedly, I would check the house where Mr. Rice lived. Towards the end of August on a Saturday afternoon, I again checked where Mr. Rice lived, and to my surprise, he was home.

I introduced myself, and began to relate my thoughts and feelings about Sam. To my surprise he said that he just let Sam run, because he could not do anything with him. He also said that Sam had been in jail – picked up by the animal enforcement officers several times – and that if I wanted him, I could have him.

Sam was there when this happened, so I thanked Mr. Rice and called to Sam, and without hesitation, he came to me and we both got into the car and drove away. That was one of the most fulfilling days of my life. Monday morning, I took Sam down the mountain to the veterinary clinic. Since Mr. Rice was not sure about any shots that Sam should have had, I wanted some professional advice. The doctor examined Sam and aside from being a little dirty, he appeared to be in good health. He estimated that Sam was

Chapter 35 – Sam

about two or three years old, and perhaps a cross breed with a Saint Bernhard, yet he had all the colorings of a German shepherd. A schedule was set up for Sam to have whatever shots that necessary: he also had a bath that day.

From that time on our relationship began to grow, much as a small sapling grows tall and strong. Sam was accustomed to running so when I went to work, I would let him run until I came home. The first time I did this, I wondered whether or not he would be there when I came home. He was not always there, but sooner or later, he would come home. From the onset, he seemed to know this was where he would live now. As time went on, Sam seemed to know the sound of my car and would come running. On other occasions when I wanted him home, I would call, but he wouldn't come. I found out that if I jingled my car keys, he would come running, but being a street-smart dog, he soon learned the jingling of the keys did not mean a ride. I could catch glimpses of him looking from behind the trees to see if I was getting in the car. If I didn't, he might or might not come home.

We spent many hours on the mountain hiking and on weekends cutting and splitting wood. By this time Sam had become totally dependable. I would never have to call him; he was always there. He demonstrated an uncanny sense of danger. I can remember on one occasion we were hiking and came to an old abandoned mine. I began hiking to the opening of the mine and Sam ran in from of me barking and jumping as if to prevent me from going into the mine. I did go into the mine, but Sam would not follow: he just barked and jumped at the opening, and because of this I came out, and he settled down. Several weeks later I learned that there was some old dynamite in the mine, and it exploded. Nobody knew for sure why this happened.

It was a year later when I decided to leave California. So, I packed whatever was necessary and Sam and headed to South Dakota. As we traveled and stopped for the night, Sam again seemed to know what

Chapter 35 – Sam

was expected of him as far as social skills were concerned. I did not have any problems with him at any of the motels. We spent about a year in South Dakota, some time at Deadwood and Lead (where the Homestake Gold mine is located) and some time in Sioux Falls.

I had been working in law enforcement in California and I wanted to get back to work, but I decided against South Dakota, so we moved to Montana. I again became involved with law enforcement in Montana, yet I had never thought of Sam as a police dog.

This is a true story about a dog named "Sam." Sam had the markings of a German Shepherd, but a much larger body because he was also part Saint Bernhard. His right ear would never stay up, the top kind of dropped, although he may have lacked in show dog status, he possessed wisdom, cunning, and tenacity beyond belief. Without any training, Sam developed social skills form his keen sense of perception, he seemed to always understand what was expected of him. We spent many hours hiking in San Bernardino National Forest. On weekends when I could cut and split wood Sam would always linger by, chasing a squirrel or a bird. We would share whatever lunch I would bring, but he loved pepperoni, salami and Mexican food. Occasionally he would wonder off, because he had been accustomed to running free. I soon found when I could not find him, if I drove about ten miles down the mountain, he would be at the migrant labor camp panhandling tortillas or enchiladas. When I would find him, he always appeared to have an embarrassed look on his face, he would put his head down and jump into the car.

When I went to work in law enforcement, I had no idea Sam would one day be working with me. This occurred one day while working at the maximum-security prison; we were looking at some dogs trained for this purpose. I happened to have Sam with me, and the trainer-handler of the other dogs began playing with Sam. He suggested to me that he

Chapter 35 – Sam

thought Sam had the potential – with some training – for this type of work. So, we went off to a training camp for twelve weeks. The trainer was correct. Sam proved he had all the ability and eagerness needed for this type of work. When we completed training, Sam and I developed an even closer relationship.

Sam would sleep at the foot of my bed, and when I would get up in the morning, he would watch to see what I would put on. If I put my uniform on, he would get the car keys off the desk and wait for me. If I didn't put my uniform on, he would lay back down. In the years that we worked together I would be disingenuous if I didn't admit I learned more from him than he did from me. Sam was not only my partner: he was my friend. At times I would talk to him, and he would sit and look at me, if I stopped talking, he would get up and nudge me with his nose as if to say, "I understand." When I polished my leather and badge, I always polished his little Deputy Sheriff's badge which he wore on his chain. I think I did this because of the pride he always seemed to demonstrate. As I said earlier, through his body language he taught me never to stand face-to-face with a potential suspect. I wore my weapon on my left side, so I would turn my left side away from the subject. I also noticed Sam would have his front legs slightly bent in anticipation of a leap. I learned to stand with one leg slightly bent to accomplish the same purpose. I also learned to follow Sam in any potentially dangerous situation, my response would have been to go straight forward, but Sam always took a different route as if to assess the entire picture.

We worked together in rain, snow, sleet and 20 degree below zero weather. If I didn't eat, Sam wouldn't, and he never whined. The climax of our relationship occurred one night in August. I did not have air conditioning in my car, so I had the windows down. About 11:30 p.m., I received a call a 211 in progress at a liquor store. (A 211 is an "Armed Robbery in Progress") Running Code Two

Chapter 35 – Sam

```
lights, no siren, we arrived in about six minutes.
Just as I rolled up and got out of the car, a
subject came out of the liquor store, turned in my
direction. With this Sam jumped from the car in
front of me as I heard a shot fired…
```

So many aspects of this story (or stories) strained belief. One point missing from this particular narrative was that Daniel told many people he had been in the California Patrol when in Riverside. He also implied the entire Sam story happened during this period to some. I know for a fact, he worked in the prison and seldom outside, though he tried to get involved in outside chase cases on at least one occasion. From every account, he was a very good employee at the prison, but none of the exploits in this did or could have happened. I found it interesting that he completely removed his then-wife, Margaret, from the narrative. I do know they ended up in South Dakota for a while, but the time spent there doesn't sync with public records showing their last known time in the San Bernardino mountains, South Dakota, and their eventual appearance in Montana. I have voter registrations showing them in San Bernardino in 1964, and Margaret listed as a nurse and Daniel listed as a supervisor at Big Sky Linen Supply, R812, Cook Ave, Billings Montana, in 1965.

Another point in the story with the casual mention of being in law enforcement were two conversations I had. One with a close friend of the family and one with the Deputy Warden. I specifically asked if Daniel had previous law enforcement in his background. Both said that never came up. The selling point for Daniel to apply at the prison was being ex-military. They had found a higher level of success with ex-military people vs. civilians.

Chapter 36 – Escape Report

Daniel kept some documents from 1971-1972, which was a pivotal year for him. Rising rather quickly in the ranks at the prison in Deer Lodge, by 1972 Daniel was living in officer's quarters, Margaret having been a respected nurse at the local hospital (until an injury necessitated her retirement), and for all intents and purposes, they were in a very good place. However, this was when Daniel's behavior started to become more erratic. For whatever reason, he kept a few items from 1972 that I've included in the coming pages.

```
April 24, 1971
Incident Report
    At approximately 8:00 p.m. 4/24/71 I was on
special duty with officer R.S. in the Rothe Hall
area. At about this time I received a radio message
from Sgt. M that some inmates had left the dairy in
a prison truck without any lights on. Visibility was
very poor due to overcast and drizzling rain.
    I drove to the end of the VMC parking lot and
stopped on the road. Sgt. M radioed that he could
hear the truck but could not see it. A short time
after this call, I saw a faint shadow cross the road
about 100 yards in front (north) of me. I asked
Officer S if he had seen anything and he said he had
not. I radioed the Captain to stay put as I wasn't
sure if the shadow I thought I'd seen was real or
imaginary. Officer S and I got out of the car and
could neither see nor hear the truck.
    After several minutes passed without any signs of
the truck, I proceeded down the Ranch #2 road,
headed south. I drove about three miles at very high
speed and upon rounding a tight corner near the
Ranch #7 turnoff, I saw the truck, a yellow 1952 REO
(Montana state-owned, License number M-3589) ahead
of us running without lights. I turned on my four-
way flashers, put the headlights on high beam, and
when I was about 20 yards behind the truck, I blew
the horn. The truck sped up. I then drew my .44 S. &
```

Chapter 36 – Escape Report

> W. revolver and fired a warning shot which hit the left rear tire of the truck. The truck did not stop, so I fired another shot into the tires. The truck kept going with no indication that the driver intended to stop. I followed the truck about 100 yards further and then ordered Officer S to open fire on the truck with the Thompson sub-machine. I fired two shots from my revolver and saw glass fly from the rear window of the truck cab. Smart fire eight rounds with the .45 Thompson.
>
> The truck then slowed to a stop. Officer S and I then ran to the truck and removed the three inmates:
>
> M, J. #23010
> S, W. #22992
> K, S. #22820
>
> The above men were employed at the prison dairy, were absent without legal authority, and had stolen the truck they were in. Inmate K was the driver.
>
> Sgt. K.S.
> R.L.
>
> PS: Immediately after removing the inmates from the vehicle we shook them down to check for weapons and to insure they were not injured. I also informed them of their legal rights at that time.
>
> KBS

And another report from Daniel:

> April 26, 1971
> Escape Report
> Captain Daniel Andrews
>
> To Whom It May Concern:
> On Saturday, April 24, 1971, working in the capacity of Duty Officer, I made a few rounds and talked to a few people. I picked up some information in reference to a possible escape from Rothe Hall. Considering the source of the information I contemplated the course of action if any to take. About 1:00 p.m. Saturday afternoon I received a call from Lt. D who informed me of the same information.

Chapter 36 – Escape Report

I then decided there could be credibility to the information received. I called Warden E and Deputy Warden B and informed them of what I had heard. Requested permission from them to secure the services of necessary personnel to set up course of action. Sgt. M, Sgt. S, Sgt. S, Officer R.S., Officer D.M., and Sheriff C were called and requested to come to my house. Checking the map of the area we all agreed that if a vehicle was going to be used in this escape attempt there were only three (3) ways out of the area. With this thought in mind Sgt. M and Sgt. S were assigned to the Conley Lake area; Sgt. S and Officer S were assigned the Ranch II Road. Officer M and I covered the road by Ranch I with the assistance of Sheriff C. The stake-out was begun at 4:00 p.m. and progressed without incident until approximately 6:00 p.m. I then heard several calls from the radio-room at the registrar's office for see if I could be of any assistance. They informed me that Mr. F. H. had called them to inform them that an escape attempt would be made from the dairy. We did not proceed to the dairy based on the face we did not know what inmates would be involved in this attempt. With this we proceeded to continue our surveillance. At approximately 8:10 p.m. I received a call from Sgt. M, and he stated from his vantage point a vehicle had started up and was proceeding out of the dairy without lights. Sgt. S and Officer S upon hearing this report moved their vehicle to the V. M. C. area, we in turn moved our vehicle closer to the Conley Lake Road. At no time were we able to see the moving vehicle without lights. We could hear the vehicle moving but could not determine in what direction. Approximately five (5) to ten (10) minutes elapsed. Sgt. S informed me by radio that they thought something had moved past them heading towards Ranch II. He then proceeded to head in that direction – at approximately 8:35 p. m. we received another call from Sgt. S that they had overtaken and apprehended a state vehicle with three (3) inmates. Upon hearing this Officer M and myself

Chapter 36 – Escape Report

headed in that direction. Upon arriving we found a state vehicle – three (3) inmates laying on the ground face down. It was at this time that Sgt. S informed me that efforts were made to stop the vehicle to no avail. Several shots were fired into the vehicle from the back to front. We proceeded then to skin search the three (3) inmates who were: S.K. B-22820, W.S. B-22992, and J.M., B-23010. After the skin search was completed, they were cuffed, placed in the cage car and brought to the inside institution where they were then placed in the disciplinary cell.

                              Respectfully submitted,
                              Captain Daniel Andrews
                              DA:ss

Chapter 37 – Letter(s) from a Convict

Also, among Daniel's personal belongings were two typed letters. He had them in a photo album, protected by plastic covers. Why he had and kept these isn't readily obvious. From what Father Nikolaev shared, Daniel was on a first-name basis with many of the "big name" convicts who came through Deer Lodge. Knowing he most likely skipped out of Detroit with automatic, or semi-automatic weapons likely that were affiliated with organized crime, there was probably much more behind his keeping these letters. I do know Daniel was both a law and crime groupie. I've always thought but for the grace of God or timing, instead of being Captain of the outside guard, Daniel probably would have been on the other side of the bars.

```
Thursday, June 22, 1972
Joe (Barboza):
   First of all, I don't expect that you are going
to be too happy over me in any case, but I remember
a couple of things you said in 1970 and 1971 - once
you said to me that we had common enemies in these
people, meaning Gerry and the others; then in a
letter to the newspaperman here you said that in the
"end they will abandon (William) Geraway too, as
they helped put (William) Geraway in prison. I find
that it is all too true. You're no bargain, Joe,
neither one of us are, but compared to these people
and the things they promote, and the double-crosses
- I have counted 14 major ones - we aren't as bad as
it would appear.
   Let me establish who I am to you so you will know
this letter isn't being written by a fed or one of
the Italians. Ted's Ace - Ted's Base - Ted's Case -
   I know that nothing cancels out how you must feel
about me and your trial - but even the worst of
enemies sometimes join for the sake of mutual
convenience to sink a common enemy. I may be going
before the Pepper Committee - if so, I don't intend
to do you any harm. I intend to bury Angiulo and
```

Chapter 37 – Letter(s) from a Convict

Chisholm. By the way, Chisholm had the information on the Wilson thing before ANY law enforcement official had it. Chisholm and Angiulo tried the same thing with me that they did with you, and Bailey is just dying to confirm a few things, and as you thought in the beginning, they want Patriarca in prison and just Limone out. All of my major negotiations were with Gerry through Cassesso and often Limone-Cassesso told me of one particular incident, and I can pass a lie test on it, where Billy Stuart the cop gave a police report to Gerry on Romeo Martin giving him information on the Deegan murder; Gerry then ordered Romeo killed, Cassesso said he personally gave the word also and drove the car and paid for the wake and funeral and that if anyone wanted to testify against him and Angiulo on that particular murder. Also, Bailey intends to move as soon as they can get by Forte – but you – I'll go all out against them, and I'll list the double-crosses. I used to think you were exaggerating when you told me of all the double-crosses, but I see now, my sister sees, what they have done and haven't done. So, I'm as vindictive as they are – I remember those four words – and that would be plead the fifth – intentionally setting up a privilege to be broken is unethical to say the least. That four word code, which I'll recite before the committee, is going to keep Bailey off the stand for good; and Chisholm is going to be finished – I'd like to nail Gerry if I could, but I only have half of the case, you would have to give the other half. Until that long series of arguments, we had some good hours, and some good mutual friends like Joe Keyes. It is too bad that everything becomes twisted. But remember this – you were with these people, went to the government, and it hurt you – then you came back to help people, went to the government, and it hurt you – then you came back to help these people but finally realized that they wouldn't keep their word, and where you are speaks for itself in a way. I've been used by both sides. But at least it appears that the

Chapter 37 – Letter(s) from a Convict

government keeps their word, while these people don't. I tried to help these people, I really did – and there are 14 double-crosses and it is my understanding that Gerry wants me out of the way because I might foul up the Bailey deal. There is a lot more, but before I go into it I want to hear from you – nothing incriminating – if you want to get back at the bastards that used you – and me – if you want to stop Bailey, let's work together and let the future bring what it may. They said they had two men with you or around all the time ready to take you out of the picture if they gave the word. One was Dr. Zorba (Nicky). You know the other.

    Let's both put our personal griefs and bitterness aside, as strong as yours must be, and let's nail Bailey and Chisholm and Gerry and Peter – Let's show them that this entire issue can be reversed.

    According to your answer, which will be sent me certified mail, return receipt requested (they have to open a letter like that in front of me and can't read it, and it'll be from my sister), I'll know what steps to take next. Peter wanted me to push on a certain cop that allegedly took too much to drink and drove off the road one night – he really likes you. So, let me know. I want your answer, not someone else's. I know your writing, and it can be sent in with a letter from Louise certified return receipt, addressee only. I'm disgusted with the whole thing, and there is nothing they can do to me. Remember you always said that all it took to be a tough guy was to lose the fear of dying? Well, I'm at that stage – I don't expect a long life, but I want to be free, I want to live a little, and I want to sink these guys, especially Gerry and Chisholm – and it would be to your advantage to help prove the four-word code on Bailey.

                                                        – B –

                   (underneath in handwriting)

Chapter 37 – Letter(s) from a Convict

Remember a letter I wrote for you to Bailey on August 20, 1970?

And a short while later, another letter.

Saturday, July 1st, 1972
Hello, Joe:

   I got word that Gerry threw me to the dogs. Once you said that only a few people were justified in their actions against the criminal code of honor. You told me that you would trust me with your life. You never had a chance on the thing you are doing time for now. I betrayed you. No, I am putting you on the street, and backing up everything you said. We were friends once, that may be past. I liked you, and we have common enemies. Get a fed or lawyer and I will get you out of prison, you have my promise. I'm sinking Angiulo.

   You were good to me when no one else was. I know the TRUE story on your case, and will be free in a short time, and we will sink Angiulo and everyone else. Get someone to me or my sister and you will on the street. Let Angiulo take his best shot. I'm getting you out. Notify your lawyer – I was offered $200,000 for sinking you. I will definitely put you on the street.

   F – k the mafia and let's give them their best shot.

Joe's Ace,
Billy

You will be out, free this summer.

Chapter 38 – Drugs

Another interesting bit of writing was found in a notebook dated September 20, 1972. Again, written by Daniel by hand, I have no idea if this was part of a class, self-help, personal research, or quite what the motivation was. Based on his very erratic behavior at this point in time that led to his being asked to leave the prison, I suspect it was self – directed research to see if he could find a way to modify or adjust his personal drug intake.

(As written by Daniel)

```
(top of page - 72 Ford Martin Olson L/D 815 Penn #1)
Sept. 20, 1972
1. Wan, Econ. Drug Uses (Topics of importance)
2. Biological Revolution since 1950
3. Need to create new drugs.
   Changing our culture (result of new drugs)
1. Communicable Diseases under control #1
2. Drugs, Sulfa, Penicillin, Broad Spectrum
   Antibiotics
   a. Body _ World War #2 (Increases Longevity)
3. Advent of Tranquilizers 1950 wider 1954 (Mind)
   a. Drugs to affect the mind (restore to normal
      mental health) (1957 to 1967 Decrease of
      mental patients by 33%)
   b. Anti - Depressants
   c. Oral contraceptives (over 8 million women use)
      Social Convenience (teenage morals)
      Credit Card Pleasure (Extending the dependency
      of children)
   d. Development of Euphoriants - Mood Elevator
      Dexedrine Amphetamines - Instant Reaction
      Chemical Control of Moods
   e. Pills to learn faster
   Next decade active use of Psycho Active Drugs
4. Why people take drugs?
   a. It is a learned behavior through the culture.
      Behavior will persist if it increases pleasure
```

Chapter 38 – Drugs

```
         Or decreases tension
    b.   Take drugs that are accepted by the culture
    c.   Multiple causes for people taking drugs
         Generic environmental past experiences
         Present environment
    d.   Drug taking is not unique
         Persists in taking an action that does not
         resolve the problem
                                            10-4-72
```

There were *many* more pages of these types of handwritten notes. From everything I had learned drugs were (and most likely at this time, still) a big part of his life and functioning. I couldn't find any indication of this being part of his training at the prison (as this would have taken place about the time everything started to unravel), or if this was an independent course of study he sought out.

I have also harbored a theory that Margaret was probably procuring drugs for Daniel, which was probably the main reason she lost her nursing licenses over the years. With her injury and retirement from nursing, this may have created a crisis and turning point in Daniel's drug use and the sudden unavailability of them to "maintain" in a stressful environment.

But between the story about Sam, the letters from convicts he had kept, and the notes about drugs, I was gaining more insight into who he was and his thought process.

Chapter 39 – 2013…

We were now into 2013, and many other things were going on in our lives. We became involved with a contentious homeowner's association (aren't they *all* contentious?) to a much larger extent than we anticipated or wanted, as well as my freelance graphic and web design work, and releasing my fourth (and fifth) album(s) under the moniker Munich Syndrome.

After Dave's mother's health declined to a certain point, and after some thought and family meetings, it was agreed that we'd move his mom from Sun City West to Dave's brother's home in Huntington Beach. We were making regular visits down to Southern California now. With the close proximity to Garden Grove and other places in Southern California, I took opportunities to research in the libraries. The Garden Grove Library had several city directories from the era I was looking at. While these city directories are no longer published, they are a treasure trove of who lived where, and also listed occupations.

It was one thing to see a location on a map or even look at street views, but it was entirely different going to the actual locations. While my adoptive parents had moved with me to Garden Grove when I only a few months old, Dinah's family had remained in Long Beach, so we had taken many trips there when I was young, and I was very aware of the city and its surroundings. I was very stunned at how close my adoptive parents and Daniel and Margaret lived to each other, both in Long Beach, and then in Garden Grove. Walking distance was an understatement. While my adoptive father stayed very vague about the lawyer who brokered my adoption, from the tidbits that would come out, I got the impression his office at that time was also within a close radius. My father knew far too much about the lawyer, his family. There seemed to be much more going on than just a couple randomly finding a lawyer and randomly adopting a child.

Going to the house Daniel and Margaret moved to in Garden Grove was very jarring. This was obviously the same builder who had done the streets I lived and grew up in. It could have just as easily been the street I knew so well growing up. The house was a one-story rambler, stucco with a small

Chapter 39 – 2013...

amount of wood trim, and a white-rock roof, exactly like our home. While I wouldn't say it was walking distance, it was very close, and I honestly couldn't rule out not having been on that street at some point as a child.

I explored some of the downtown areas I'd frequented as a child and realized how close everything was to everything else. I flashed on the picture of Daniel holding a bowling trophy in what was obviously the backyard on Pinto Drive. My parents were both avid bowlers, both in leagues separately and together. There weren't that many leagues in our city. While it's possible they didn't have a social relationship (or more?) in Long Beach, they most definitely would have intersected in the smaller social circles they now found themselves in. Another point of reference came to me when I recalled Delores saying Daniel had mentioned dancing classes in Southern California. Both my parents regularly attended Arthur Murray dance classes, as well as going out dancing. Again, the overlap and potential for interaction seems probable. I started culling through my memories now. Going to the park by myself or with friends, going to the movies, hanging out at the mall… Had I encountered them? Were they watching me? I have no idea. There was always the possibility I had encountered Daniel's brother Donald Andrejewski as well.

Chapter 40 – 2013-2014

As 2013 continued, so did the rather relentless emails and calls from Delores. She finally established her own separate residence and seemed to be going for the final divorce from her husband. It was with some surprise she announced that not only were they reconciling *again*, they were now purchasing a new home together. This was worrisome (for me), as Delores had always had her own home to return to when things went south. Now that would be sold as part of the down payment for the new home. At first it was all sweetness and light. A new place, a new start, everything new in their home. But small criticisms started creeping in. Then small complaints became larger complaints. A new tone of despair and unhappiness clouded all our communications. After far too many complaints, in the gentlest way I could summon, I said "Delores, it seems to me you've made some poor choices in terms of husbands and mates."

I never heard from her again. I sent a couple more emails and a birthday card but received no reply. I called a few times, but it always went to voice mail. I felt bad she no longer responded but did not regret finally saying what had been obvious to me (and probably everyone else she knew) from the start. She made, and was continuing to make, poor choices.

The year became very overwhelming with Dave's Mother passing away just shy of her 85th her birthday, and his younger brother passing just a couple of weeks later. Another responsibility that had fallen upon us was Dave's Aunt had been diagnosed with severe Alzheimer's back in 2012. At the time, they said she wasn't well or expected to last long, and she was put on hospice care. We found an exceptional, albeit expensive, facility for her, and under their care, she was still going strong in 2013 and her money had run out long ago, so this was also an ongoing concern.

Our obligations and involvement with our HOA reached a crisis point early in 2014. Certain events caused us to re-evaluate if it was the best place for us continue to live, or if the timing was right to look for something better. By April we made the decision to move, done a fair amount of research, found our "forever" home, and closed on it by the end of June. It was a

Chapter 40 – 2013-2014

much bigger undertaking than either of us anticipated, but well worth it once the bigger items were addressed.

Another good thing that was happening since talking with Danni every day was her improved sense of self. She used to call, quite frequently, after her son called her. These calls *always* ended (and more often than not, started) with her in tears. She was astute enough to realize her son only called when he was on his way home from work. There was never a call from home when his wife might be around. The gist of most of these calls were of him being angry with Danni for being ill. He complained she was exaggerating or making up her ailments and conditions. As he hadn't actually laid eyes on her in person for *many* years once he fled New Hampshire, it made it even more offensive. I told her, repeatedly, if he's going to call and be openly abusive and disrespectful, hang up. Even better, don't answer at all. Let the calls go to voice mail. See what he has to say before you engage. While there wasn't an instant change in her attitude, she stopped engaging, refused to take the abuse, and there was a significant decrease in calls where she'd be inconsolable due to the sobbing. There was a time she blamed herself for this behavior, but I explained he was a (very) grown man, and it's his choice to man up and stop throwing temper tantrums because *Mommy* isn't there the way he'd like her to be or not.

Chapter 41 – Brother from Another Mother

With the new house finally settled and set up, 2015 had a feeling of new starts all around. A few months into the year, I went downstairs and logged into my email while the coffee was brewing. The first email from was from 23andMe saying I had a half-brother! With the amount of detective work, research, and interviews I had done, this just didn't seem possible. I logged into my account there it was: half-brother. I don't know how long I sat there, but I had to reheat the first cup of coffee. I sent a message via 23andMe and received a response almost immediately. John was a couple of years older than Danni. He was born and placed for adoption in New York. Instantly, I knew this was correct as Sue Ellen had referenced Daniel spending time in New York, which predated his time in Chicago where he met and married Mary (Danni's mother).

We exchanged a few emails, and John was certainly the exception out of all of Daniel's children. John was the only one of us raised without any knowledge of or even marginal interaction with Daniel. Also, unlike the rest of us, his upbringing had been remarkably stable and loving. Unlike the various issues the rest of Daniel's children experienced, while his family of course knew he was adopted, he was never made to feel different or question it. It turned out he had a son, also adopted, who had given him the 23andMe DNA kit for Christmas. It had apparently sat untouched for quite a while.

Unlike what I and Daniel's other children went through to find out about our Father, I was able to give John a succinct overview and summation of his Father's side of the family. The information he had on his Mother was very slim. All he had was a last name that was not particularly common. We ended up communicating more through email than the phone as he's definitely a (very) late-night person and I'm an early riser, combined with the 3-hour time difference between coasts.

I updated Sue Ellen, with whom I wanted to double check the info regarding Daniel living in New York. I had the New York part of Daniel's narrative correct. I could almost hear her head shaking as she said, "I wonder how many more are out there?" Danni was more intrigued and echoed the

Chapter 41 – Brother from Another Mother

thought that there could be many more half-siblings waiting to be discovered.

Not long after the discovery of John, I was rather surprised to receive an email from Audrey. She made vague mention of us falling out of touch, but the biggest item was her update of her mother, Delores. Delores had taken a shotgun and killed her husband, then called 911, telling them what she had done, and turned the gun on herself! As shocking and upsetting as this was, I wasn't all that surprised. Delores had previously mentioned that she wasn't afraid of dying on several occasions. She had mentioned having a gun at hand most of the time. I had also heard and seen her flashes of anger. It could be quick and pass as quickly as a thunderstorm. But this one obviously hadn't. I felt very badly for Audrey (and Arlene, though Audrey didn't mention or reference her), and a sadness that I'd never get to speak to or hear from Delores again. I let Audrey know about John.

She replied one last time saying "The whole Daniel Andrews thing is such a mess... I wouldn't even know what to say."

I replied with – what I *thought* was – a humorous remark, "Well, you could drop him a note and say, 'Remember that time we were shared DNA material?'"

I received no reply from Audrey after that. Sadly, Delores had fulfilled her self-proclaimed prophecy of being the *black sheep* of the family. I shared the information with Danni, John, and Sue Ellen.

Another medical issue that had been ongoing with Danni was her opioid use. Having the massive medical history and the overall pain she was in; the doctors had started giving her Fentanyl quite a while back. As time went on, the doses became larger and larger. The patches would last for a couple of days. There was a consequence to this. Many days I'd call she'd fall asleep mid-sentence, or be so out of it, she didn't even recall us having spoken. It was getting worse and worse, and Alex was very concerned as well.

With the discovery of John, Danni's diminishing health, and the various people now involved, a plan began to have a family *'union'* (as opposed to reunion) in Colebrook towards the end of the year. As time went on, September was agreed upon by all parties. What came as a surprise (for most of us) was suddenly Sue Ellen and her daughter Karen said they were joining us as well! While welcome, it was unexpected.

Chapter 42 – Washington & New Hampshire

While plans were coalescing for everyone to meet in New Hampshire, Henry's health was declining. As we entered September it was looking like this would be the end, so we went up to Washington to visit. Henry was in a nursing facility, holding his own, but not doing well. We stayed for several days, and when visiting, I was trying to steer conversations towards end-of-life and what / if there was anything he wanted to discuss. I point-blank asked him some questions about my adoption, and he brushed the questions aside with "I don't know." He would drift off or stare at the TV with banal game shows and briefly the news, but we didn't discuss anything meaningful. No longer eating, he still maintained. As the trip to New Hampshire entailed too many people and had been prearranged, I finally said my goodbyes and we headed East.

We flew to Boston and rented a car. We thought Sue Ellen and Karen might arrange their arrival so we could drive up to Colebrook together, but the details of their arrival didn't sync, so we agreed to meet them up there. John and his lovely wife Yumeko were driving up from New York. We had previously stayed at the Northern Comfort Motel but knew Danni would have more limitations now being wheelchair-bound and with a larger group of people. We had found a place online that looked like it would be a large suite with two bedrooms, that would be a good central meeting spot for the visit. As it turned out, it was not handicapped accessible, and after talking with Alex, we settled on the Colebrook Country Club Motel. John and Yumeko were already checked in when we arrived, and we were finally able to meet in person. While John has much darker hair, Dave said he could see the resemblance. We agreed to drive out to Alex's and try figure out where Sue Ellen and Karen were later.

Prior to the visit, Danni tried to get out of bed and had hurt her foot and leg. Days before we arrived Alex had taken her to the local hospital, and it was confirmed it was a break. A bad break. We might have suggested we all meet in town, but with this new injury, we went out to them. Alex met us out front and briefed us on Danni's condition. She had been napping. I went in first and tapped her shoulder gently.

Chapter 42 – Washington & New Hampshire

She rolled over, squinted, looked at me and said, "It's nice to meet you, John."

I broke out laughing and teased she didn't even recognize me from our first visit and all the pictures we've shared with them over the years.

She got flustered, but kind of laughed. John and Yumeko were great. They went over and introduced themselves, hugging her and sitting by her. They weren't standoffish or stiff. They just started talking and got to know Danni and Alex. I sat back a bit, as Danni (and Alex) and I talk almost daily. After a while, I got to spend some time with Danni while they talked with Alex. One of the things I knew was John wasn't big on foul language, and I knew Sue Ellen and Karen frowned on it, too. Danni, on the other hand, would let loose with anything, so when the others were on the other side of the room I leaned in and whispered "Fuck you, fuck you, fuck you" and Danni grinned and whispered back "Fuck you, fuck you, fuck you, too…" and we both laughed and hugged.

About an hour after we were there, Sue Ellen and Karen made their way to the house. Both were dressed much more fashionably than what you'd generally find in Colebrook. Their arrival brought in a much higher level of energy that wasn't quite matched by everyone in the room after we had been there a while. This was the first time Sue Ellen and Karen had met Danni (and Alex) in person, despite speaking on the phone for years. It was a very nice moment having everyone assembled in the living room, despite Danni not being anywhere near her best while still recovering from the break. After visiting, Danni said she was in too much pain and too tired to join us for dinner, so the rest of us headed back to the hotel. John's room was next to ours, but Sue Ellen's was a bit further down. After a certain amount of everyone recalibrating, we made our way out for our first meal together at the Black Bear Tavern. Sue Ellen and Karen were very interested in John and Yumeko, so most of the conversation was directed their way. It was somewhat obvious to all that we weren't local, and our waitress enquired where we were from. I explained the group dynamic and that we were visiting our sister, Danni. She said she knew Danni and Alex and was actually a childhood friend of Danni's daughter April. It shouldn't have been

Chapter 42 – Washington & New Hampshire

surprising to run into people who knew each other there. We said we'd regroup in the morning.

As it turned out, everyone got up at different times, and Sue Ellen and Karen were definitely getting in a fair amount of sight-seeing while up in this region. John and Yumeko joined us to go back out to visit with Danni and Alex the next day. Danni was still not doing well with the broken ankle. We spent some time with her before giving her a chance to rest while we explored the town.

We wandered into a gift shop on the main street that had a room in the back with artistic photos of some of the sights from the region. There were some photos of the Balsams. The Balsams is a sprawling hotel that was apparently the inspiration for Stephen King's *The Shining*. Alex had worked there and regaled us with stories about it. According to him, they had planned on shooting the movie version of *The Shining* there, but the hotel declined as they had a golf tournament or some event happening. At this point in time, the place was completely closed with plans to renovate.

As I was pointing to the pictures and relaying the stories Alex had shared, a woman who worked (owned?) the shop came and asked if we needed anything. I mentioned a relative had worked at the Balsams and she brightened and asked, "Who?" I then explained it was Alex, and that John and I were Danni's brothers. The woman's face closed up and she turned and walked away! Alex had mentioned that after the accident people had stopped coming by or calling. I was not inclined to spend a penny in that shop after that reaction.

On our third day in Colebrook, Danni had a follow-up appointment at the local hospital. She asked if we could go with her. Yumeko was a nurse, so having her input and presence was greatly welcome. I noticed the tone of their treatment when they first went in was not one I would appreciate. We were asked if all of us wanted to be present for the follow-up and we all said yes except for Sue Ellen and Karen, who opted to sit in the lobby.

The doctor came in and said based on the nature of the fracture, she recommended surgery and putting pins in. Danni completely lost it, sobbing hysterically that she NEVER wanted another surgery again as long as she lived. The doctor seemed poised to press her case, but when the four of us

Chapter 42 – Washington & New Hampshire

stood up and explained the VERY EXTREME and long-standing medical issues she's already endured, she immediately dialed everything back relenting, saying she understood and would look for the best options to avoid surgery.

It turned out everyone's departure schedules were different. Sue Ellen and Karen were the first to leave, with John and Yumeko set to drive back the next day. That left Dave and I there for one final dinner. Danni was doing better, and after gentle prompting, they agreed to go out to dinner with us at the Black Bear Tavern. Having a much smaller group we were enjoying our meal when my cell phone rang. It was my sister's (then) husband letting me know my father had passed that afternoon. While it wasn't good news, being with this group made things a bit easier. We finished dinner on a somber note. We went by their place the next morning to say our goodbyes and headed home to California.

Chapter 43 – 2017

One of the mysteries of Daniel's family tree was his mother: Beatrice Bagnowski. From the time of my first efforts on Ancestry.com up until the present, new data, primarily Census reports were now available. From the data of the 1930 Census, Paul Andrejewski had left the household, leaving his wife Beatrice as the head of the household with four children. As Daniel had been born in 1927 this would negate his claims that he had been orphaned. The 1940 Census shows another large shift. Beatrice was no longer in the household. It was Eleanor (Daniel's aunt) was the noted as the head of the household.

Around this time, I was matched with a 3rd to 4th cousin on one of the DNA sites. I messaged her and she said her mother would be the one to talk to. Her mother, Barbara, was on Facebook and I sent a message. We friended each other and after many messages back and forth we set a time for me to call her. Barbara was a delight and filled in a lot of blank spaces explaining what happened with Beatrice. It looks like Beatrice met Paul in the 1920's in Detroit. In the nicest way possible, Barbara indicated Beatrice was a "party girl" and while I didn't want to spin something that wasn't there, I pressed, and it was confirmed she was a prostitute. While the exact story of why she left the family isn't known for certain, Barbara did confirm Beatrice met a mobster in Detroit, married him and had a son. This would have been around 1935. By the 1940 Census Beatrice was listed as the head of the household with a five-year-old son, Donald McIntyre. Barbara indicated by this point in time, Beatrice was trying to get away from her husband, Donald McIntyre Sr. and was going under the last name of Rose.

Barbara recounting visiting Aunt Beatrice, saying she was enjoyable and fun to be around. Apparently, she loved going through the large department store in Detroit trying all the perfume and cosmetic samples. Sadly, Beatrice contracted tuberculosis and passed away in 1960. It was the same tuberculosis ward that her son Daniel and his wife Mary were in about 10 years previously. Barbara wasn't sure what became of her son, Donald. She believed he had worked as a hospital orderly, but after Beatrice passed, he more or less vanished from the family.

Chapter 43 – 2017

When I relayed this story to Danni, she remembered a story about when all the Andrzejewski children were small. Kathleen (the oldest child) was apparently attempting to make pancakes one day. The problem was, they looked (and probably smelled) strange. It would seem no adult supervision was around at the time. Kathleen went next door with her failed plate of pancakes asking the neighbor what was wrong. To the neighbor's shock and dismay, it appeared Kathleen was attempting to make pancakes with Ajax, instead of flour. The assumption was that Beatrice was not around, so the authorities were called. When Beatrice finally arrived home, the authorities informed her that they'd be taking Kathleen into protective custody. Apparently, her reply was "take all of them."

This definitely played into Daniel's narrative that he was an orphan. What he left out of the narrative was not much time passed before his aunt Eleanor quickly brought all four of the Andrejewski children under her roof. Based on Census reports, it would appear their father Paul resided with them at certain points as well, but it was Eleanor, along with her sister Alexine, who took over the responsibilities of caring for the children.

Looking at the trauma having not one, but both parents, walk away from a home must have been overwhelming. Throw in the poverty of the Great Depression, the impact on all of the Andrejewski children had to be immense.

Another mystery was that of the oldest son, Donald. From all accounts he was well liked and loved. He went off to war, but when he returned, he was changed. What would probably now be considered PTSD, at the time, wasn't commented on. He had met a woman in Italy and expressed a desire to marry her. Eleanor apparently had put her foot down and strictly forbid him from doing this. Shortly afterwards Donald vanished. Most of his belongings were still in the home. Posters were placed around Detroit and there was even a notice on local TV looking for him and his whereabouts. The family never knew what happened or became of him.

While I have no information about his state of mind, between city directories, Census reports and public records, Donald went to Southern California, living in and around Anaheim. It would appear he was married and divorced 3 times. He passed away in 1981, and the last information had him passing in Orange California and buried at a military cemetery.

While I had this information early on, Sue Ellen had told Myrtle that I knew what had become of Donald, she never reached out for that information. Knowing what I did about her parents and family history, I now understand why Myrtle never wanted to speak to me. These were obviously deep and painful hurts that she obviously did not want to revisit or reopen.

And in looking at where Donald ended up, I do believe Daniel ended up in Southern California because that's where Donald was located. I have no idea if Daniel was in communication with Myrtle during his time in California, but I suspect Daniel and Donald never knew of their parents passing.

Chapter 44 – 2018

So many things were happening between our visit to New Hampshire in 2015 and 2018, aside from keeping in touch with John, Sue Ellen, and of course Danni & Alex, a part of me felt the birth search had reached a natural and (possibly) final conclusion. During the years after it started, I'd relate the story to friends and acquaintances and without a miss, I'd hear, "You *have to* write this story! I'd read it!" I had sat down several times attempting to memorialize it, but it just didn't seem to flow, and I'd push it aside.

Another very good thing that happened was after getting far too close to the edge with her Fentanyl use, after an emergency hospital stay, Danni was able to stop her use of the very dangerous opioid! It took a lot of courage and effort, but she was able to turn something around many have been unable to do!

Somewhere around the middle of the year John contacted me that Audrey was on 23andMe! I found this quite odd and surprising as she had never expressed much (if any?) interest in any of the family history, had never followed up contacting John (I sent her his email back in 2015), or much of anything else. I looked and there she was. After about three or four weeks, I received a "sharing request" for DNA information, which I allowed. John then told me he had received a note from her. I had already shared everything I knew with him regarding the entire family and said to keep me posted, if he wanted to. About two weeks later, I received an email from Audrey! She was all, "*Can you believe it? We have another brother?*" She went on to say she didn't really know why she never responded to my last email back in 2015, said she had a new family, and seemed excited about getting to know John.

I replied and reminded her that I had told her about John, along with his email *three years ago*. I wished her well with her new endeavors and family and hit "Send." The email immediately bounced. She had obviously blocked my email back in the day and had either forgotten or was this the ultimate in passive-aggressive behavior? I used a different account and sent her the same reply. This one did not bounce, and I heard nothing more. I noticed she

Chapter 44 – 2018…

withdrew her public profile on 23andMe shortly thereafter. As far as I know, she never got back in touch with John again.

As 2018 was ending, we received a Christmas card from Sarah Durand. She mentioned she was still waiting for the story, and the clock was ticking. As the story and history unfolded chronologically as each discovery was made or happened, that's how it now felt right to finally lay it all out.

Another change was at the end of 2018 we signed up for a third DNA study. This time through Ancestry.com. One of the main drivers was I had been contacted by a gentleman claiming we were matched on a DNA site but could not find his name or any such identifier among the two I was on. He had mentioned Ancestry.com, but while we had family trees there, we had never joined the DNA study. We did, and between the three DNA sites, I have been matched with several hundred people on my birth mother's side. Sadly, with her being adopted, none of us have been successful in connecting the dots. A cousin from Dublin showed up and using that as a springboard it would appear either of Margaret's grandparents may have come from Ireland. It would be nice to explore those roots but being able to link them through the proper family lines would be necessary. I now really wanted to connect those dots. I knew my birth father's lineage very well, but my birth mother's lineage was still a cypher. Also, the person who claimed we were related did not show up on Ancestry.com at all. I have no idea if it was misplaced information on his end, or a possible scam? This started me on the path to research not only how to obtain my own unredacted birth certificate, but also how to obtain my birth mother's.

Chapter 45 – 2019

Having spent the lion's share of 2017 and 2018 working on my eighth album (under the moniker Munich Syndrome) and creating a YouTube channel with over 65 videos (and counting), January felt like it was the right time to block out time every day for starting to memorialize this story. The first order of business was to pull out the various boxes and folders with the notes, phone numbers, photographs, official documents (birth, death, marriage certificates), as well as paper calendars detailing the years and dates, we were in the various locations. I had a few moments of panic when I thought I had misplaced a very important cache of documents, but with the last move, they had been put in another box.

Once I started at the beginning, it began to take shape. But as with many times in this search, things came up in real time to change things. One of the most unexpected surprises was my husband was able to get one, then two, and finally three contracts in Oklahoma. This was where my Uncle Lloyd and his wife Janine lived. Also, Lloyd's daughter, Samantha, who was (and IS) very much into genealogy and family history. Samantha and I had talked on the phone and exchanged emails as well as chatting on Facebook but had never met in person. With the first contract in Muskogee, we booked the trip so the last few days we could stay with the family in Norman and catch up. I realized there were some points in their shared history with my birth mother I'd like to revisit.

Lloyd and Jaime were VERY welcoming, and Samantha very kindly opened her lovely home to us and let us stay with her. What was interesting was talking to Samantha one-on-one and hearing her take on their history as opposed to the version Lloyd liked to present. We had a very nice visit, and as it turned out, we would be back in two weeks for the next contracts Dave had. We made plans to end our trip in Norman again. Samantha had already made plans to return to Michigan, but again, kindly let us stay in her home.

Lloyd is a wine connoisseur and had planned on a road trip with his wife that week. It turned out Dave's contract work wound down quicker than he had planned, so we asked if we could join them. It turned out to be a good thing for us, as well as for Lloyd and Janine. Lloyd will be turning 90 and is

Chapter 45 – 2019

still driving. (He probably shouldn't be, but that's another story.) He had meticulously laid out the route, places and arrival times. The problem was, he had them all documented on paper maps. When we were available, we offered to drive. Almost instantly we were confronted by many streets, highways, and lanes closed for construction and/or repair. Having GPS capabilities on our phones allowed us to navigate the patchwork of closures and detours without too much hassle.

The one time an issue occurred, and GPS could have helped. We were driving towards the first winery on the list, and without warning (or visible signs) the road ended, and we were on a bare dirt and rock road. The rate of speed we were traveling had been about 40 mph and the sudden departure of the asphalt had a jarring effect, like suddenly being in a "Dukes of Hazzard" episode. Two things also compounded this turn of events. We were in a rental car and did not want to return it pock-marked from flying rocks, but worse, a big off-road truck was directly behind us (going much faster than we had been) and obviously wanted to get around us. I was determined NOT to let that happen and have this truck throw all the debris up at us, so I kept at a higher rate of speed than I would normally have. Lloyd kept 'suggesting' I slow down, but until we hit the turn off and the truck was no longer on my tail, I maintained my speed. Thankfully, we arrived safe and sound, the car unblemished, with only a semi-heavy coating of dust to show where we had been.

During this particular week in Oklahoma we drove over 1,000 miles and saw a vast quantity of the state. We were also able to have some nice conversations over lunches and dinners, as well as stay at a lovely bed-and-breakfast that was also a winery. One thing I did notice was Lloyd and Janine were less inclined to dismiss the wild (to them) stories Margaret had shared with them in 1980 when they last saw each other. When I first met Lloyd and Janine their attitude was 'she was just talking all this crazy stuff' and pretty much dismissed that last interaction. This time around Lloyd seemed a bit more interested in hearing more and Janine certainly paid attention. I wasn't completely sure getting on these topics would be upsetting, but it seemed to end well.

Chapter 45 – 2019

In between our second trip to Oklahoma and a trip to London, we also went to Seattle to attend a 60th birthday for a very good friend. While there we made the drive down to Olympia to visit with Lloyd and Janine's son, Rob and his wife Nancy. We had stayed in touch after meeting them with Lloyd and Janine back in 2008. We had visited them when they lived in Port Orchard, and they had come by and visited us when we lived on the Peninsula and again after we moved. Both are VERY creative, smart, funny, and involved. We had a very relaxing afternoon during which Nancy provided a sumptuous feast. We got to talking about the story I was working on, and Rob's folks.

We sat out back in Rob and Nancy's backyard. Rob shared an interesting side story to the last time my birth mother interacted with her brother. The story, as I then currently understood it, was Margaret and Lloyd's mother had passed, Margaret had shown up and was instantly confrontational and abrasive. On this point, there seems to be a group consensus. But Rob expanded upon this and said he and his older brother had picked Margaret up at the airport. Rob shared that his older brother was instantly combative with Margaret, saying inflammatory and negative things to her. It was obvious she felt outgunned and outnumbered before she set eyes on her brother. It's not to say everything would have been sweetness and light had the day not gotten off on a negative footing, but it certainly didn't help.

Our final trip to Oklahoma got off to a rocky start and between extreme weather, less than a sweet suite at the hotel (no dresser, no table lamps, no chairs for the table, it looked like someone had robbed the room) and some other issues, this trip seemed ill-advised. Thankfully, by the time we got to Norman, the cloud (literally and figuratively) seemed to have passed. One thing that I have no idea why I didn't realize earlier: I had never talked to Janine one-on-one about growing up with my birth mother. They were best friends since Janine's family moved next to Margaret's when they were 10! Thankfully after going out for lunch on Thursday, Lloyd said he had things he wanted to do, so we dropped him off at their home while Janine came back with us to Samantha's, and we had a chance to talk one-on-one. It seems they had a pleasant enough childhood, but Janine did comment that Margaret's mother was extremely demanding. If something was out of place,

Chapter 45 – 2019

a paper doll session left some clippings somewhere, she'd come in and scream at the top of her lungs. For Janine's upbringing, while her own mother might yell, she'd NEVER do it while guests or friends were over. Margaret's mother had no such constraints.

I asked about that last time they were all together and Janine was bit reticent, but said Margaret was very complimentary to her, but was openly antagonistic with her brother and mother. Samantha was also present for part of this visit. I had noticed that both her parents were dismissive and somewhat put off by Margaret bringing a large 20-gallon trash-sack full of medication and medical devices. Samantha felt that her parents just didn't (or couldn't) grasp the fact that Margaret and her husband were living (well) below the poverty line. At this point in their lives, they were living on the "poor farm" in Anaconda on land from an abandoned copper mine. Very shortly after this last visit, they were being required to move as the land and water was contaminated by arsenic from the mine. But there was sense that everyone was (very) put off by Margaret wearing a cheap polyester suit that could have been a waitress uniform, and big floppy straw hats. Margaret was very proud that her husband had given them to her, but while it was nothing anyone at the funeral would be caught dead in, there was no realization by the others that what Margaret was wearing was the absolute best she could do with the resources available to her at that point in her life. Samantha saw this, but I don't think the realities landed with Lloyd and Janine.

Chapter 46 – Less than…

One of the bigger surprises for me in documenting this journey was how I had distanced myself from it emotionally while it was happening. Over the years in sharing the story I've encountered people who ask if I was sorry that I began my birth search, or if I regretted many of the negative and sad things I uncovered. The answer is always a steadfast, "No." But as I was now reviewing, and in many ways, reliving the past 12 years, certain emotions were coming to the surface. The most surprising was anger. Not only did I have anger at Daniel and Margaret for the trail of destruction and unhappiness they left in their wake, anger at Margaret's adoptive parents and how it changed and damaged her, and most unexpected, anger at my adoptive parents.

It was surprising to realize how little I had ever really thought about my upbringing. Like so many things, it was there, and when you're a child, there's really little you can do to change or shift things. My parents who adopted me had a very passive-aggressive form of parenting. And "love" was an interesting word. It was said, *but* the way it was said, you could just have easily exchanged it with any other word. Another phrase that was thrown my way more than a few times was, "You have unconditional love," but I now realize that was *not* the case. It was VERY conditional, right up to the very end. And with that, it wasn't love, but approval, and the approval was withheld to obtain control.

Being adopted, I felt as though I was hired for a job I never applied for. People are looking for a part of themselves to carry on, and in their children, looking for a reflection and legacy. In my adoptive parents' case, they couldn't have children. When the only option was adoption, out came a whole Pandora's Box of psychological issues they frankly weren't mentally or emotionally capable of recognizing or acknowledging.

My Father had never been demonstrative and spent next to no time with me. The only real times I can recall interacting was when he was already in a bad mood when he came home and would lash out at my mother, then me. The rest of the time, he'd come home, pour a drink, sit down in the living room, and act as if nothing else around him existed. On one birthday (I

Chapter 46 – Less than…

believe I was 6 or 7?) I had opened a few packages and one was a T-Rex model I had wanted. The note on the package said "Love, Dad".

I'm not sure why, but when he came home, I ran up to him excited, package in my hand, and I said, "Did you really get this for me?"

He looked at me, looked at the package, paused and said, "No" and walked away never having wished me a happy birthday or showing the slightest bit of interest in me or the day.

In my case, things *seemed* fine (but then, what did I have to compare them to?) in the early years, but this was when a subtle (too often extreme) anxiety manifested itself as a stomachache, that has never completely gone to this very day.

As I became more "me" getting older, the disapproval increased as did my parents indifference. Around second grade I made a request that was met with abject horror: I asked for a Ken doll. (I wasn't stupid enough to swing for Barbie) To my surprise and delight, I did "earn one" when I agreed to disassemble the large fantasy world that had come to overtake my bedroom. I did notice this Ken was the most uber-masculine version available and all the accessories were sports related. It was also around this time my parents pretty much eliminated my birthday from their calendars. "*Something*" always came up on, around, before, and just after each birthday. In my teen years, after living in the Bay Area, my Mother would always schedule the family vacation back down to Southern California to take place the week of my birthday, and *alwa*ys say, "We know you'd prefer to have the house to yourself for a few days, so you don't need to worry about coming along with us." Another aspect of my birthdays that manifested itself around age 11, was they'd give me a card with a check in it. I was 11! What was I going to do with a check? It felt very dismissive and impersonal, and I threw it away. They continued with the check giving until I was in my early 20's. I never cashed a single one. And only once did my father inquire about it being uncashed. I told him I felt the check(s) were impersonal. He just looked at me and that was that. As it was, I always had (and actually still have) a hole in my stomach when my birthday comes around. I marvel at people that not only revel in their birthdays, some extend it into a birthday week, and more than one person I've been acquainted with has stretched it into an entire month. (I'm waiting for that "birthday year" to happen any second.) To say I've always felt diminished by these events is an understatement.

Another testament to their parenting was when I started to edge into adolescence. I went from having natural sun-bleached hair to lank, oily hair that got darker, along with starting to get blackheads on my nose. My father would angrily pull me into the bathroom and forcibly squeeze the blackheads, causing extreme pain, and then snap, "Keep them that way!" He also made snide comments if I let my head rest on side window of the car: leaving any kind of oil mark enraged him. To say I was self-conscious was an understatement.

What now puzzles and angers me is *WHY* my parents would go to the time, effort, and expense to acquire a child (though "selling" a child is illegal, adoption is nothing more than a regulated form of child commerce), and then be so completely removed and disinterested in what it entails. To be fair, my parents never put much effort or thought into pets, hobbies, friends, or anything else, but still... I understand all children (possibly most?) aren't planned. They are born into their families who may (or may not) be ready or equipped for the addition. But for people to try – it was probably the most effort either of my adoptive parents ever put into anything in their respective lives – it is a REALLY DIFFICULT process to "acquire" a child, their passive-aggressive disinterest, while hurtful at the time, has left me with levels of anger I often find hard to dissipate.

Moving into adulthood, the area of high school I excelled in the most was art. This was pretty much ignored by my parents. I graduated high school on the Dean's List (most due to the extra credits I piled up taking art classes) and when I enrolled in college, it was as a Fine Arts major. When I informed my adoptive parents, I was starting college, they shrugged and said, "That's fine." After three years, I told them I needed to take a break and once again I got, "That's fine." I was working fulltime at a large department store in their display department. They had two display "specialists" who were in charge of mannequins, dressing and outfitting them, and sundry things associated with that. What I was tasked with, and excelled at, was building the display props and lighting in the store. After proving myself in a very short probationary period, I was left to follow my own creative urges. If I

Chapter 46 – Less than…

wanted to build 4' high castles on top of the jewelry department cases I could (shades of the fantasy worlds I used to create as a child) or hang massive pieces of driftwood from the ceilings and cover them in white twinkle lights. In many ways this was the best job I had, but it was also the poorest paying.

I can only recall once in five years my parents actually making the drive down to the mall to see my handiwork, and once they were there giving a very non-committal, "That's nice" and immediately left. Around 1980, I felt the need to better myself, so I returned to school, this time with a commercial art major. To afford this, I also started driving for a delivery company, and went to school full-time while working full-time. By the end of my program, I graduated with a double degree in Fine Arts and Technical Arts & Graphics, along with a departmental recommendation, and was on the Dean's List. I submitted five items into the Technical Arts & Graphics show that year, and won First and Second prizes, as well as three Honorable Mentions. My parents attended, but once again, said absolutely nothing. My instructor was standing by them and said, "if he had entered more, he would have won more." Sometime after that I asked my mother why they never said anything about my degrees or finishing the program and her reply was "Well, you didn't go to the graduation ceremony." I replied, "I WAS WORKING THAT NIGHT."

As it turned out, I was making more with the delivery company than I could make in commercial art at the time, and it was only then that my parents showed even the slightest bit of approval.

During all this, my love of music had never abated, and with the money from the delivery job, I was able to buy my first synthesizer. While I enjoyed it, I was hearing "more" in my head, and soon bought a second one (to play the bass parts on) and a drum machine. Now with these components I made another purchase of a four-track recorder, and then a mixer. Little by little, every night I'd come home and teach myself how all these things worked and little by little, started fleshing out songs. After many months I had a complete song, written, played and performed by myself. I invited my parents up to listen. They both sat there stony-faced. When the song was over, my father just got up and left. My mother sat for a moment longer and said, "why can't you do something happier, more upbeat?" I replied this was

Chapter 46 – Less than…

what I had intentionally written. She then got a very worried look and said, "You're not going to quit your job, are you?"

(Thanks for the support…)

A few years later, I left the delivery service and transitioned (rather quickly) into being a Creative Director for a couple of e-commerce start-ups, as well as doing web and graphic design. My pay level more than tripled. Yet oddly, my parents (and especially my mother) expressed regret I was no longer at the delivery company. Moving forward I started writing and recording under the moniker Munich Syndrome. My parents never inquired about it, and as far as I know, never actually listened to the albums I had sent them. When my mother was nearing the end of her life, I had just completed a song I was VERY proud of. It was more melodic and had harmony vocals. I asked if she wanted to listen to it and put the headphones on her. She dryly looked at me and said, "I don't give it a rave."

In this and in coming out as a gay man, I received no support. My parents didn't disown me as much as just ignore that aspect (as well as anything else that didn't fit into their world view). They pretended it just didn't exist. But two events stuck out in my mind. In my early 20s I was dating a guy fairly regularly and one night my mother asked where we went out to.

She said, "Do you and Stu pick up girls at a disco?"

Exasperated I said, "NO. I'm gay and I'm dating Stu."

She got flustered and said, "Was it something I did?"

I paused, smiled, and said "YES!" The subject wasn't brought up again for many years.

But I didn't realize what an alternate universe she was living in until my husband moved in with me. She was shocked and surprised, and said, "If it's a matter of money, I could send you $20 a week!" This showed me she'd rather me be alone – not "Are you happy?"

A lot of these things I had swept aside or pushed to the back of my mind. But I realized, had they had ANY semblance of a nurturing nature, they would (should) have recognized my passions for art and music and encouraged that. As it was, I became me despite them, not because of any support or encouragement.

Chapter 46 – Less than…

Oddly, a validating fact came up doing the Ancestry.com research. Finding the Census Records from 1920 and 1930 I discovered my grandfather on my father's side was a professional musician, as were his two brothers. They all played piano in Detroit during the 1920s and 1930s. One of them also taught music.

Chapter 47 – All Men are Created Equal ... Unless You're Adopted

When my search started back in 2007, I knew access to unredacted birth certificates would be challenging. It happened my search angel, Martha, had access to data in California. When I enquired about her assisting with obtaining my birth mother's in Michigan, she gave me a very firm "no." With the vast number of matches on the three DNA sites, I really wanted to (and still do) connect the dots on Margaret's side. I started looking online to see what the protocol or steps would be to obtain my original birth certificate. Starting on the state level, I was finally able to find how these requests were handled on a county-level. After going through several pages, several layers down, it appeared only a court can order the unredacted birth certificate to be released. The court has to take into account the age of the petitioner and any other circumstances.

This then led me to several days of searching and reading to come up with two options: I could petition the court in the county I currently reside in or I could petition the county in which the original adoption took place. Armed with this information I called the court in the county I reside in. After the usual voicemail hell of options, I finally found a person to talk to. I lucked out with the woman (whose name sadly escapes me) who answered. She had obviously worked in the court system for quite a while, and my request didn't seem that challenging. She put me on hold several times, and I suspect she left other calls unanswered at some point, but eventually came back saying "I'm stymied. I thought I knew where forms for this would be, but I'm not able to locate them." She put me on hold again, while she tried another avenue of search. We were probably on the phone for quite a while when she said "I think it's best you talk to the law librarian for the State of California. Here's the web address. And good luck!"

I went to the website and finally figured out this would be a live chat session. I explained what I was trying to do and what guidance I had received from the courthouse. There were times I thought the conversation had been terminated as 10 or 15 minutes would pass with no activity showing in the chat window. Finally, the librarian came on and said they could find no

Chapter 47 – All Men are Created Equal… Unless You're Adopted

specific forms for the county I was trying to petition. After another lengthy break, they directed me towards two PDFs from two separate counties. I was advised to review both forms and basically create my own form.

Two days and several conversations and web chats later, I was basically told the State of California does NOT have an official form to petition the state for this particular request: each county creates its own form if it feels a need for such a form. I was sharing my frustration with a friend who works in government, and she was dumbfounded. She said the state has forms for EVERYTHING. There are forms to request forms! My feeling is, the state does not want anyone asking for an unredacted birth certificate, and as such had created no clear path in the hopes the request will be forgotten.

I downloaded both forms, and my husband and I compared the two and attempted to parse the information into one coherent form. This took a couple of days, but we finally had the information we felt the court would require. To play it safe, we went and made two copies and had both notarized. I also included a copy of my passport and driver's license to show who I was. With both copies in hand, I made my way to the courthouse. The woman who was VERY helpful on the phone instructed me to go upstairs to the Family Court line. She said it's the long one, but it's the one I'll need to stand in. I got to the courthouse early, and sure enough, there was a very long line already in place. I can say, if Disneyland is the happiest place on earth, this was its antithesis. Everyone seemed to have clumped together trading their family court tales of woe. Drug addiction, child abuse, vanishing spouses. I was in line for about 35 minutes when a patient, but tired looking, woman started going down the line to make sure people were in the right line and had the correct paperwork. The man in front of me shared his tale of having to come back from Germany, where he is currently deployed, to file the right paperwork in order to get visitation with his daughter. It was rather heartbreaking when the woman got to him and informed him, they had guided him to the wrong forms, and he would need to get a separate set and get them notarized. To his credit, the man didn't get angry, but the look of tired resignation was heartbreaking.

The woman got to me, and I explained what I was seeking. She said I was in the wrong line. She then proceeded to give me directions that led me

Chapter 47 – All Men are Created Equal… Unless You're Adopted

through two lefts, a right, and three doors down, one being unmarked. I made my way through this maze and was somewhat relieved to see there wasn't the long line I had been in. I went into what I thought was the right door and stood behind the one counter with one woman in front of me. I was standing there for possibly five minutes when a voice from across the desk, behind a wall asked if I needed help. I recognized the voice as the one I spoke to on the phone. She remembered me as well. She told me I needed to go one more door down and wished me luck.

There was a very long desk with windows, but only one woman at a window at the very end. While seemingly nice enough, she had that kind of dead-eyed look government employees can get. I explained what I was trying to do and had the forms. She looked at me, looked at the forms, looked at me again, then the forms one more time. She looked at me one more time, and then walked away, throwing glances over her shoulder. She went behind some file cabinets into what seemed like an office and I could hear the low rumble of conversations but couldn't make out what was being said. Ten minutes later she returned.

She paused and said, "Chris says this is fine, but you need to change this bit of information at the top to be your personal information."

Keeping in mind, we had set this up to mirror the forms used in two other counties, I asked, "Does this mean I need to leave, redo these forms, get them notarized again, and bring them back?"

It felt like an eternity while she just stared at me. Finally, after blinking a few times she said "Well, you could white it out and write it in, if you want to leave it here now?"

I told her that would be preferable to going through all the effort to get things notarized and returning to the court. I made the adjustments and she informed me, "Chris will get back to you in a couple of months." and advised me to modify my copy of the documents.

I left, but I had no feeling of certainty I'd receive the information I was seeking, or that I'd even get a reply. As she didn't ask for a court filing fee or give me any sort of receipt, I had a feeling the paperwork could just as easily be tossed into the trash.

Chapter 48 – Michigan Records

Having gone this far into the legal options to obtain my own birth certificate (now into May of 2019) and having had reasonable success talking with the woman at the courthouse here in California, I decided I would make an attempt with Michigan records and my birth mother's birth certificate. I knew the city and area my birth mother's parents lived at the time of her adoption and looked for the phone number for Human Services and dialed. I got the expected voice mail chain and was told to leave a voice mail in what I hoped was the right extension. To my utter surprise, my phone rang five minutes later. A VERY nice woman told me I was in the right area as I explained my plight and what I was trying to accomplish.

She sighed and said I might want to try to do this through the courts in California. I explained what a trial (no pun intended) it had been just to get to a point of having the court accept my homemade form. I explained my birth mother was adopted as was I. She then informed me I had no standing to request the unredacted certificate. She asked if my birth mother could apply for it. This confused me as I was under the impression the states did not want to give the unredacted certificates out. She then said, "If there's someone with standing, like a parent or sibling, then the court can relay the information on the unredacted certificate, but not release the actual document." For the states that have closed adoption laws, original birth certificates cannot be released until 100 years after being issued! I told the woman my birth mother had a living brother, and she said he would have standing. I took the name and address to send the request to and thanked her.

This coincided with our trips to Oklahoma visiting Lloyd and Janine, and after running it by Samantha, I approached Lloyd asking if he would petition the courts in Michigan for Margaret's unredacted birth certificate. I didn't get an immediate response but was relieved to get a note back saying he'd more than happy to assist. Part of this request also meant digging into his own history, as the state would need verification that he had 'standing' to make this request. This would entail providing documents showing both he and Margaret were adopted by the same parents, his birth certificate, and *also* showing the changing of his last name.

Chapter 48 – Michigan Records

Dave and I pulled together a request based on the information I received on the phone with the woman in Michigan as well as modifying the form we had created for my court request in California. When we next went back to Oklahoma, Lloyd had all the necessary documents, and we made digital copies and printed them all out into a package. We sent the bundle for Lloyd so all that would be necessary was for him to get the papers notarized, include a copy of his ID and sent them out, which he very kindly did.

Chapter 49 – State of California Reply

On July 3rd we went to the store and had run into friends who invited us to join them for the July 3rd parade. We made tentative agreements and went on with the day. Around 4:30 Dave ran out to get the mail and he came back with a large manila envelope from the court I had petitioned – now more than three months previously. Upon opening the envelope, I was surprised to find 70 pages enclosed!

On top was a photocopy of my birth which was redacted (exactly what I was NOT asking for in the request). However, it was a full birth certificate instead of the official short-form birth certificate I've used for anything official. Everything dealing with my birth parents had black squares covering their names (which I've now known for 12+ years, addresses or anything else identifying). When I saw this, I was *very* disappointed. The next two pages were copies of the petition I had submitted.

Following these pages, I was given a case number with the attached documents: EF COPIES OF PETITION FOR BIRTH RECORD INFORMATION AND ORDERS and ALL DOCUMENTS RECEIVED FROM STATE OF CALIFORNIA, DEPARTMENT OF SOCIAL SERVICES

What surprised me was they had a document dated July 17, 1997 stating:

```
Dear Mr. Roundsley:
July 15, 1997
    Per your recent request, enclosed is a copy of
the nonidentifying background information that was
sent to you in April 1991.
    If you have any questions, please contact the
Adoptions Policy Bureau at the above address or
telephone number.
```

While I did request this information back in 1991 (and subsequently misplaced it during three moves), I have zero recollection of requesting this information a second time.

Chapter 49 – State of California Reply

STATE OF CALIFORNIA - HEALTH AND WELFARE AGENCY
=================
DEPARTMENT OF SOCIAL SERVICES
744 P Street, M.S. 19-31
Sacramento, CA 95814
(916) 322-3778
April 18, 1991
Dear Mr. Roundsley:

   This is in response to your request for information concerning your adoption.

   Enclosed is all the available information obtained at the time of your adoption that we are able to provide from our file. The Department of Social Services (DSS) does not maintain contact with parties to an adoption after it has been completed. However, we will place your letter and address in our file to note that you made an inquiry.

   If the Department of Social Services or an adoption agency receives notarized waivers of confidentiality from the adult adoptee, from one of his or her birth parents, and from one of his or her adoptive parents (or proof of death of both), then a meeting can be arranged between the parties. If siblings, separated by adoption, are over 21, and both send in notarized waivers of confidentiality, names and addresses of each may be exchanged. However, adoption agencies cannot solicit such waivers. DSS waiver forms can be obtained by a request to the Department.

   DSS or an adoption agency can receive, maintain, and release designated nonidentifying letters, photos, or other materials to adult adoptees, birth parents, and adoptive parents of minor adoptees upon request.

   You may request a copy of your amended birth certificate from the State Registrar, Department of Health Services, 304 "S" Street, Sacramento, CA 95814. The service charge is $12.00.

   You may be able to obtain the original sealed birth certificate by petitioning, under Health and Safety Code Section 10439, the superior court in

Chapter 49 – State of California Reply

your county of residence or the county of adoption. The judge has the discretion to decide whether or not the record will be unsealed.

Other documents are in the closed adoption record filed with the office of the county clerk. Under _Civil Code Section 227, they are open to inspection only by an order of the judge of the superior court. Identifying information may be deleted. I realize the information we are sending to you may not answer all of your questions. However, this is all of the information that we are permitted under law to provide.

```
                        Sincerely,
                        - name redacted -
                        Adoptions Systems Unit
                        Enclosure(s)
```

First page -
Person Requesting Background Information: Adoptee
Adoptee David Roundsley
 - Birth Date: redacted
BIRTH MOTHER (Source: Birth Mother)
Descent - Race; German
Age at Birth of Child: 23
Religion: Protestant
Education: She completed high school and nurses' training.
Occupation: Nurse
Physical Description: She was 5 feet 5 inches tall, with green eyes and light-brown hair.
Special Interests: Not reported
Were Birth Parents Married to Each Other? Yes

(a lie)

Parents of Birth mother: Her parents were deceased.

(A lie, if she's referring to her adoptive parents, but had she sought out her birth parents and found them deceased?)

Chapter 49 – State of California Reply

> Siblings of Birth Mother: None (a lie, she has a brother)
> Marriages of Birth Mother: This was her only marriage.
> Siblings of Adoptee: None
> Health: She was in good health. Her mother died at 47 of a stroke. Her father died at 55 from a heart attack.

(This was VERY specific and didn't seem to be a random fact that would have been pulled out of thin air. As Margaret's adoptive parents were still very much alive, had Margaret searched for, and found, her birth parents??)

> Birth Mother's Health at Birth of the Child: She was in good health. There were no complications of pregnancy or delivery. Child's Health at Birth: You were full term, weighed 6 pounds 10 ounces, and in good health.
> Circumstances of Placement: Your birth parents stated that they were so much in debt that they did not know where their next meal was coming from; they were afraid that they would have difficulty feeding you. Their doctor referred them to an attorney who assisted in arranging the placement.
>
> BIRTH FATHER (Source: Birth Father)
> Descent – Race: German
> Place of Birth: Michigan
> Age at Birth of the Child: 27
> Religion: Protestant (?? He was raised Catholic)
> Education He completed high school and some college
> Occupation: Vending machine salesman
> Military Service: Not reported

(This was false, as he had served in WWII.)

> Physical Description: He was 5 feet 10 inches tall, weighed 140 pounds, with brown eyes, light-brown hair and a tanned complexion.
> Special Interests: Not reported

Chapter 49 – State of California Reply

```
Extended Family: He did not know his family
background as he was an orphan. (A falsehood; his
birth father had left the family by 1930 and his
birth mother turned the children over to child
services sometime between 1930 and 1935. Their aunt
Eleanor and Alexine were to raise them, with the
longest duration they could have been in care was 6
months)
Marriages of Birth Father: This was his only
marriage.
```

(This was a lie, with a previous marriage to Mary Badora documented)

```
Health: He was in good health.
```

The next page puzzled me for a moment, but in looking at the date, I realized it predated the adoption of my younger sister by about four months. My parents requested a summary from an independent adoption study that I was unknowingly was a part of, and this information was to be used to assist in my sister's adoption. What's also interesting is the date coincides with the time Daniel and Margaret left Buena Park to begin their migration north.

```
August 14, 1963

Mr. John Gary, Executive Director
The Adoption Institute
1026 So. Spaulding Ave.
Los Angeles 19, California
```

(A web search showed The Adoption Institute was *shut down* by the State of California not long after this letter. Information posted on Adoption.com from two users indicated the Institute dealt with **'black market'** adoptions and the information on at least one adoption was mostly fabricated).

```
Dear Mr. Gary:
    We are happy to send you the following summary
from our independent adoption study relating to the
adoption of David Roundsley by his parents. In view
```

Chapter 49 – State of California Reply

of the fact that this was an independent placement (arranged by a doctor and attorney through the request of the birth mother), the study is not as complete as in a typical agency adoption.

David Roundsley was born (redacted) in Long Beach and placed with the petitioners August 19. He was a healthy baby who developed well in the home, and the adoption was granted (redacted).

David's natural parents were a young couple still struggling with attaining an education and trying to get established in the world and felt they could not take on the responsibilities of parenthood at the time. The natural mother was born in 1932, in Michigan, of German descent, Protestant faith. She had completed high school and some nurse's training. She was 5'5" tall, weighed 110 lbs., and had green eyes and light brown hair. Both of her parents were deceased, the mother at age 47 died of a stroke, and the father at age 55 from a heart attack. The natural father was born in 1927 in Michigan, of German descent and Protestant faith. He was described as being 5'10" tall, weighing 140 lbs., with brown eyes, light brown hair and a tan complexion. He had finished high school and some trade training and was temporarily employed as a salesman for a vending machine concern. They impressed the social worker as being sincere and thoughtful in trying to make the best plan for the baby.

The adopting parents had been interested in adoption for some time and had applied at the Children's Home Society but had never received an appointment. They learned of the availability of the child through contacting an attorney on the suggestion of another adoptive couple.

The adoptive father was born (redacted) in New Mexico, of English descent and Protestant faith. His father died in a mine explosion and his mother was living and in good health at age 62, in (redacted). An older married sister lived in (redacted) and had a boy 17, and a younger sister lived in (redacted) and had girls age 3 and 4. The medical report indicated that the adoptive father was in good health. The social worker described him as being 6' tall, weighting 170 lbs., with hazel eyes and wearing glasses, and with medium brown hair. He had had many job experiences, served in the U. S. Army from 1942 to 1946, was honorably discharged, and attended the College of Commerce for two years on the GI Bill. He became interested in accounting and worked part-time at Baker's Appliance Company and decided to work full-time after 1949 in lieu of completing college. The owner as Baker's Appliance Company indicated that he was the office manager, earning $500 per month.

The adoptive mother was born (redacted) in Illinois, of English descent and Protestant faith. She had two brothers and one sister, all older, all married, and with several teenage children amongst them. Her parents had been divorced, with the children raised by the mother. At age 81 the father was a retired carpenter and the children had remained in touch with him. Her mother, age 73, lived with the adoptive parents and the social worker reported that there were good relationships between the adoptive mother and her mother and the adoptive father with his mother-in-law. The adoptive mother was in good health as reported by her doctor, and although they had been advised by doctors that they probably would not have their own children, no specifics are included in the record. The mother completed one year in secretarial course at Santa Ana Junior College and was employed in various office work positions during the years until such time as they took David into their home.

Just prior to the adoption the family had purchased a new, bright, attractive home in Anaheim. All the family members were happy with this acquisition, and it was being well cared for.

The four references, including friends and a neighbor of long standing, reported favorably concerning the couple and their care of David.

Chapter 49 – State of California Reply

The social worker's summary evaluation reads as follows:

This appears to be an average American couple. While they appear considerably older than their actual years, their marriage appears secure and stable. They have a good understanding of each other. There seems to be a smooth relationship between woman petitioner's mother and woman petitioner and woman petitioner's mother and the man petitioner in the home. It does not appear there is any distinction over this situation. There is no question that the petitioners are devoted to the minor and will offer him a great deal of love and security and opportunities and that in all probability this will offer a normal home for a child."

We hope the above information will be helpful to you in working with this couple in the connection of their desire to add another child to their family at this time.

>   Very sincerely yours,
>   J.G.
>   (redacted), Chief
>   Bureau of Adoptions and Licensing
>   BC:LJ
>   # 2158

The next page was an authorization for release of information:

This is your authority to give to The Adoption Institute, 1026 So. Spaulding Ave., Los Angeles 19, California, any information in your files concerning the undersigned (if applicable) the above-named child, including both medical and social history and the result of any tests or examinations which have been given.

The information is necessary in a study being made by the above agency for a proposed adoption.

Chapter 49 – State of California Reply

The next page was a tad baffling, as many of the facts and dates didn't add up. The reason my parents said they went through a private adoption was they had applied to Children's Home Society and had never heard back. Also, it lists their address as Anaheim, when in actuality, it was the city of Garden Grove.

```
To: Mr. Manuel Siegel, Area Supervisor
Children's Home Society of Calif.
1505 North Broadway
Santa Ana, California

Fr: State of California
Department of Social Services
Case No. OR 1947 AD (redacted area)

This department is investigating a petition filed by
(Name of Man Petitioner) and (Name of Woman
Petitioner) of (Address) in the Superior Court of
Orange County to adopt a child. It is our
understanding that they made application to your
agency for a child on July 1953 (Date).
Will you please give us information in regard to
them, using the form below, one copy of which may be
retained for your file.
State Department of Social Welfare
Was application accepted by you?  Yes X  No __
Was application investigated?  Yes __  No __
Significant information obtained in the
investigation:
Application accepted 6-30-54 and transferred to
Santa Ana office 9-30-55 at which time we felt they
showed the kind of family that could give good
consideration to adoption. However, before we could
go on, we learned of their independent adoption
planning and consequently closed the situation.
A child was placed in the home on _____.
A child was not placed in the home for the following
reasons: _____
Significant material on the agency's experience with
the home: _____
```

Chapter 49 – State of California Reply

```
Return one copy to:
  State Department of Social Welfare
  616 K Street, Sacramento
  948 Market Street, San Francisco
  145 South Spring Street, Los Angeles
Form: ADOP m66, April 1949
```

The next page was surprising, yet unsurprising. For whatever reason, someone in the process felt Margaret and Daniel had lied about being married. A telegram was sent to the County Clerk in Cook County, Illinois, and received the following response:

```
EDWARD J. BARRETT
COUNTY CLERK
COOK COUNTY, ILLINOIS
CHICAGO 2
(REDACTED AREA DATED 7-2-54)
PURSUANT TO THE INFORMATION WHICH APPEARS AT THE
RIGHT-HAND CORNER OF THIS LETTER (REDACTED AREA),
THIS OFFICE IS UNABLE TO LOCATE THE RECORD REQUESTED
BY YOU.
SHOULD YOU HAVE ANY ADDITIONAL INFORMATION, WE SHALL
BE GLAD TO RECHECK OUR FILES.
I ASSURE YOU OF OUR DESIRE TO BE OF ASSISTANCE.
VERY TRULY YOURS,
EDWARD J. BARRETT
COUNTY CLERK
```

A large MARRIAGE stamp was at the bottom of the page, April 16, 1954.

This page was followed by two "Adoption Work Sheets – For Agent's Book".

The assignment was filed October and due the following April with the names of the two lawyers who brokered the adoption. Several boxes were checked, but it was also filled with redacted squares.

The next page was the social worker's report:

```
Redacted - Roundsley OR 1947 AD
```

Chapter 49 – State of California Reply

Date redacted: Called in home by appointment. Saw both the man petitioner, and the woman petitioner, the minor, and the woman petitioner's mother. Housing and Household – Petitioners are living in their new home in a new subdivision. They moved in here in Date Redacted. They have three bedrooms, a living room, a dining room and kitchen. In the home are the man petitioner, the woman petitioner and the woman petitioner's mother who is 73 years of age, and the minor. The petitioners occupy one bedroom, the minor one bedroom, and the woman petitioner's mother the third. The mother has lived with them for some little time as she is divorced from her husband. She pays the petitioners $30 per month for board and room. She is quite healthy and has her activities and interests. While she had a stroke 2 years ago, she seemingly has completely recovered from this. There appeared to be a very good relationship between both the petitioners and the mother. Needless to say, she is devoted to the minor. The home was attractively furnished in new good furniture. The house is unusually attractive having the bright colors so frequently used in the kitchens nowadays. The kitchen is in the front of the house and the living room has a large window opening on the back. The yard is not yet landscaped as the petitioners are doing the work themselves. They first plan to fence the back yard.
Placement – Petitioners report that they had a long wish to adopt a child as doctors had told them it was very unlikely that they will ever have their own. They have seen several doctors on this over a period of years. They had applied to Children's Home Society of California but have never received an appointment with them. The man petitioner works in the office of an appliance shop in Long Beach and apparently a machine had been sold to a customer and when some difficulty was encountered with this machine, a service man had been sent out to check it. Previously to this, the petitioner had had conversation telephonically with the customer and an

Chapter 49 – State of California Reply

acquaintanceship was struck up. The service man noted that this customer had two adopted children and she told him that she had also arranged for her neighbor to adopt some children. The service man commented that the petitioner who this customer had become acquainted with telephonically wished to adopt and asked the woman how it could be accomplished. Subsequently, this customer, over the telephone, gave the petitioner the name of the attorney, Henry C. Shriver, in Long Beach and suggested that he call him. The petitioners contacted Mr. Shriver and about one month later, were notified by the attorney that this baby was available for adoption. IT was their understanding that the natural parents were a young couple who were attending school and just did not wish to be bothered with the baby. The petitioners expressed quite a bit of concern as they have received a bill for $600 from their attorney, stating this is payment of all charges involved. They have asked their attorney for an itemized statement upon several occasions but have not received one to this date. They did state that their attorney told them that his fees would only be $150, and they had questioned where the reset of the money was being spent as they had checked with several friends and felt that the remaining $450 was rather excessive for doctor and hospital bills. However, it was plain to realize that the petitioners are not making too much questioning as they do not want to do anything that would upset the completion of the adoption. They reported that they had been given no background information and are interested in obtaining this. Agent promised to get in touch with them after the parents had been interviewed.

Minor – Minor, who is now seven months old, is reported to weigh 17 pounds 14 ounces. He is a healthy-looking youngster, has rather a square face, blue eyes and reddish-brown hair. He has no teeth yet, but it is very obvious that he is cutting teeth now as he drools constantly. He sits up very well.

He was attractively dressed in a little yellow corduroy overall and a blue sweater. The petitioners report that the baby sleeps well, going to sleep about eight o'clock at night and sleeping to 7:30. He has slept throughout the night since he was three months old. He has two naps during the day, one in the morning and one in the afternoon. He is eating all of the baby foods and has about 24 ounces of straight milk during a day. He has been very well since the first. He did have colic then.

Petitioners – Man petitioner verified information on the questionnaire and supplemented it. He reported he is six feet tall, weighs 170 pounds. He has hazel eyes and wears glasses. He has medium brown hair. He is rather sleepy, slow-moving individual though pleasant and apparently has quite a bit of warmth and quiet strength. He attended school in Van Houten, New Mexico, and graduated from high school at Raton, New Mexico, at the age of 17. He worked for a while and then came to California and entered aircraft school in Glendale. This was civil service work and he was there for about a year before entering the army in Long Beach on October 17, 1942. He received his discharge at Camp Beal on March 18, 1946. He had one-year overseas' service primarily in Arabia and Egypt. He had no disabilities. After coming out of the service, he worked at odd jobs mostly in and around Long Beach. He worked in the oil field supply for 2 ½ years and then went to the College of Commerce in Long Beach for two years under the GI Bill. At this time, he took up accounting and worked part time during his schooling at Baker Appliance Store in Long Beach. Following his completion of his schooling, he devoted his full time in this work continuously since that time where he is an accountant.

His father died at the age of 52, following a mine explosion, where he had been an electrician. His mother is 62 and lives in (Redacted). He has two sisters, one older and one younger. One sister lives in (Redacted), is married and has a boy 17. The

Chapter 49 – State of California Reply

other sister lives in (Redacted), is married and has two girls, age 3 and 4.

Woman Petitioner – Woman petitioner verified information on the questionnaire and supplemented it. She looks much older than her reported age. She is 5' 7 3/4" tall, weighs 145 pounds, has very sparkling dark brown eyes and auburn hair, with a medium complexion. Her hair looks dyed but claims this her natural color. She was rather heavily made up and was dressed in a rather fussy manner. She was not as poised as man petitioner but appeared big-hearted and warm endeavoring not to be nervous. She said she came to California when she was a year and a half old and obtained all of her schooling in Long Beach and Garden Grove, graduating from the Garden Grove High School at the age of 18. She took a secretarial course at Santa Ana Junior College for one year and then went to work for Douglas. She worked there for three years. She traveled with her husband while he was in the States, working at various places. This was primarily in Texas. While he was overseas, she returned to Long Beach and worked there. Her last employment was with the Federal Housing Administration in Long Beach and she worked there up until taking the baby. She has worked practically her entire married life doing office work in various concerns.

Her father is 81 years of age, is a carpenter, living in (Redacted). Her mother is 73 and lives with them. Her parents were divorced when she was seven or eight. She lived with her mother who remarried when woman petitioner was about nine. While she has lived with her mother and stepfather, she was never adopted and never used their name. She has two brothers, both older than herself, and a sister also older. They all lived with their mother but retained their relationship with their father. One brother lives in (Redacted) and works for Douglas. He is married and has four boys, ages ranging from 14 to 19. Her other brother lives in

Redacted and has one boy 17. Her sister lives in (Redacted,) and has two boys, age 16 and 21. Activities and Interests – Woman petitioner reports she has always been interested in music and used to belong to the Singers' Workshop in Long Beach and appeared in several operettas. She is not taking any active part in this at the present time. Petitioners report that they usually take a trip to San Francisco when they have any time off. In discussing their plans for the minor, they state they have no church connections though probably will eventually join a Methodist Church as they seem to feel that is the best church in their area and they definitely plan to send the minor to Sunday School, believing this is part of a child's training. They will send him to public school and definitely plan to send him to college. Petitioners report they would like to adopt a second child but they do not have any great hopes of being able to locate one and accept the fact that they do not believe that an agency would place a child with them as they had become so discouraged previously.

Finances – Petitioners presented papers which verified their home purchase. The original purchase price was $16,000, purchased on a Federal GI Bill, with only $300 down payment. Their monthly payments are $103. This is carried by T. J. Bettes Company in Los Angeles. Agent reviewed the papers which showed there is a balance due of $15,962.58. Petitioners have a joint checking account in the Long Beach First Western Bank. On Redacted, their statement showed there was a balance due of $480.88. Agent also reviewed their six Series E Bonds which had a face value of $25. Agent reviewed their insurance papers. Man petitioner has a $2,500 policy with Manufacturer's Life Insurance Company. This was taken out in February of 1954 as a whole life pay. This is a rather odd varying policy of carrying a continuous $2,500 a value of $4,192 which reduces in twenty years to $1,208. He also has another $2,500 life insurance policy with the Manufacturer's Life,

Chapter 49 – State of California Reply

taken out at the same time. The entire family are covered under Blue Shield and that is, the minor will be covered as of 4-10. In discussing their financial status, the petitioners report that they borrowed $1,000 on a personal loan from the Bank of America and are paying this back at the rate of $40. This is primarily to meet the payment of $650 to the attorney. They own a 1953 Dodge and a 1956 Plymouth both clear of indebtedness and they report their furniture is clear.

Agent discussed with the petitioners their rather limited financial status in view of the fact that both of them had worked for the last fifteen years and apparently had lived in rented property during this entire time. They seem to feel they had done fairly well in acquiring their furniture and their car and man petitioner does not believe that he will have difficulty in meeting the rather large payment on his house. He states his job is permanent and he feels that he will always make at least as much as he now is making and that from now, they will be able to save as well as meet their current obligations.

Further Discussion – Petitioners particularly requested that agent furnish them with background information as they are interested in this for the baby's sake.

Agent's Evaluation – This appears to be an average American couple. While they appear considerably older than their actual years, their marriage appears secure and stable. They have a good understanding of each other. There seems to be a smooth relationship between woman petitioner's mother and woman petitioner and woman petitioner's mother and man petitioners in the homes. It does not appear there is any distinction over this situation. There is no question that the petitioners are devoted to the minor and will offer him a great deal of love and security and opportunities and that in all probability this will offer a normal home for a child.

Chapter 49 – State of California Reply

Date (Redacted) – Interviewed the natural parents in the office of the State Department of Social Welfare by appointment. Agent talked with the parents together briefly and then the father stepped out. Agent talked with the natural mother. She was extremely interested in information regarding the petitioners and when this information seemed to vary greatly with that which had been furnished her by the attorney, she requested that her husband come back into the room. Agent discussed the situation with them together, then left them alone for a few minutes and returned. There was considerable further discussion at this point.

The natural parents reported that they had been married two years and had come to California from Chicago. They had been unable to secure work when first coming to Los Angeles and they feel this was primarily because they had such a short residency. They state they are now working and are managing to pay their bills and are looking forward to getting ahead. Both parents impressed agent as being an extremely serious, sincere young couple and they were quite sincerely disturbed at the information given them regarding the petitioners. They report they were so badly in debt that they did not know where their next meal was coming from and just felt they could not take on the responsibility of a child as they were afraid that actually they would have difficulty in feeding it. The father spoke up and said he had been raised in an orphanage and he knew what it was to see other children with toys and clothes and not able to have them himself and he felt he could not wish this on a child of his. However, in reviewing the petitioners' circumstances, they both commented that it looked to them as if within the next ten to fifteen years, they would be able to do a great deal more for the child than the petitioners would. They stated they had learned of the petitioners in this manner. They were caring for a motel that was owned by a Los Angeles City policeman. He knew of the natural

Chapter 49 – State of California Reply

mother's pregnancy and their disturbance over what to do and he referred them to a doctor. This was in the seventh month of the mother's pregnancy and she had not been to a doctor up to that date. They went to the doctor who in turn referred them to this attorney. They went to the attorney's office. They report they were given information on several different couples. However, they reported the information that they were given as to the couple who took the baby did not correspond with the information on several different couples. It was this fact that caused them to consider seriously before signing consent. After discussing it at great length, they decided that it would not be fair to reclaim the child now, saying that the petitioners had gone into this apparently in all honestly and sincerity and they felt that it would be too great a tragedy to inflict on the petitioners. Agent was impressed that they were sincere in this reasoning. The parents in discussing the placement said they had been asked by the attorney how much money they wished for the adoption and they said they did not wish anything, that that was not their reason for placing the baby for adoption. The mother reports that they inadvertently received a hospital bill for $85 which they turned over to the attorney. She belies this was the full hospital bill as she was only in the hospital for two days. She said she saw the doctor twice, once in the seventh month of her pregnancy and once again at the time of delivery. She volunteered to send these bills into the office. Both parents gave full background information. The mother said she was a factory worker at first as she felt this was a disguise; however, she is a trained nurse and now working in this profession. The father is working as a salesman for a vending machine concern and eventually hopes to own his own vending machines.
The parents were informed of their rights and responsibilities and were told that once consents were signed, they could not be withdrawn without

```
court approval and this would be a matter for the
individual court to determine, that nothing could be
guaranteed. They thought the matter over well and
while both being disturbed over the misinformation
which had been given them, finally decided the only
thing to do at this point was to consent to the
adoption freely and willingly signed joint custody
consent.
                                    Hoobyar: mr
                                    Date (Redacted)
```

A lot of this was news to me, and I was able to reframe answers I had received from my adoptive parents over the years. One thing that was much clearer, was my adoptive parents weren't prime candidates to adopt (and I can attest to that well after the fact!) and from reading between the lines the doctor, lawyer, and agency involved were obviously for profit, and not a first choice for people who were legitimately eligible and qualified to adopt. Despite the window dressing of social worker reports and the like, this was buying and selling transaction, dressed up as something better than it actually was. I found many of the statements from my birth parents to be disingenuous, and from the fact that they were in debt and didn't know where their next meal was coming from to suddenly own a brand new home in Garden Grove less than a year later, I think it's safe to assume some (probably all) of the disputed $450 from my adoptive parents found its way into their pockets. At one point, many years ago (knowing this was a private adoption) I asked my father directly how much the adoption (essentially 'me') cost. He said there were no costs. There's no way to go back and find out what was so disturbing to my birth parents about my adoptive parents, but there was enough concern or interest for them move to a closer proximity.

I will say, I was somewhat dismayed at the fact that my birth parents were disturbed and troubled by whatever information came to light about my adoptive parents, but it didn't bother them enough to rethink alternate options regarding me. The comment that it would be upsetting to my adoptive parents underscores "the child" (me) was nothing more than an item that was transacted upon. More importantly, I feel money, the money

Chapter 49 – State of California Reply

they now had in their pockets for a sizeable down payment for a not inexpensive brand-new home might be threatened. I can say any sympathies or understanding I might have had for Margaret had all but evaporated as I read these documents.

I had also asked Sarah when I first met her if Margaret had ever mentioned looking for me and she said Margaret had said "it's best we leave that alone." I completely understand that now.

The following pages included legal releases from all parties, with the information (redacted) relating to my birth parents.

What came up next in the packet was yet another telegram. Again, from Chicago it said:

```
(M CD499) 17 COLLECT 1 EXTRA NOT AT STATE BLD G=
CHICAGO ILL 2 1010AMC=
MARY HOOBYAR, STATE DEPT SOCIAL WELFARE=
108 WEST 6 ST RM 400 LOS A=
NO RECORD OF MARRIAGE ON FILE BETWEEN (REDACTED) AND
(REDACTED) JULY SECOND 1954=
RAY J WELSH DIRECTOR BUREAU OF VITAL STATISTICS=
```

Why was this an issue they kept going back to and trying to verify or disprove?

The next telegram showed they were interested in something more:

```
WESTERN UNION:
FROM LOS ANGELES, CALIFORNIA MARCH 30, 1956
COUNTY CLERK
COOK COUNTY COURT HOUSE
CHICAGO, ILLINOIS
VERIFY MARRIAGE (REDACTED) AND (REDACTED), CHICAGO,
7/2/54. WERE ANY PREVIOUS MARRIAGES NOTED? REPLY
COLLECT.
MARY HOOBYAR
STATE DEPT. SOCIAL WELFARE

OFFICIAL MESSAGE – TAX EXEMPT
CHARGE TO:
```

Chapter 49 – State of California Reply

```
STATE DEPART. SOCIAL SERVICES
402 CAIRNS BLD.
108 W. 6TH STREET
L.A. 14
MHM AD 8:45 A.M.
```

While no further telegrams resided in this pile of papers, something I've never been able to ascertain is "when" or "if" my birth father Daniel Andrews actually divorced his first wife, Mary Badora. I found their marriage on 29 April 1949 in Chicago. I "thought" I had found the subsequent marriage of Mary and her last husband on Ancestry.com, but no such records are there either. Daniel did marry Margaret on 20 October 1956 in Las Vegas, Nevada, and divorced 12 June 1975 in Red Lodge, Montana. Daniel married Delores 6 November 1976 in Cody, Wyoming. They divorced in 1979. I am not sure that either Daniel or Mary were actually free to marry.

One page that was a bit surprising was the health report. It showed them checking for syphilis (both me and my birth mother). This is definitely standard now, and probably was then, but after hearing the lurid stories of multiple partners, I found the page a bit chilling.

The remaining body of papers were the waivers, agreements, and final adoption paperwork which was completed and signed off on eight months after I was born.

Chapter 50 – The End?

Reading the various reports, comparing this with the various narratives fed to me by my adoptive parents over the years, and now filtering this through everything I had uncovered during my search, I found myself feeling like I was in state of suspended animation. One of the lies told by my birth parents, and then relayed to me as I got older was the fallacy that my birth mother's parents had both died relatively young, and my birth father was an orphan. For my adoptive parents, this was fact and part of my birth parent's history. What this telegraphed to me was, neither side of my birth families lived long. Following this line of fact and logic, I had a feeling I was not destined to live a long life, and as such, didn't plan for one. Instead of a firm scholastic goal and plan for my life, my attitude was to follow my instincts and enjoy what time I had. I know the choices I made early on would have been radically different had this information not been given to me.

While my adoptive parents were still alive, I had always sensed their answers were evasive, and their replies, while mostly based on a fact, were made to cast themselves in a better light than the facts might warrant. After reviewing the full reports from the state and reading between the lines it took a few days for it all to resonate. Some of the lies I understood, such as my adoptive father (later in life) claiming to have obtained a higher degree of education than he actually had. I've seen this trait in many people. However, the one I couldn't wrap my head around was the story he gave me about the lawyer contemplating adopting me himself. Why he would make this up, I have absolutely no idea. It was also clear there was never a point in time when child abandonment was filed against my birth parents. Telling me they had me for a year before finally going to court was yet another embellishment. Perhaps it was to make themselves seem more noble than they actually were? The adoption was approved in April, seven months after I was born. It was also clear Margaret did not waver about the adoption. If anything, she came across as more determined to make the adoption happen than Daniel did. And any questioning about my adoptive parents might have been a ploy if she and Daniel realized they could make much more from the adoption than was originally brokered.

Chapter 50 – The End?

While I was grateful and appreciative to see all these reports and files, it left me feeling rather deflated and somewhat let down after the effort and time put into this search and journey.

Postscript

After thinking about the contents of the reports, I had gone back and noticed a number on the cover page with a name saying if I had any questions to call. A few days later I did. This was the court clerk who received my initial petition. As briefly as I could, I explained why I wanted my original unredacted birth certificate and explained I currently had no standing to request my birth mother's, even though she had been deceased for 14 years. She helped me draft a court order for her to submit to the judge.

To my shock and utter amazement two weeks later a court order was granted allowing me to receive my unredacted birth certificate from the state. While nothing new was listed on the document, after such a long and protracted fight, it felt like a massive win.

My uncle Lloyd had submitted a request with the state of Michigan (on my behalf) in May of 2019. At some point near the end of the year he said he had received a call from Michigan Department of Health and Human Services that was a bad connection. The bad connection compounded with his diminished hearing resulted in him having no idea what the call was trying to convey. I assumed with an incomplete call there would be some type of written follow-up via mail or email. But none was forthcoming. I began to think the call might have been one indicating they could not, or would not, help in this request.

And then, just as I was putting the finishing touches on this book, Lloyd forwarded me an email from the caseworker in Michigan. The email said there was no adoption on record in Kent County! This baffled both of us. As I now had my original birth certificate, I let Lloyd know I'd take over and contacted the caseworker. To my utter shock and surprise, she informed me that if I sent her my original birth certificate (which thankfully, I now had), she could release the information from my birth mother's adoption! I emailed a copy, and within minutes I was holding the paperwork from my mother's birth.

It indicated that my mother was born to a young girl, Liana Siegrist, from Kalkaska, Michigan, who was not yet 15 when she became pregnant. Liana's mother placed her in the Salvation Army Home for Unwed Mothers in

Postscript

Grand Rapids, Michigan. It listed my mother's father as "unknown" but the fact that Liana gave my mother a name, Adalia Siegrist, indicated she wanted to keep my mother. The paperwork shows Liana's mother exerted her rights as parental guardian and placed my mother for adoption two months after she was born.

Having the name of my maternal grandmother allowed me to connect a LOT of dots with DNA matches and in looking at matches that weren't on my maternal grandmother's side, allowed me to finally connect more dots and figure out who my mother's father was. There were two potential candidates who fit the age and location who were connected via DNA. After working with several people, the matches were narrowed down to Paul McGrath. Paul's mother, Mary O'Brien, was born in Limerick Ireland and married a McGrath. In looking at the pictures of my mother I always sensed an Irish connection and it was now finally confirmed. In talking to family members related to Liana Siegrist, I also confirmed the scenario my mother had discovered: her mother was from a poor farming community. Family members were aware a child had been placed for adoption early in her life, but the details were never discussed.

Over the course of 13 years I know there were some people who were upset or unprepared to deal with the past (and truth), but I found my search also brought closure and healing to much wider group of people. All of this was much more expansive than I could have ever imagined.

However... one thing kept bothering me. The comments that Margaret had always wanted to have children with Daniel always lurked in the background. One of the earliest questions I asked Sarah was if Margaret had ever considered finding or contacting me. She said Margaret said that was best left alone. Father Nikolaev also said the same thing. He had said Margaret was SO excited when the tea leaf reader saw her in a house with many children. She always wanted a child with Daniel. Never once was there "we had a child but had to give him up." Also, after things were over with Daniel, Margaret railed about being taken advantage of, all the injustices, and being taken for a ride. She complained about this to several people, yet oddly a very potent complaint would have been "...and Daniel forced me to give OUR child up for adoption." Yet, she NEVER shared this with anyone, except possibly Sarah. Not even when she was confronting her adoptive mother and brother about the woes and injustices she had endured. Taking into account of all the statements she made to a wide variety of people, I now realize, not only did Daniel not believe he was my father, but NEITHER DID MARGARET! Daniel made a very telling comment to the private investigator that Margaret was involved with several men at the time of my birth. I believe that was truthful. What was left out of that statement was Daniel was involved with them as well. The extent of their swinging and group sex was to such an extent, both of them questioned who the father was. And based on their activities and number of partners, both felt it was more likely that Daniel was NOT my father. The detective said Daniel had a slight tear when he presented my photograph and informed him that Margaret had passed. At the time, I took the tear to be strictly for Margaret. I'm now thinking, it might be at that moment he realized he DID have a son and had let the opportunity pass. One of the first things Eleanor told Danni very early on was Daniel REALLY WANTED A SON, and when a daughter was born, he had no interest. Based on everything else I've uncovered about Daniel, I have absolutely no idea why having a son would have been so important to him. There is zero evidence of paternal or nurturing instincts with the man.

Another theory put forth by several people I talked to over the years was that if not gay, Daniel was most certainly bisexual. Margaret was not only his beard, but also his gateway to participate with other men. She provided the caveat that he was "just swinging" as his wife was present. And I do believe Margaret was sufficiently smitten and under his spell, that she would take him on his terms under any circumstances, including sex with other men (and maybe women), acquiring drugs, and doing anything and everything to please him and make him happy. Being married and displaying large wedding rings was always something that seemed to be very important to Daniel throughout his life.

Putting me up for adoption not only provided Daniel and Margaret with a "clean slate" but also endowed them with the money for a brand-new home in a brand-new city and gave them the ability to reset everything that came before: fleeing Detroit with semi-automatic weapons, drug use, the cloud hanging over Daniel for his abuse of Danni, probable crime affiliations, and possibly feeling they needed to distance themselves from swinging, now the reality of unplanned pregnancy entered the picture. The fact they married in October after settling into their new home was also part of the reset and new beginning as well as a reward for Margaret. I also now believe Daniel and Margaret moving as close to me as they did, had little to do with my specifically. I now believe proximity to Daniel's brother was the bigger influence on that decision, and Margaret probably had a cursory interest (at best) on 'the child' she had, and possibly by observing me she could point out to Daniel the children they could have together when they were ready.

I also picked up on the comment in the report that they were working at a hotel managed by a Los Angeles policeman. It noted Margaret's distress about the pregnancy. My feeling now is the distress was because they were swinging, and she found herself pregnant and firmly believed it could have been any of a number of the strangers they had been involved with. And for all I know, activity at the motel might have been more than recreational sex. This might have been a way for a young couple to find employment at an uncertain time.

I now know there was and could never have been a point of reconnection (or connection) with either Daniel OR Margaret. And I have every confidence neither would have been willing or able to tell me truth, had that opportunity been available. I recognize that people can and do change. From all accounts Margaret was a true and wonderful friend after Daniel left and was an amazing aunt and surrogate mother to the Durand children. But it also needs to be noted that she was a willing participant in her 20 years with Daniel: transporting semi-automatic weapons from Detroit out west, scoring drugs, and losing her nursing license many times in the process, willingly moving in the dead of the night and skipping out on paying rent, and also being a willing participant in whatever sexual interests and needs Daniel had. And she was the one easily and willingly lying to the state regarding her marital and work status during my adoption process. Again, the statements made to the state about not knowing where their next meal was coming from to suddenly affording a brand-new home, underscored the duplicity both my birth parents were capable of. While there was regret at not meeting

Margaret, I now know not only would she probably not have welcomed meeting me. I feel she either would have given a reply similar to the one Daniel gave to the private detective or would have spun her own tale of nothing being her fault and how she was blindly led down the garden path.

For anyone considering a similar search and journey, it's clear there is something they need to know, discover, or find out about themselves and their origins. While many of the things discovered were unpleasant (okay, just about all of them), my only wish was for the full and unadorned truth to have been revealed earlier. The only advice I would offer anyone considering such a search and journey would be to be open and honest with everyone you meet and be prepared for some cold, hard truths. To research each and every lead, regardless of how improbable or inconsequential it might seem. For me not knowing the truth left a void that was filled with distortions and conjecture. While none of this search has been pleasant, it's given me insight into "why" everything happened as it did. Being able to confirm and discover all the threads of my biological family tree has given me a sense of self, closure, and peace I was unsure would ever exist.

Also, "The answer is always 'NO' if you don't ask."

Selected Song Lyrics

Words & Music by David B. Roundsley

The Only Path

Most of the time you go with the flow
And let life take you where it wants you to go
But sometimes you have to take a stand
And grab the lead with a guiding hand

I didn't know who I was or fit in
I knew there was a start but never a begin
Trying to make sense of a kaleidoscope of lies
Having knowledge doesn't always make you wise

> Through the pain I've learned how to live
> Through the anger I try to forgive
> To find the thread some things unravel
> But this is the only path I can travel

Sometimes the lessons remain hidden
And access to the truth is sometime forbidden
But on occasion a clue will emerge
And suddenly all pathways do converge

> Through the pain I've learned how to live
> Through the anger I try to forgive
> To find the thread some things unravel
> But this is the only path I can travel

This was written just as I was starting to write the book. While I wasn't consciously addressing the book at the time, in looking back, I can see the seeds of the book had been planted.

Reprinted by permission – Syndrome Sounds / ASCAP
From Munich Syndrome's 8th album, Electro Pop 2 (Deluxe Edition)

Suburbia

When I was young the suburban myth, was nothing as it seems
It's as if everyone had given up, on their hopes and their dreams
I lived too long in a black & white world, everything faded and sad
A life with no expectations, everyone angry and mad

The dreariness of time, like punishment for crime,
    everything was left unsaid
Pretending all was good, doing what we should,
    facing each day with dread
It was an effort just to get through,
    no matter what we said, or tried to do
At the end of the day everyone was looking for escape…

    The starched linen curtains couldn't hide the secrets and lies
    The TVs turned up loud to muffle the yelling and cries
    Broken homes and promises happen every day
    Life in suburbia was a golden cliché

Hypocrisy and drinks on the menu every day,
    when the men go off the women did play
At the bowling alley flaunting the affairs,
    ignoring all the whispers and unwanted stares
Bullies in the schoolyard bullies at church,
    words and a fist for a target they search
Battered and bruised hollow to the core,
    everyone looking for escape…

About my childhood and time growing up in and around Southern California and the hypocrisy that touched and tainted everything.

Reprinted by permission – Syndrome Sounds / ASCAP
From Munich Syndrome's 8th album, Electro Pop 2 (Deluxe Edition)

Android Dreams

Every night, I surrender, to a world of dreams
Memories, sounds and colors, nothing's what it seems
In a room from another life, a faded affair
I hear the music on a radio, that isn't there

A different place, another era, memories to reclaim
A time, vaguely familiar, new and yet the same
Colors faded like an old photograph, echoes of another day
Like a slow-motion movie, waiting to replay

Waves of unconsciousness, wash over me
Leading to an altered state reality
Moving forward, touching time
Fragments of a dream, moments sublime
Every night I surrender, to a world of dreams...

Written around 2011, I felt like I was living in concurrent time-streams, almost seeing and sensing events that happened in the past but were replaying like an old movie.

Reprinted by permission – Syndrome Sounds / ASCAP
From Munich Syndrome's 4th Album Robotika

Watching You

Acquiring satellites, looking from the sky
For deeper meaning, the reasons why
A blip on the radar, phantoms in the night
Some things are hidden, hiding in plain sight

Looking for answers only finding questions
Secret rumors and indiscreet suggestions
Stories hidden and tales told
The price of silence, bought and sold

>We - are - watching - you
>We - know - everything - that - you -do

Scouring the data looking for a trace
Of the evidence that puts you at the place
The scene of the crime, crimes of opportunity
No free pass, no immunity

>We - are - watching - you
>We - know - everything – that - you -do

This was written when my birth father was still alive but rebuffing my efforts to contact him. Resorting to online searches and eventually a private detective, surveillance was happening in the background.

Reprinted by permission – Syndrome Sounds / ASCAP
From Munich Syndrome's 3rd album Electronic Ecstasy

Always Walking

Forever walking, always on the run
For a karmic debt over what's been done
A coin was tossed, sometimes a losing bet
Necessity will rule, without regret

Spur of the moment, bad deeds were done
Before the dust can settle, it's off on the run
Too many names on the casualty list
Hoping none of them will ever be missed

> Forever walking, from this karmic debt
> Forgetting to remember, remember to forget
> Forever walking, from this karmic debt
> Forgetting to remember, remember to forget

The ends always justify the means
Even if it all falls apart at the seams
Cognitive dissonance, a screen made of smoke
Deadly serious, like a killing joke

> Forever walking, from this karmic debt
> Forgetting to remember, remember to forget
> Forever walking, from this karmic debt
> Forgetting to remember, remember to forget

Reprinted by permission – Syndrome Sounds / ASCAP

Bad Blood (The Ballad of a Bad Man)

There once was a man who'd look you in the eye
As he tells you one hell of a lie
An orphan he said, from birth
A man of god, not one of this earth
A self-made man, as it was told
The narrative was bought and sold
Doing everything just to fill a hole
Where most people have some kind of a soul

The sex was always easy, there's room for more
The dirtier the better, he knows what's in store
With showers golden, and room for a drink
Please leave the evidence in the sink
Drugs kind of sand the edges so smooth
When the shit gets real, in the night he'd move
When partners falter, they're tossed to the side
Time to find another ride

> Burning down the memories, so daunting
> Casting off the ghosts that, come haunting
> Sometimes it all comes back in a flood
> But there's no denying that bad, bad blood

His momma didn't love him, neither did his dad
It made him so very hard and sad
A coldness that could never melt
That's when he put on his bible belt
Poisons in his bloodstream, a sickness of the soul
The need for subservience and control
Unpleasant memories from the past
Need to be torched, not built to last

Reprinted by permission – Syndrome Sounds / ASCAP

Goodbye

I saw a balloon go up into the sky
As it vanished, I whispered goodbye
To a past, that was never really there
Pretense and fantasy, tenuous as air

No longer tethered to all of the lies
At the finish line, there was no prize
No more sadness over what should have been
Just a punchline from the comedian

> Yesterdays are so over, no more backwards glances or pain
> Say goodbye to the past, and its indelible stain

Always kidding, now the butt of the joke
Finding fire, where there's smoke
No more sadness over what should have been
Just a punchline from the comedian

> Yesterdays are so over, no more backwards glances or pain
> Say goodbye to the past, and its indelible stain

Reprinted by permission – Syndrome Sounds / ASCAP

Munich Syndrome Discography

Sensual Ambiance
2006

Electro Pop
2008

Electronic Ecstasy
2010

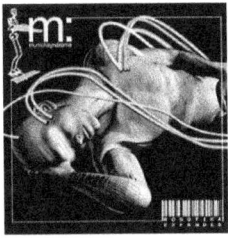
Robotika (Expanded)
2012

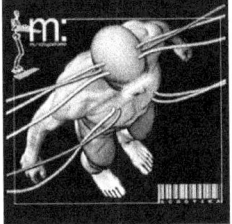
Robotika (VIP)
2013

Atmospherics 1: Urbania
2016

The World of Tomorrow
2016

Electro Pop 2 (Deluxe)
2019

The Best Of
2019

GRAY/SCALE
2020

Bad Blood
2020

We want to thank everyone who made the Kickstarter Campaign a success allowing both the book and the album to be published:

Andrew Hanuman	Karen Nierhake
Andy Jordan	Kev & Shaza
Anthony R. Cardno	Leanne & Stephen Sims
BackerKit	Lisa Swift
Bennie Henderson	Lori Okada
Brenda Burhance	Marilyn Kanes
Carrie Moran	Mary Hansen
Crystal, Karen, & Paul	Mary Mannion
Danielle & Kumar	Michael & George
Darren W. Faragher	Paul Moloney
David L. Hatt AKA D3	Randall Watkins
Frank Schildiner	Rob Early
Gretchen Roundsley	Sarah Betz
Gretchen Ward	Sheila L. Ashbeck
Jacob (Jack) Wicks	Sheryl Youngblood
Jacqueline Lepley	Shirley Howell & Jay Holm
Jake Wicks, Adoptee	Stacy Shuda
Jeffrey & Patty Norman	Stephen & Debbie Rowe
Jen & Don Iles	Suzanne & Brook Isola
Jen Greenhalgh	The Chamberlains
Jens & Dawn	Tom Martinez
John & Phyllis Farrell	Tom McIntire
Julia "Babs" Mensing	Tours of the Tales
Julianna Sockol	Wayne & Sherrie Trotman

www.ingramcontent.com/pod-product-compliance
Lightning Source LLC
Chambersburg PA
CBHW072148070526
44585CB00015B/1037